Strangers in the City

Strangers in the City

*Reconfigurations of Space,
Power, and Social Networks Within
China's Floating Population*

Li Zhang

Stanford University Press
Stanford, California
2001

Stanford University Press
Stanford, California
© 2001 by the Board of Trustees of the
Leland Stanford Junior University

Printed in the United States of America
On acid-free, archival-quality paper

Library of Congress Cataloging-in-Publication Data
Zhang, Li.
    Strangers in the city : reconfigurations of space, power,
and social networks within China's floating population / Li
Zhang.
        p.   cm.
    Includes bibliographical references and index.
    ISBN 0-8047-4030-5 (alk. paper.)—ISBN 0-8047-4206-5
(pbk. : alk. paper)
        1. Rural-urban migration—China—Beijing. 2.
Migrant labor—China—Beijing. 3. Urban policy—China—
Beijing. 4. Social change—China—Beijing. I. Title.
    HT384.C6 B459 2001
    307.2'416'0951156—dc21   2001020611

Original Printing 2001

Last figure below indicates year of this printing:
10   09   08   07   06   05   04   03   02   01

Designed by Janet Wood
Typeset by BookMatters, Berkeley in 10.5/13 Bembo

For my parents and for Mark

Acknowledgments

In the course of researching and writing this book, I accumulated enormous personal debts of gratitude to many individuals and institutions. My field-work in 1995–96 was graciously funded by the Fulbright-Hays Doctoral Dissertation Research Abroad Fellowship, the Committee on Scholarly Communication with China, and the Wenner-Gren Foundation for Anthropological Research. Two preliminary studies in Beijing were made possible by the President's Council of Cornell Women, the L. T. Lam Award for South China Research from the East Asia Program at Cornell University, and travel grants from the Mario Einaudi Center for International Studies and the Peace Studies Program at Cornell University. The writing was supported by Cornell's Sage Graduate Fellowship, the Marion and Franklin Long Fellowship in Peace Studies, and the An Wang postdoctoral fellowship at Harvard University. My home institution, the University of California at Davis, was also of great help by granting me time off during the first year of my appointment to accept the postdoctoral position at Harvard, and by providing me with a faculty research grant and a junior faculty book publication grant from the Dean's Office (College of Letters and Science). I thank all of these institutions and agencies for their generous support.

I am deeply indebted to the Wenzhou migrants in Beijing, who kindly shared with me stories of their life experiences and struggles, which were filled with courage, hardship, inspiration, and joy. It was through them that I began to enter and understand a very different world formed on the margin of urban Chinese society, a world that was imbued with intense business competition and cooperation, social conflict and group solidarity, and profound hope and uncertainty. While in China, I also received indispensable intellectual and moral support from Professor Yuan Fang in the Department of Sociology at Peking University.

This book is a revision of my doctoral dissertation, which was presented to the Department of Anthropology at Cornell University in 1998. I would like to express my profound gratitude to my dissertation committee members—Benedict Anderson, John Borneman, Elizabeth Povinelli, P. Steven Sangren, and Dorothy Solinger—for their advice, sustained interest in my project, and unflagging academic and personal support throughout the years. I am especially grateful to my thesis adviser, P. Steven Sangren, who set a high standard of scholarship and provided constant encouragement and guidance during my graduate study at Cornell. During my exchange study in the Department of Anthropology at the University of California at Berkeley (1996–97), I benefited greatly from the dissertation-writing seminar organized by Stanley Brandes, in which many of the ideas presented in the book were encouraged and discussed extensively. I thank Stanley and all the seminar participants, especially Jay Dautcher, David Eaton, Glen Etter, David Hughes, Sandra Hyde, John Leedom, and Ann Russ, for their close engagement with my work and for their friendship during the otherwise lonesome writing process.

Many other people offered critical comments and useful suggestions on portions of the earlier versions of the book. Among them I especially want to thank Ann Anagnost, Deborah Davis, Sara Friedman, Stevan Harrell, Gail Hershatter, Emily Honig, Jennifer Hubbert, Lida Junghans, John Kennedy, Matthew Kohrman, Beth Notar, Jean Oi, Elizabeth Perry, Lisa Rofel, Joshua Roth, Vilma Santiago-Irizarry, Mark Selden, Vivienne Shue, Kellee Tsai, Liu Xin, and two anonymous reviewers for Stanford University Press. I appreciate several long conversations with Aihwa Ong, which were crucial in framing some of the key theoretical questions in the final version of the book. Marc Miller and Anne-Marie Broudehoux helped me prepare the diagrams and the Beijing map respectively.

Dorothy Solinger, Xiang Biao, and Jong-Ho Jeong, who were all working on closely related topics regarding the floating population at about the same time, shared many ideas, observations, and fieldwork experiences with me throughout years. I am especially indebted to Xiang Biao, a Wenzhou native and graduate student at Peking University at the time, who introduced me to the Wenzhou migrant community in Beijing, which became a crucial starting point for my fieldwork. Dorothy Solinger was both an excellent mentor and a kind friend, whom I could always count on for constructive critique and insights pertinent to my project, often on very short notice. I thank them all for their friendship and intellectual companionship. I am also grateful for James Ferguson, Liisa Malkki, and Leo Chavez at the University of California at Irvine, who nurtured my initial interest in anthropology and the study of migration and displacement when I first arrived in the United States from China.

I was fortunate to spend a year (1998–99) as an An Wang postdoctoral fellow at the Fairbank Center for East Asian Research at Harvard University. Without the luxury of time and the intellectually stimulating environment I found there, this book would not have appeared so quickly. While I was at the center, I benefited from discussions with and support from James Watson, Rubie Watson, Elizabeth Perry, Ezra Vogel, Hue-Tam Ho Tai, and Merle Goldman. In particular, James Watson was extremely kind to me and took the time to read my entire dissertation and offer sound suggestions for revision and publication. My thanks also go to Nancy Hearst and Pam Summa for their editorial help. My colleagues at UC Davis, especially Susan Mann, Roger Rouse, Suzana Sawyer, G. William Skinner, Carol Smith, and Aram Yangoyan, have been a reliable source of intellectual companionship and provided a pleasant environment as I completed this book. In particular, I am grateful for G. William Skinner's close reading of the entire manuscript and for his detailed, thoughtful comments.

My writing also benefited from productive discussions with faculty and students at the following institutions where I presented various parts of my work: the Jackson School of International Studies at the University of Washington, the Department of Anthropology at the University of Chicago, the Department of Anthropology at the University of California at Davis, the Center for East Asian Studies at Stanford University, the Fairbank Center for East Asian Research at Harvard University, and the Asia-America-Pacific Research Group at UC Santa Cruz. Muriel Bell and Matt Stevens, my editors at Stanford University Press, were extremely attentive and supportive in guiding me through the book preparation and production process. I am especially grateful to Muriel Bell for her enthusiasm about my project and for bringing fresh anthropological studies on Chinese society to the public.

Finally, I owe a great many personal debts of gratitude to my families in China and America for their unconditional support and understanding. I can never repay the lifelong love and inspiration my parents provide me. My deepest appreciation goes to my husband, Mark Robert Miller, who has been a constant source of encouragement and emotional support. He accompanied me to China for the fieldwork and spent an enormous amount of time reading, editing, and offering critiques and suggestions on my work at every stage of the writing process. Most important, his unceasing curiosity about the world has greatly enriched our lives together.

Contents

List of Illustrations

Strangers in the City

Introduction

In early December 1995, snow had just fallen on Beijing and the temperature was minus ten degrees centigrade. Amidst the freezing cold of winter, some ninety thousand rural migrants living in the city's southern suburbs were undergoing a life-shattering event. Under pressure from a government campaign targeted specifically at them, these people, mostly petty entrepreneurs and traders from rural Wenzhou in Zhejiang province, were suddenly forced to abandon their homes and leave the city. Over a period of less than two weeks, about half of these migrants were driven into Beijing's remotest areas and surrounding rural counties. All of their forty-eight large housing compounds were demolished, flattened by yellow government bulldozers and turned into piles of debris. A once lively migrant community with a flourishing private economy suddenly resembled the bombed-out remnants of a war zone.

This government campaign to clean up a prominent migrant community in Beijing was part of a larger fierce and ongoing battle over space, power, and social order. With rapid commercialization and a booming urban economy in the post-Mao era, nearly 100 million peasants have left the rural hinterlands to seek employment and business opportunities in China's urban centers.[1] This enormous group of people on the move is known as the floating population (*liudong renkou*), a by-product of economic reform and China's entry into the orbit of global capitalism.

Although the floating population consists of people with diverse socioeconomic and regional backgrounds, their primary goals are the same: to make money and get rich in the cities. Some of these rural transients are able to bring a small amount of capital with them to start small businesses and exploit the huge potential of the urban consumer market. Indeed, some of them have accumulated a considerable amount of new wealth. But the majority of peasant workers who come to the cities have nothing but their labor to sell. The lucky ones manage to find temporary menial work in construction, restaurants, factories, domestic service, street cleaning, and other jobs that most urbanites are not willing to take. Still, there are many others who cannot find anything to do and thus drift hopelessly from place to place. Even though rural migrants are not entitled to the same legal rights as permanent urban residents and are subject to pervasive discrimination and periodic expulsion, large numbers of them arrive in the cities every day to pursue their dreams of prosperity.

While emerging market forces open up new ways for peasants to break through the constraints of the household registration (*hukou*) system to work and trade in the cities, multiple layers of social and political tensions exist between migrant newcomers, the state, and urban society. Despite the fact that the cheap labor and services provided by rural migrants are in high demand in cities, migrants are regarded as a serious social problem by urban officials and residents. The floating population is seen as a drain on already scarce urban public resources and is blamed for increased crime and social instability. Too far away to be reached by rural authorities but not yet incorporated into the urban control system, rural migrants are considered "out of place" and "out of control." The very existence of this large, mobile, and unmanageable population has called into question the old Chinese socialist control based on a relatively stable population fixed in space. Moreover, the recent formation of "congregating zones of floaters" (*liudong renkou jujudian*) is even more disturbing to top leaders and city officials, who believe that the "political vacuum" formed in such places can easily become fertile ground for the growth of social vices and nonstate political forces. Therefore, as mass migration led to the formation of community-based migrant power, the state developed new strategies to regulate the migrants.

This book is an ethnographic study of the development, destruction, and eventual reconstruction of an emerging nonstate-organized migrant community under late socialism. By "late socialism" I mean the historical moment in which Chinese society is undergoing a profound transformation under multiple socioeconomic forces: accelerating marketization and privatization, entrenchment of global capital, and lingering socialist institutions and practices.[2] The community I focus on in this study is Zhejiangcun (Zhejiang Village), the largest migrant settlement in Beijing. The majority of migrants living in this southern suburban community are peasants-turned-entrepreneurs whose family businesses specialize in garment manufacturing and trade. By examining the politics of the making, unmaking, and remaking of this migrant community, I seek to explore how space, power, and identity-reformation intersect to reconfigure the state-society relationship in a period of increased spatial mobility and marketization. Therefore, this book can be also read as an ethnography of changing Chinese state-society relationships under late socialism.

More specifically, the book addresses the following interrelated questions: How does the late-socialist state attempt to turn rural migrants into a distinct kind of subject for new forms of control and regulation? What kinds of social networks do rural migrants mobilize to create their social space and popular leadership in the city? What are the social and political ramifications of the informal privatization of space and power within the migrant population? How can we reconceptualize the reform-era Chinese state in order to make sense of the dissimilar responses from diverse state agencies to profound social and spatial changes brought by migrants?

I probe the above questions in the following ways. First, I place the production of social space by migrant entrepreneurs at the center of my ethnographic inquiry to illuminate their struggle to negotiate a third kind of state-society relationship in China, one that is outside the strictly rural or urban mode of state-society dynamics. I argue that it is primarily through the spatial and social production of a migrant community (manifested in the construction of private housing and marketplaces) that a new form of migrant power and leadership has emerged and developed. Put in more abstract terms, the production of social space is conditioned by the existing power relations and itself constitutes a vital source of power. But as I show in the chapters that follow, although locality-based migrant power no doubt challenges the state monopoly of production, trade, and community life, it is nevertheless deeply intertwined with officialdom through informal patronage ties.

Second, this book provides an ethnographic account of how pervasive clientelist alliances developed between three vertically positioned groups: local officials, migrant leaders, and ordinary migrant families. In this emerging realm of commercial and political clientelism, migrant leaders act as "local bosses" or "political brokers" to regulate market order and communal life, while negotiating with the state for migrants' rights to live, work, and trade in the city. I maintain that the making of such triadic clientelist ties in migrant communities is not merely a revival of traditional forms of social networks such as cliques and gangs; rather, these clientelist alliances created by migrants are highly commodified and have enabled a new mode of governmentality in managing a third kind of subjects—the floating population (neither strictly rural nor urban) in China. Here I use the term "governmentality" to refer to the art or strategies of governing practices that aim to shape, guide, and affect the mind and conduct of persons through multilevel social domains such as the family, community, discourse, and other social institutions (see Foucault 1991 and Gordon 1991; see also Ong 1999).

Third, while analyzing the ongoing reconfiguration of social and spatial relations within this community and its relationship with the state, I situate a locally grounded analysis in the larger geopolitics of the capital, Beijing. The geopolitics of Beijing is determined by its unique political and symbolic position in the Chinese national order of things. A number of questions are germane to political leaders' concerns: How should residential communities be organized and on whose terms? What kinds of private capital, production, and trade should be allowed in a place like Beijing? How should the relationship between political control and economic gains be balanced to ensure greater political stability? These questions are derived from the state's increasing concern about how to maintain its political control and implement its vision of a new socioeconomic order in a rapidly changing world where the prospects for socialist states are largely gloomy.

Thriving unofficial migrant communities have exacerbated bureaucrats' political anxieties about their ability to sustain the power to regulate emerging regimes of private economy and alternative residential communities. This is because, based on kinship and native-place networks, many migrant groups have constituted themselves as separate communities with their own leadership and a strong sense of regional identity. Further, with the increase of housing demands and capital accumulation, some larger, wealthy migrant groups have constructed semipermanent housing and marketplaces, which has profoundly altered the spatial organization and power dynamics in parts of Chinese cities. Such informal privatization of power and space within the migrant population creates multiple local centers of power that compete with the once-monopolizing state power.

In the early 1990s the perceived political danger from the migrant settlement Zhejiangcun was particularly acute because of its location only five kilometers from China's political center—Beijing's Tiananmen Square. Moreover, sweatshop-like, labor-intensive cottage industries operated by Wenzhou migrants and their fortress-like housing compounds appeared too messy and disorderly to city officials. The enclave was thus deemed incompatible with the type of development that the post-Mao regime wished to promote in the capital: that is, high-tech development, large corporate commerce, and managed foreign investment. In other words, rural migrants' cottage industries ran counter to what I call the "late-socialist urban aesthetics" promoted by the state to attract foreign investment and international and domestic tourism.

Fourth, this study focuses on migrant entrepreneurs rather than migrant workers. Migrant entrepreneurs can be compared to what Gates (1996) defines as "petty capitalists" because they operate family-based businesses by using preaccumulated small capital and extended kinship ties.[3] In contrast, migrant workers (*dagongde* or *mingong*) have nothing but their labor to sell and depend heavily on the urban labor market for work. As small manufacturers and traders with economic resources, the entrepreneurs have a distinct advantage over migrant workers in that they are able to create native-place-based enclaves, better social connections, and business flexibility.

Using the politics of migrant community-making as an aperture, the larger aim of this study is twofold: to explore the culturally specific rearticulation of power, spatial politics, and changing state-society dynamics in late-socialist China; and to suggest how these changes can deepen our understanding of postsocialist transformations. My account of Chinese migrants' production of social space and creation of clientelist networks challenges two assumptions frequently echoed in popular Western discourse on postsocialist transitions: "the retreat of the state" and "the triumph of the market and capitalism."[4] These assumptions present a vision of (post)socialist transition as a progressive and unilinear move toward a known end: liberal capitalism and democratic polities. They further assume that the disintegration of socialist regimes and their opening up to market capitalism will automatically lead to a withering of state power (usually represented as evil and oppressive), and that such a retreat will necessarily lead to the formation of egalitarian and democratic social spaces.

Recent scholarship on Russia and Eastern Europe questions this monolithic vision of postsocialist transformations by emphasizing the complexities and uncertainties in the culturally specific reconfigurations of the economy and power relations in these rapidly transforming societies.[5] Recent experiences from many parts of the world clearly indicate that a free-market economy itself is not a simple remedy for the diverse social and political problems that have long existed in different societies; at times the market can even exacerbate latent social, economic, and political tensions. As Verdery (1996) has pointed out, when "the visible hand of the state is being replaced by the invisible hand of the market," what we witness in some regions are political anarchy, military dictatorship, ethnic cleansing, the rise of the Mafia, and (re)emerging modes of social domination (see also Handelman 1993; Humphrey 1991; Ries 1998; and Verdery 1991).

A closer look at post-Mao China shows that the assumptions regarding a withering state and market triumph are fraught with empirical and analytical problems. Drawing on my ethnographic research, I argue that the Chinese party-state, understood as an internally divided regulatory regime, continues to play a salient role in shaping people's everyday lives, social spaces, and identities, despite accelerating market forces; but at the same time, the ways in which state power operates have indeed changed. In this context, unofficial migrant enclaves do not exist in the vacuum of an absent state power; rather, they become new sites for contesting the control over space, identity, private economies, and alternative modes of city life.

Therefore, rather than asking *how much* state power is implicated in everyday life, I propose to examine how the mode and focus of socialist governmentality have changed over time in China. I highlight two significant changes in the management of the migrant population. One was the gradual shift toward deregulating migration and then intensifying the regulation of migrants at their urban destinations. A second change was the gradual appropriation of the popular migrant leadership as a social force to control the rural migrants.

The continuing salient role of the state that this book reveals has also been observed by other China scholars in different contexts (see Perry 1994; Walder 1986; Oi 1989; Solinger 1999a). For example, in her 1988 study of Chinese state processes, Shue expressed deep skepticism about the notion of a dwindling socialist state power in the reform era. Her more recent study of a small city in northern China shows that the "thinning" of intrusive, oppressive, and restrictive modes of state power is often accompanied by a simultaneous "thickening" of a regulatory and facilitating power, buttressed by the expansion of local bureaucratic apparatuses (Shue 1995). Anagnost (1997) reminds us that the Chinese party-state retains a dominant role in reconstituting the postrevolutionary subject as "civilized citizens," while Rofel (1999) shows that the state does not necessarily operate against market forces but uses them to construct a postsocialist modernity that many Chinese aspire to embrace.

The persistent relevance of the state and its ability to adapt to new conditions in reform-era China problematizes the master narrative of retreating state power in the postsocialist world. Therefore, on another level, this book is an attempt to demonstrate how the experiences of China's migrants speak to the complex reconfiguration of power and space in countries that have departed from socialism. It argues against a unilinear, progressive metanarrative of socialist transformation as a triumph of one epochal stage over another, good over evil, capitalism over socialism, and democracy over totalitarianism. The tale of Chinese migrants' struggles shows that although the social spaces they have created challenge the established social order and state *thesis* domination, they are far from becoming civic grounds that will nourish democratic politics. The migrant world I have come to know is built on pervasive hierarchical patron-client networks that enable new kinds of social domination and exploitation.

In what follows, I situate the themes of this book as outlined above in the larger fields of anthropology and sinology. In addition to briefly discussing how my own thinking about these issues has been shaped by relevant theoretical developments, I suggest how this study can further contribute to a more dynamic and fuller understanding of the relationships between space and power and between state and society.

Space and Power

Space has been largely left out of anthropological analyses of local politics and social change because it is often regarded as external. Instead, time and temporality are assigned a privileged position in explaining social and political processes. Yet, as theorists of cultural geography have argued, social space is not merely a passive locus or "container" of human activities and social relations; rather it is deeply implicated in all social processes (see Harvey 1989a, 1989b; Soja 1989; Massey 1994; Watts 1992). On the one hand, space is constituted through practices and power relations; on the other, social relationships and political domination are also spatially constituted and transformed. In Foucault's words, "space is fundamental in any form of communal life; space is fundamental in any exercise of power" (1984: 252). By theorizing about the intimate connections between spatial formation and the techniques of power, Foucault sheds light on how modern subjects came to be created and disciplined (1972).

My attempt to articulate the relationship between spatial production and migrant power in China is particularly influenced by the French Marxist thinker Henri Lefebvre. In *The Production of Space*, Lefebvre examines how real, lived social space (as opposed to empty "physical space" and abstract "mental space") is produced by concrete human practices and serves as a powerful tool in shaping people's thoughts and actions. He highlights the centrality of space in social and political struggles under capitalism in the following terms:

> Space is becoming the principal stake of goal-directed actions and struggles. It has of course always been the reservoir of resources, and the medium in

which strategies are applied, but it has now become something more than the theater, the disinterested stage or setting, of action. Space does not eliminate the other materials or resources that play a part in the socio-political arena. . . . Rather, it brings them all together and then in a sense substitutes itself for each factor separately by enveloping it. (Lefebvre 1991: 410–11)

Two of Lefebvre's insights are germane to my thinking about how the social production of space shapes the politics of migrant community-making. First, Lefebvre sees space as a central component of the capitalist mode of production and social domination. He writes, "in addition to being a means of production it [space] is also a means of control, and hence of domination, of power" (ibid.: 26). Social space can be conceived of as a fundamental means of production because it provides places necessary to the reproduction of the family, the production of labor power, and the maintenance of class relations. Viewing social space as the underpinning of production is extremely useful for understanding why Chinese migrants' appropriation of urban space constitutes an essential part of their social and economic struggles.

Second, Lefebvre suggests that if we agree that space is socially produced, our primary task is to examine the production of space rather than observing things in space. Thus a focus on spatial processes does not mean that the study of social space rejects the notion of time, since it deals precisely with the history and temporality of space. By integrating time and space in the same analytical framework, this study of Zhejiangcun does not treat the spatial organization of the community as a static container for local politics. Instead, I believe that it is through the temporal contestation of space that local power dynamics and migrants' negotiation with the state get articulated. I thus focus my ethnographic lens on the ongoing process of making and remaking this migrant enclave over time.

Although the mutually constitutive relationship between space and power has been explored by some anthropologists in the context of capitalism (see Harvey 1989b; Gupta and Ferguson 1997), it has not received enough attention in studies of socialist and postsocialist countries. With this study I hope to add new ethnographic insights from late-socialist China to the ongoing theoretical discussion. If, as Lefebvre has pointed out, socialism tends to create larger centers of production and greater centers of political power, recent informal privatization of space and power within some migrant groups in China responds to this tendency by establishing other locally based centers of production, trade, and power.

In the early anthropology of China, little attention was paid to the productive role of space (especially urban space) and its intrinsic link to power in larger political-economic contexts. One of the few exceptions is G. William Skinner's now classic analysis of China's regional structure as a hierarchy of town- and city-centered local and regional systems (1964–65, 1977a). Skinner's work moves anthropology on China beyond village studies by providing invaluable analysis of the distinct spatial patterning of the Chinese political economy, but we still know little about how people appropriate physical space in their everyday struggles for social power. In more recent years, anthropologists have become increasingly concerned with changing social relationships, state power, gender relations, and cultural politics in urban and translocal settings (see, e.g., Anagnost 1997; Brownell 1995; Yang 1994). Although these studies have provided a much-needed anthropological understanding of rapidly changing urban Chinese society, the role of space in shaping these social and political processes remains largely underdeveloped and undertheorized.[6] In this book, by focusing on space, power, and migrant subjects, I aim to fill this empirical and conceptual gap and thereby contribute to the development of a multifaceted urban anthropology of China.

I analyze the dialectical relationship between spatial practices and the production of power within the floating population in three ways. First, I show how increased spatial mobility has made it possible for millions of Chinese peasants who were previously tied to the countryside to obtain jobs and develop business opportunities in the cities. As a form of spatial practice, migration thus became a vital way for these impoverished peasants to accumulate some wealth. Second, I analyze the ways in which the specific forms of spatial reorganization of the migrant household and the family business have had salient effects on the value of women's work and have thus reshaped gender and domestic relations among rural migrants (see Chapter 5). Third, and most important, I detail how, by turning part of the urban space into their own place, Chinese migrants began to gain control over their communal lives and the economy. Without their own physical space, migrant entrepreneurs would not be able to create their own community and successful businesses in the city. Although members of the floating population have virtually no means of owning land in the city, they are able to challenge and manipulate land-use regulations through clientelist ties with local officials.[7] The informal privatization of space in migrant communities reinforces the power of a popular migrant leadership. In sum, by focusing on "the active—the operational or instrumental—role of space, as knowledge

obj ective

and action, in the existing mode of production" (Lefebvre 1991: 11), we can better understand the ways in which spatial mobility and place-making constitute a critical part of migrants' struggle for power, local control, and residence rights in the city.

Finally, in this study I conceptualize power as a relational process rather than a thing possessed only by the dominant class. I analyze how power operates through both discursive and nondiscursive everyday practices, and through both visible, formal state apparatuses and social institutions and informal, diffused social networks. I seek to explore a more nuanced understanding of power that takes into account cultural specificities. For example, in the Chinese language there is no generic word for "power." Instead, my informants usually used two specific Chinese terms—*quanli* and *shili*—to refer to their struggle for power and social control. *Quanli* refers to bureaucratic power determined by one's officially appointed position; *shili* alludes to locality-based social and political influence, which is determined by one's wealth, social networks, and personal traits. Even though people frequently draw from both types of power simultaneously in everyday life, they have very different social and political bases and thus cannot be collapsed analytically.[8]

State-Society Rearticulations Under Late Socialism

In most cold war–era studies of Chinese society, political scientists analyzed the Chinese state primarily as a monolithic, repressive, totalitarian regime.[9] In this picture, state domination appeared seamless and static, leaving little room for consideration of how citizens could also assert their agency to influence the trajectory of Chinese politics. Later, informed by vehement power struggles among political leaders during the Cultural Revolution, some scholars began to question the totalitarian model, instead favoring a pluralist approach to highlight the internal divisions and conflicts within the top leadership (see, e.g., Nathan 1973). Yet, because of its focus on top-level politics, this pluralist approach offered few insights into the differentiation and fragmentation of the Chinese state on nonelite levels.

Research in the post-Mao era has become increasingly critical of the rigid dichotomy that defines the state and society as discrete entities working against each other.[10] Scholars used their research in diverse Chinese contexts to highlight the deeply entangled relationships between local state agents and social elements. For example, in analyzing the reconfigurations of state-business relationships during the economic reform period, Pearson (1997) and Wank (1999) have identified two increasingly important modes of state-society relations, namely "corporatism" and "clientelism." In both modes, state elements and private businesses are more deeply enmeshed with each other than they have been in the past.

Since the late 1980s, anthropologists working on China have become increasingly concerned with the question of state power, placing it at the center of their ethnographic inquiries. Rather than analyzing epochal political events, the bureaucratic structure, or state policy-making, they focus on everyday practices and symbolic processes through which state power works in different social domains.[11] While examining how the state exerts hegemony in everyday life, these studies also examine how state hegemony is constantly contested and sometimes subverted by subordinate groups.

This study aims to deepen this trend of anthropological inquiry into the state through an ethnographic approach. I suggest that what differentiates an ethnographic account of the state from other approaches is not just the scale of analysis but the very conception of the state. Rather than taking the state as a given political entity, an ethnography of the state begins with how the state is imagined, encountered, challenged, and reconstructed through everyday practices (cf. Gupta 1995). In other words, we need to shift from an institution-based analysis of the state to a practice-oriented analysis. Foucault's notion of "governmentality" is particularly useful for moving beyond the dichotomy of state versus society. Governmentality, or the art of governing activities, is articulated through processes both inside and outside the state. A variety of social institutions and informal social networks can all function as regimes of power that shape people's sense of self and conduct. Examining modes of governing strategies in diverse social realms is essential for my project because, as I will show, turning rural migrants into subjects and mobilizing the campaign to clean up migrant communities were made possible both by formal state agencies and by other social elements.

To deepen our understanding of late-socialist state-society dynamics, I do three things in this book. First, unlike most existing scholarship on Chinese state-society relations, which has largely focused on relatively stable and well-established rural or urban communities, this ethnography focuses on how the newly emerged floating population encounters the state in everyday life. Migrant enclaves, with very few established power structures, offer a unique situation for examining the process by which alternative forms of power and authority have emerged to challenge state domination. Solinger's book *Contesting Citizenship in Urban China* (1999a) explores the relationship among the state, markets, and peasant migrants. Her analysis is placed on a macro, structural level, whereas this ethnography delves more deeply into the microprocesses through which the relationships among space, power, and the state are actually played out in the making and unmaking of a migrant community.

Second, my account of Zhejiangcun pays special attention to how the relationship between economic gain and political control was conceived differently by the governments of different places (for example, Beijing and Wenzhou) and by officials on different bureaucratic levels. It has been widely acknowledged that Chinese state-society relations vary greatly across regions, settings, and time, yet such spatial and temporal variations have not been sufficiently analyzed (Perry 1994). I believe that revealing the dissimilar attitudes and actions of different state agents will deepen our understanding of the politics of migrants' space-making activities.

Third, I provide detailed accounts of patron-client networks within the migrant community and analyze the importance of local bosses who function as "political brokers" to mediate the often problematic relationship between state agencies and ordinary migrants.[12] Although the entangling of state and society has long been part of Chinese political history (see Perry 1994), I argue that the degree and forms of informal alliances created between state agents and other social elements have greatly increased and diversified in the era of marketization and commodification.[13] Scholars have made it clear that clientelist ties tend to emerge in a context where the distribution of resources and opportunities is unequal (see Eisenstadt and Roniger 1984; Flap 1990; Foster 1963; and Schmidt et al. 1977). Patronage networks, formed on the basis of personal loyalty and obligation and implicit coercion and exploitation, are especially important for migrant entrepreneurs in China because their noncitizen status in urban society prevents them from gaining access to resources and business opportunities through legal channels. Their informal networks thus undermine the monopoly of state control, foster competition within the bureaucracy, and help migrants gain local protection and urban resources. But at the same time, such ties can be appropriated by officials to extend their indirect control to migrant communities.[14]

Since I will frequently refer to a number of government agencies that Wenzhou migrants directly or indirectly interact with, and it is important to differentiate these agencies by administrative level, specific function, and region, I offer a diagram here as a point of reference (see Figure 1). Each level of government has a similar set of branch offices, which I have not included in the diagram to avoid redundancy. The four that are most relevant to migrant life are the offices in charge of industry and commerce, taxes, police,

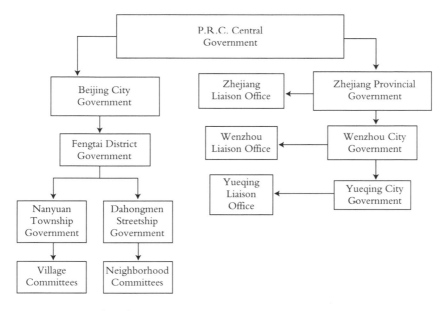

1.   Hierarchy of government agencies

and city planning. Throughout the book I use "upper-level government" to refer to the central, provincial, and city governments; "lower-level government" refers to district, subdistrict (*jiedao*), and township governments.

Discovering Zhejiangcun

This study grew out of sixteen months of anthropological fieldwork in Beijing and Wenzhou in the summer of 1994 and from June 1995 to September 1996. I also made two follow-up research trips in January 1998 and July 1999 to track more recent developments in this community. Beijing is one of the major magnets for rural-to-urban migration in China. By 1994 the Beijing municipality (including its suburbs) already had 3.29 million transient people in addition to its 12 million official permanent residents (Beijing Municipal Planning Committee Research Team 1995). Yet this city has received little attention from Western scholars working on Chinese internal migration. As the capital, Beijing has a unique position in geopolitics, which affects the meaning and consequences of migration there. For these reasons, I decided to study the politics of migration in Beijing.

During the summer of 1994 I first learned from some Beijing residents

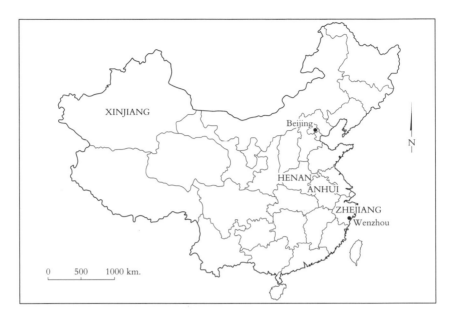

1.   People's Republic of China

that the so-called floating population was not always as mobile as the media reported. Indeed, many relatively stable migrant enclaves were thriving on the outskirts of the city at that time. Urbanites called these socially and spatially demarcated migrant enclaves "villages" (*cun*) after the dwellers' common provincial origin. I became fascinated by this new social phenomenon, which had been virtually absent during the Mao years in which I grew up. I was determined to seek out these unofficial migrant communities. Although most people in Beijing knew of the existence of migrant "urban villages," few could tell me their precise locations. After making numerous inquiries over a period of two weeks, I was able to locate the four most well-known migrant villages—Zhejiangcun, Anhuicun, Hunancun, and Xinjiangcun—created by migrants from Zhejiang, Anhui, Hunan, and Xinjiang provinces respectively (see Maps 1 and 2). Unlike most squatter settlements in other Third World countries, Chinese migrant urban enclaves are not occupied exclusively by migrants.[15] These so-called migrant villages are often inhabited by both permanent suburban residents and migrants who rent rooms from the locals.

Zhejiangcun is the largest and best established migrant settlement in Beijing.[16] In 1995 it had nearly 100,000 migrant residents. The majority

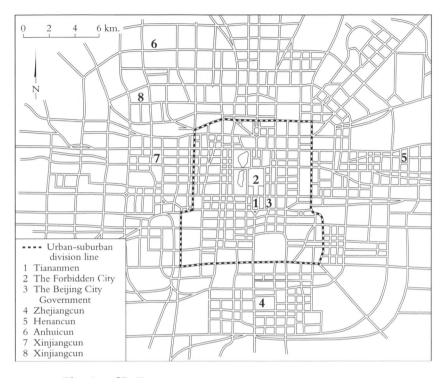

2. The city of Beijing

came from the Wenzhou region (once a prefecture, now officially classified as a municipality) in Zhejiang province—one of China's more advanced provinces (see Map 3). More specifically, Wenzhou migrants came predominantly from two largely rural areas—Yueqing and Yongjia, both of which were within the administrative boundaries of the Wenzhou municipality (see Map 4).[17] Although in the early 1990s Yueqing was reclassified as a county-level city, like Yongjia it still consisted of vast rural areas. Wenzhou migrants in Beijing are mostly self-employed petty entrepreneurs and merchants in the informal garment industry.

Because Zhejiangcun was largely stigmatized and had been "cleaned out" several times by the city government, migrants there were highly suspicious of "outsiders" (non-Wenzhou people normally identifiable by their dialects) who wanted to do research among them. A researcher without personal connections with Wenzhou migrant families could be viewed as someone sent by the government to collect information, or a reporter who could

3.   Zhejiang Province

write unfavorable things to demonize them. Given this situation, I was introduced to the Wenzhou migrant community by a friend who himself was a Wenzhou native and had done extensive field research in Zhejiangcun. In the first month of my fieldwork, he accompanied me to the community many times and introduced me to several key local bosses as well as ordinary migrant families. Through his friendship and mediation I was able to transform myself from a stranger into a friend of the Wenzhou migrants. Once several families had accepted me as their frequent guest, it was relatively easy to extend those personal connections to other migrant families. When some of them found out in our casual conversations that my mother was born and

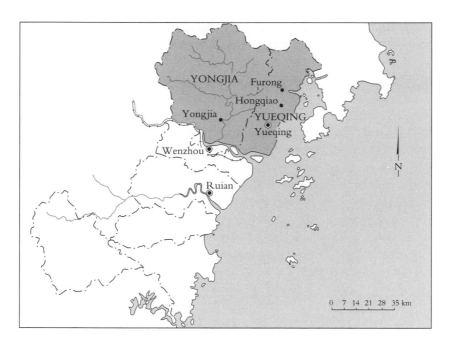

4.   The Wenzhou Municipality

grew up in Hangzhou, the provincial seat of Zhejiang, they were delighted and began to consider me a *bange laoxiang* (a half-native fellow). Thus native-place identity (with its fluid geographic boundaries) was a powerful means for establishing rapport with Wenzhou migrant entrepreneurs.

In all, I interviewed about 110 migrants from seventy households and had numerous informal conversations with migrants from diverse socioeconomic backgrounds. The majority of the interviews were conducted either in my informants' houses or at their stalls and shops while they worked. Two kinds of places became the primary sites for my research. One was the market-place, where Wenzhou migrants conducted their garment wholesale or retail businesses. Because the majority of migrants living in the housing com-pounds were engaged in garment production, marketplaces provided me with the opportunity to talk to migrants who specialized in trading as well. Marketplaces also allowed enough anonymity for me to interact with stall keepers either as a customer or as a university student.

My other primary research site was the migrant housing compound, which hosted nearly half of the migrants in the area when I began my fieldwork. Housing compounds were also ideal places for building long-term rapport with informants because migrants there were more open and accessible than those who lived in local farmers' houses. Since families in the same compound usually knew each other well and had many daily interactions, I quickly became acquainted with the families that shared a common physical space.

But just as I had begun to enjoy the openness and convenience provided by these housing compounds, the government campaign to clean up Zhejiangcun took place. In the middle of my fieldwork, I suddenly lost contact with nearly half of my informants as they were forced out of Beijing and their homes were demolished. I was devastated by this unexpected event and spent several days pondering how to resume contacts with the widely displaced families and wondering if it would even be possible. Although I was worried about my own research, I was also concerned about the fate of those migrant families who had become my close personal friends. After brief official reports on the "success" of cleaning up Zhejiangcun were released in the newspapers, many of my Beijing friends called to ask what I planned to do next since I had just "lost" the fieldwork site. In fact, this community did not disappear for good; it actually expanded several months later, though most Beijing residents thought that it no longer existed. That impression persists even today.

One day while I was sifting restlessly through my notes, I suddenly realized that I could reestablish contact with the Wenzhou entrepreneurs by calling them on their cellular phones. Most Wenzhou entrepreneurs carry beepers and cell phones for business convenience, and many had given me their numbers. So I jumped to the telephone and spent the entire day calling my informants. By the end of the day, I had found at least fifteen families, some of whom remained hiding in Beijing's suburbs; others were in relocation sites outside Beijing.

During this period, I also traveled to rural Yueqing in Wenzhou and stayed with two migrant families for half a month during the Chinese New Year. My goal was to understand what kinds of social and economic ties Wenzhou migrants maintained with their homeland. The shifting and unstable aspects of my fieldwork site demanded that I question the often taken-for-granted notion of "community." In this case, the migrant community was not a natural, fixed, eternal place; rather, it was constantly made and remade through political and economic struggles in space and time (see Malkki 1995).

Now let me turn to three notable and distinct features of Zhejiangcun.

First, the community has no fixed geographic boundaries and is spread over several large suburban neighborhoods in the Fengtai district in the southern part of the city. People disagree about where Zhejiangcun begins and ends. Some believe that it refers to a cluster of some twenty-five preexisting local villages now densely populated by Wenzhou migrants. Others insist that it refers to the entire region where these migrants can be found, which extends to the third ring road north of the city, the Nanyuan township airport to the south, Majiabao to the west, and Xiaohongmen to the east. Some even told me that Zhejiangcun is not a particular place but refers to any cluster of Zhejiang migrants in the city. The indeterminacy of its boundaries suggests that Zhejiangcun is a fluid social group capable of asserting itself over the preexisting communities and transforming them into their own place.

Second, the enclave is dynamic and open. It is the largest center for private manufacturing and trade of inexpensive garments in northern China, thus constituting a major part of Beijing's emerging "secondary economy."[18] The commercial activities of migrants living there extend far beyond this single locale in Beijing, reaching other cities and provinces and even other countries, such as Russia and parts of Europe. Therefore, this place is not as isolated as it is portrayed officially: as "a little closed kingdom."

Third, the community has a diverse social composition. It is not as homogeneous as most urban residents and officials believe. Several social groups reside together in a large area, including Wenzhou migrants (56,000), local Beijing residents (14,000), and migrants from Anhui, Hubei, Henan, Shandong, and Sichuan provinces (40,000). Most non-Wenzhou migrants are wage laborers who perform sewing, sales, or security work for Wenzhou employers (see Ma and Xiang 1998). Since the Wenzhou migrants constitute the majority, as a whole they are economically more powerful than the locals and migrants from other places.

Finally, the name of the Wenzhou migrant community deserves a closer look. The name Zhejiangcun first appeared in the late 1980s and was coined by Beijing residents to demarcate the social body of Wenzhou migrants from the rest of urban society (see Xiang 1996, Wang 1995). The first part, Zhejiang, is the name of the province from which these migrants come (rather than the name of their region—Wenzhou). The second part, *cun* (village), has a number of important social connotations. The word *cun* in this context not only marks the ruralness of this social group but also signifies a sense of social isolation and spatial boundedness of this community. A "village" within the city thus stands as an anomaly, something out of place and incompatible with the existing urban order of things. That image has largely shaped the popular urban imagination of migrant settlements in negative terms. In short, Zhejiangcun is a misleading and alienating term that was virtually forced upon Wenzhou migrants by urbanites. Most Wenzhou migrants do not like this label because, as one migrant explained, "it gives people the impression that this place is dirty, parochial, uncivil, and even antagonistic toward Beijing society."

Organization of the Book

With this ethnography I hope to integrate time and space in my narrative of the Wenzhou migrants. The organization of the chapters therefore reflects the temporal progression of this social and spatial development, rather than presenting a snapshot of the community. The chapters are largely in chronological order, but each also has its own thematic focus and addresses a specific set of questions.

Chapter 1 is a broader analysis of how the Chinese party-state attempted to transform rural migrants into a new kind of subject by creating a new social category (the floating population) and by adopting strategies to monitor and discipline migrants through everyday practices. In this dual process of subject-making (or what Ong [1996] has called "being-made and self-making"), I show how rural migrants have also come to subvert and revalorize the meaning of the category "floating" and the negative images associated with it, while creating alternative modes of social life and multifocal community life beyond a single, fixed geographic location.

Beginning with Chapter 2, I move to a specific account of space, power, and the state in the formation of the Wenzhou migrant community in Beijing. I trace how a distinct historical commercial culture and petty capitalist economy nourished Wenzhou migrants' current economic and spatial practices. I then chart their migration passages and highlight the centrality of family and native-place networks in this process. Chapters 3 and 4 examine the simultaneous processes of informal privatization of space and power in Zhejiangcun. In Chapter 3, I document how Wenzhou migrants appropriated land in local villages to create large residential compounds and analyze the social and political meaning of this new kind of spatial formation. Chapter 4 is an account of the social and spatial bases of a nascent popular migrant leadership and of its mediating role in policing the local order. In Chapter 5, I explore the interplay between changing gender and domestic relations and the spatial reorganization of Wenzhou migrant households and production. Chapter 6 examines crime and criminality by comparing two competing interpretations of the origin of crime and disorder provided by Wenzhou migrants and by official discourse and the mass media.

In Chapters 7 and 8, I examine how the privatization of space and power in this migrant community led to an open political conflict between the upper-level governments and Wenzhou migrants and local residents. Chapter 7 details multiple-level social conflicts and popular resistance during the campaign, highlights the disparity and instability within the state, and analyzes the motivation behind the campaign. Chapter 8 documents the exodus of Wenzhou migrants and their subsequent return to Zhejiangcun. It focuses on how these returning migrants rebuilt their economy and communal life by forming new commercial alliances with closed-down state factories and local government.

The conclusion assesses the future of the migrant population and migrant enclaves in a period of deeper structural transformations in urban China. It suggests the larger implications of this study for rethinking power, space, clientelism, and governmentality in late-socialist China and other postsocialist societies.

1. The Floating Population as Subjects

Rural-to-urban labor migration is by no means unique to Chinese society but is found in most parts of the world. Yet the conception of Chinese migrants in the post-Mao era as a floating population and the specific cultural and political meanings attached to this new kind of subject are distinct to China. How does the late-socialist state attempt to transform millions of rural migrants into a third kind of subject (neither rural nor urban) in a period of unprecedented spatial mobility? What discursive and nondiscursive practices do state agents use to achieve their subjectification? How do rural migrants respond to and subvert new modes of state domination?

This chapter explores these questions by focusing on everyday state practices that deprive the migrants of the same rights to the city that permanent urban residents have. I argue that the floating population is made possible through multiple strategies both inside and outside the state apparatus: the reworking of the household registration (*hukou*) system; cultural processes of naming, categorization, and media representation; and the invention and implementation of new regulations that govern everyday migrant life. Contrary to the predictions of some Western analysts and journalists that the *hukou* system will soon be abolished, the post-Mao regime does not intend to do away with this system; rather, the *hukou* system has been reformed and made more flexible to serve the new need to reregulate peasants on the move.[1]

The first half of this chapter traces how the category "floating population" was created and analyzes its cultural meanings and three techniques used by the dominant discourse to shape migrant subjects. It then discusses a number of nondiscursive forms of regulation specifically targeted at the floating population. But turning migrants into "internal aliens" (or noncitizens) in the cities is not a one-way process completely controlled by the state. As social agents with their own intentions, desires, and ideological histories, Chinese migrants do not simply take up or internalize the subject position offered to them by the state (see Giddens 1979). The second part of the chapter thus examines how, based on their increased economic capital and consumption power, some migrants have come to reshape the meanings of the available social categories while struggling to develop their own sense of self and social belonging beyond officially defined urban citizenship. Chinese migrants are able to subvert the meanings of the available categories (such as "floater") "not by rejecting or altering them, but by using them with respect to ends and references foreign to the system that has no choice but to accept" (De Certeau 1984: xiii). In sum, the dual process of "being-made and self-making" (Ong 1996) is the focus of my inquiry into migrant subject formation.

Naming and Categorizing Mobile People

In his investigation of the cultural and political invention of the Chinese peasantry (*nongmin*), Cohen (1993) argues that modern intellectual and political elites transformed China's rural population into the peasantry, a culturally distinct and alien "other" that the new socialist society aimed to liberate. By denaturalizing the taken-for-granted category "peasantry," Cohen further analyzes the political and social consequences of this practice in the reconstruction of the modern Chinese political economy. In a similar spirit, I argue that the floating population is a socially constructed category and that it is important to analyze how it was invented at a particular moment in recent Chinese history. So far, few studies of Chinese migrations have examined the history of the floating population and its thick layers of cultural and political meaning. By stressing the socially constructed nature of this category, I do not intend to suggest that it has no real social basis. Rather, I hope to illuminate how mobile people are conceived of as floaters and that the meanings attached to this category are an integral part of social and political struggles with real consequences.

Two important theoretical points have informed my analysis. First, categorizing and naming are inseparable from social power. "The labor of categorization, of making things explicit and classifying them" (Bourdieu 1991: 236) is a crucial mechanism for defining the meaning and order of the social world. Therefore, as many scholars have demonstrated, naming and categorizing do not simply describe, reflect, or represent social order, but also shape and reshape power relations among different groups (see, e.g., Borneman 1992; Foucault 1972; Koselleck 1985; Zito and Barlow 1994).

Second, in his study of the historical-political semantics of asymmetric counterconcepts, Koselleck (1985) argues that historically formed social concepts should not be viewed in isolation; instead, we need to trace the asymmetric structural relationship between antithetical binary concepts to denote the relations of power that produced them. Building on Koselleck's insights, I maintain that to better understand how and why labor migration is conceived as a floating population in China today, one must ask: Who did the naming and who was named? Against what and at what historical moment was this category invented and on whose terms? What political and cultural ramifications does this social category entail?

Before the implementation of the 1958 household registration rule, there was a short period of rapidly increasing rural-to-urban migration in the early 1950s (see Solinger 1999a; Davin 1999). Although the state was not entirely absent in monitoring this migration, official regulation was largely erratic, fragmented, and ineffective. As a result, many peasants had moved into the urban industrial sectors by 1954. In those days, migrants were not treated as a distinct group of subjects who needed to be put under special control and legal regulation. Neutral terms, such as *yimin* (migrants) or *ximin* (migrating or relocating people), were used to refer to relocated peasants. Other slightly different, nonjudgmental terms regarding migration, such as *qianxi* (relocate), *renkou yidong* (population movement), and *renkou liudong* (population mobility), were also used.[2]

By the mid-1950s, voluntary labor migration to the cities came to be seen as an urgent national problem. According to Selden (1979), about twenty million peasants rushed into the cities from 1949 to 1957, and these rural migrants could not be fully absorbed by urban industry, thus exacerbating the problem of urban unemployment (Walder 1984). Further, some officials believed that industrialization required the rural population to remain on farmlands so that they could continue to produce food for those working in industry (Zhang Qingwu 1988). As a result, the state passed new regulation measures to block the "blind flow" (*mangliu*) of peasants into cities to avoid the pathological growth of oversized metropolises experienced by other developing countries. Restricting people's spatial mobility was also regarded by bureaucrats as a reliable way to maintain socialist stability.[3]

It was through the reinforcement of the 1958 Household Registration Stipulations that Chinese peasants were turned into what Potter (1983) calls "birth-ascribed" rural *hukou* (household registration) holders. By requiring every Chinese citizen to register at birth with the local authorities as either an urban or a rural *hukou* holder of a particular fixed place, this system divides the entire Chinese population into two different kinds of subjects with asymmetric power. Rural *hukou* holders are prohibited from migrating into the cities and are not entitled to receive state-subsidized housing, food, education, medical care, and employment; these are reserved for urban *hukou* holders only.[4] Cut off from urban employment, guaranteed food supplies, subsidized housing, and other benefits of the city, peasants were anchored in the countryside for decades with virtually no spatial mobility. In the following two decades, nonstate-directed population movements were largely eliminated from China's social landscape.

Rural and urban residents were subsequently placed under different forms of state control and social surveillance. In the countryside, state control was made possible through a far-reaching grassroots cadre network (see Oi 1989; Shue 1988). In the cities (understood to include various levels of administrative and economic "central places" [Skinner 1997a]), pervasive state control over urban citizens was made possible through work units and neighborhood committees (see Walder 1986; Whyte and Parish 1984; Lu and Perry 1997).

During the 1960s and 1970s, however, a very different kind of state-directed, politically motivated population movement took place. To promote economic and technological development in the frontier areas, many skilled urban workers and professionals were relocated by the state to underdeveloped border provinces or minority autonomous regions like Xinjiang, Inner Mongolia, Yunnan, and Heilongjiang (see Shen and Tong 1992). Millions of urban youth and intellectuals were also sent down to the countryside to be "reeducated" by poor and lower-middle-class peasants (see Bernstein 1977). During the heyday of the Cultural Revolution, millions of floating Red Guards, mostly urban youth, traveled from place to place and eventually gathered in Tiananmen Square to be personally received by Chairman Mao (see Meisner 1977; Yan 1993). But such large-scale displacements of urban people and spatial mobility were not seen as population movements; instead, they were conceived of as political events, described in highly politicized terms such as *zhibian* (supporting the border areas by professionals), *shangshan xiaxiang* (the sending of urban youth up to the mountains and down to the countryside), and *dachuanlian* (establishing revolutionary ties among Red Guards). Those who were involved in these movements were not regarded as distinct social groups to be subjugated to special regulations as the floating population is today.

After the late 1970s, the situation changed dramatically, as mass labor migration rose on a scale unprecedented in modern China. A number of factors motivated millions of Chinese peasants to leave the countryside.[5] First, agricultural reforms initiated by former leader Deng Xiaoping greatly improved the efficiency of farming, generating nearly 200 million surplus rural farm laborers.[6] Second, a rapidly growing urban economy and the penetration of foreign and overseas Chinese capital demanded large numbers of cheap laborers. Third, the collapse of the state-monopolized "urban public goods regime" (a term borrowed from Solinger 1995b) made it possible for migrants to obtain basic resources and services through market exchange in the cities. Fourth, the gradual relaxation of migration policy allowed rural migrants to live and work in the cities on a temporary basis.

As peasant workers began to reappear in the cities in the early 1980s, they were generally seen by the urban public as temporarily displaced outsiders (*waidiren*) who would soon return to their rural origins. Rural transients as a whole were not treated as a structurally and culturally distinct group and thus were not put under a different form of systematic official control. But as more and more peasants poured into towns and cities, putting great stress on urban infrastructure and resources, they came to be regarded as a social problem despite their enormous economic contributions. Further, spatially detached from their home villages, rural migrants could no longer be directly reached by the rural authority in their places of origin. But at the same time, migrants, considered outsiders by city officials, were not effectively brought under the urban control system. Without a clear structural position in the society, migrants appeared detached from the existing social system and became a people of prolonged liminality—belonging neither to the rural nor to the urban society. From the government's point of view, these mobile people needed to be sent back where they came from or transformed into a new kind of subject through reregulation.

The state's initial response to the reemerging migration was to block and repress it. In 1981 the State Council issued a ruling intended to stop the flow of peasants into cities. A few years later, two important documents were issued: "State Council Notification on the Question of Peasants Entering Towns" in 1984 and "Provisional Regulations on the Management of the Population Living Temporarily in the Cities" in 1985, both of which took a relatively permissive stance on peasant movement into cities. This new state policy, however, was not immediately translated into local practice; conservative blocking (*du*) practices continued to be the dominant mode of governmentality in managing the migrant population at the local level. Most local officials regarded migrants as subjects of the governments in their native places, arguing that it was not their duty to regulate these outsiders even if they were temporarily residing in the city. No rules or laws were available to guide the practice of government officials in this domain. Local urban governments simply tried to keep migrants outside their own jurisdictions. As a result, migrants, then considered illegal, were randomly driven from place to place within the cities. Petty migrant entrepreneurs had to conceal their commercial activities from officials. News reports on migrants' activities were suppressed because many officials feared that publicly acknowledging the existence of mass migration would only encourage an influx of more peasants.

But official attempts to block migration did not stop millions of peasants from entering cities. As economic reform progressed, the growing urban economy needed migrant labor to fulfill low-end, dirty, dangerous jobs and to develop the service sector. Denying the presence of migrants in cities would only make it more difficult to extend government control over them. Thus, in order to bring "out-of-place" migrants back under state control, Chinese authorities began to change their strategy for managing the migrant population. A critical shift that began in several cities in the late 1980s was clearly reflected in social commentary:

> Clearly, expelling [*pai*] does not work, and blocking [*du*] does not work either. The key is to pay special attention to regulating [*guan*] so as to establish an effective social control network, formulate proper rules and laws, and eventually make the floating population part of an efficient way of ordering our society. (Chen Youquan 1988: 24)

A paragraph from the "must-know rules" (*xuzhi*) listed in more recent training materials distributed by the Beijing government to the floating population summarizes this new strategy:

> The fundamental goal of making regulatory rules is not to clean up, drive away, or disperse migrant workers as before, but to guide, control, and regulate them under the new condition of a socialist market economy—that is, to transform a disorderly kind of floating into an orderly kind of floating. (Beijing West-District Government 1996)

The reregulation of migrants accompanied a proliferation of discourse on the floating population in official documents, government censuses, newspaper reports, scholarly research, the broadcast media, and popular literature. Such "scientific" knowledge about the floaters has persisted since 1985 and has shaped the popular imagination of city dwellers about rural migrants. It also became the basis for the state's new migration policies and rules, which deemphasized suppression but highlighted the importance of local reregulation.

The Production of Discourse About the Floating Population

The first intense discussion of the floating population took place between 1987 and 1988 and the topic remains one of the most heated official and urban public discourse at this writing fifteen years later.[7] The primary focus is on two sets of interrelated issues: (1) the demographic background, economic activities, mobility, speed of growth, and spatial distribution of the floating population; and (2) the social impact of this migration and possible strategies regulating the migrant population more effectively. Almost all official and scholarly publications are obsessed with the question of how to improve the government's regulation of rural migrants.

Two typical articles written by scholars who also hold government positions are those by Zhang Qingwu (1983) and Yi Dangsheng et al. (1995). Like many others, these two articles begin with a sketch of the basic characteristics of the floating population based on data collected in Beijing and several other provinces. Then they analyze a number of "push" and "pull" economic forces and policy changes as the causes of reform-era migration. Finally, they evaluate the positive and negative effects of the floating population on urban society and propose stringent regulation strategies and tactics. In these accounts, the migrant population is portrayed as a social group with a striking gender imbalance (more males than females), a high concentration of young male laborers, and high spatial mobility. It is said that rural migrants not only "float" from place to place; they also tend to "congregate in the rural-urban transitional zones" for extended periods, and "some have formed stable enclaves where the number of migrants has exceeded that of the local *hukou* residents" (Yi Dangsheng et al. 1995: 143). The migrant population is also defined as a group of high fertility and thus as a threat to the national family planning project: "The floating population has a serious problem of excessive pregnancy and birth rates. Its floating nature exacerbates the difficulty of government regulation" (ibid.: 151). Further, the floating population is frequently accused of being responsible for urban ills such as deteriorating public security, high crime rates, prostitution, and drug trafficking. Such accounts in the name of scientific research and knowledge are powerful influences on people's image of the floating population.

In particular, censuses and surveys generate "scientific" knowledge about the floating population. On October 1, 1991, a census was carried out in fifty-eight townships in twenty Chinese provinces and autonomous regions. This census collected information on the following aspects of the migrant population: scale of the migration flow, gender, age, previous occupation, educational level, marriage status, length of migration, current occupation, income, and temporary abode of the migrants (see Zhang Qingwu 1994). In Beijing, two citywide censuses were completed on April 20, 1985, and November 10, 1994, to develop a profile of the migrant population, its impact on the city, and its future development trends. Although their sampling and research methods were seriously flawed, these censuses provided scholars and officials with ostensibly objective, scientific, and thus authoritative knowledge about the floating population (see Du Wulu 1986; Luo et al. 1986; Liu Xiuhua 1996; Wang and Feng 1986). As Anderson (1991) has suggested elsewhere, a census does not simply describe existing social groups; it reflects the state's vision for the ordering of a society. Through the production of knowledge based on censuses, surveys, and social analysis, the floating population came to be conceived of as a real social entity that is fundamentally different from the urban population, and as a social problem to be solved. As a result, the state was able to "transform foreign forces into objects that can be observed and measured, and thus control and 'include' them within its scope of vision" (De Certeau 1984: 36).

Representation of the migrants in the media and press also contributed to the popular image of the floating population. Writings by Ba and Ma (1989), Hao (1992), Zhu (1987), Du Weidong (1988), and Liu Manyuan (1993), for example, focus on the ruptures in migrants' everyday lives and conflicts in their cultural values and beliefs as they are caught between the rural world they left behind and the urban world they have just entered. The city is paradoxically portrayed as a social space with two opposite meanings—it is a source of civility that helps enlighten rural migrants, but it is also a dangerous zone of moral degeneration that turns migrants into prostitutes and criminals. In both scenarios, the floating population is defined as an inferior group to be civilized and transformed by higher moral codes set by permanent urban residents. In the following pages, I discuss three techniques of representation commonly used to construct images of the "floaters."

UNIFYING AND HOMOGENIZING

The floating population includes a wide range of mobile people with diverse migration experiences and lifestyles. Migrants are divided by place of origin, economic status, occupation, consumption power, and relation to the means of production.[8] People classified under this category often do not view themselves as sharing any fundamental common traits or class consciousness.

In fact, there are class distinctions among migrant entrepreneurs, small traders, and migrant wage workers based on their different positions in the system of economic production. For example, Henan migrants who make a living by collecting and recycling garbage told me that they felt little in common with Wenzhou migrants who have their own garment or leather workshops and carry cellular phones and beepers. The economic status, lifestyles, and social expectations of wage workers from Hubei and Henan provinces employed by Wenzhou migrant entrepreneurs are also very different from those of their bosses. (See Zhang, forthcoming, for a much more detailed account of the dissimilar urban experiences and modes of social belonging among Chinese rural migrants.)

Second, the migrant population is deeply divided by regionalism. Migrants who share local origins have created their own enclaves within many Chinese cities. These native-place-based migrant groups tend to monopolize a particular informal economic sector by excluding migrants from other places, a phenomenon common in China historically (see Crissman 1967; Honig 1992, 1996; Jones 1974; Skinner 1958, 1976; Wang Zhenzhong 1996). In Beijing, a division of labor has emerged along the lines of migrants' native places of origin: Zhejiang migrants dominate garment, leather, and eyeglass businesses; Xinjiang migrants run restaurants that serve regional specialties; Henan migrants sell vegetables and recycle trash; Hebei migrants work in construction; Anhui migrant women work as maids; and Shandong migrants work as tricycle-peddlers. Migrants from different regions thus see each other not only as economic competitors but also as social and cultural outsiders.

These class, regional, and occupational differences are salient factors that divide the floating population, but they are often obscured by official representations, which tend to portray migrants as a homogeneous group of aimless and ignorant people driven by poverty. This image of a powerless, uneducated, and low quality (*suzhi di*) group is then juxtaposed with its antithesis, permanent urban residents, who are held up as sophisticated, modern, and reliable.

DEHISTORICIZING AND DEHUMANIZING

In both official and urban public discourse, the floating population is portrayed as an amorphous flow of undifferentiated laborers without histories. Migrants are often referred to not as living individuals with their own desires, dreams, and intentions, but as flocks of raw labor that can be used or expelled at any time. Photographs in newspapers and magazines tend to focus on a few selected moments of migrant life to create the "typical" image of migrant workers as crowds of indistinguishable, exhausted bodies waiting hopelessly on the streets for jobs. This floodlike, formless image of mobile bodies driven by the market has shaped the urban public's perceptions and attitudes toward migrants and has reinforced a fear that migrants might "take over" the city.

In my interviews with Beijing residents, they frequently echoed such troubling assumptions about the floaters. One day when I showed pictures of some Wenzhou migrant entrepreneurs to several Beijing professors and workers, they expressed surprise and some dismay. One of them nearly screamed: "Look at these migrants! They do not look like floaters at all! Look, they are well-dressed and they even have *dageda* [cellular phones]! . . . They must be making money in illegal ways." The pictures obviously upset these urbanites' stereotypes of rural migrants. When asked how they thought of floaters, their answers usually included the words dirty, silly, poor, aimless, uncivil, congregating, and money-driven. Certainly not all migrants are rich; rather, my point is that the dehistoricization of floaters as poverty-driven raw labor not only obscures the important differences among migrants, but also reduces them from real human beings to an objectified commodity. It is through such dehumanizing and objectifying discourse that unequal power relations between migrants and urbanites are also encoded.[9]

ABNORMALIZING

In his study of the development of modern European institutions such as prison and of discourse on sexuality in the West, Foucault (1978, 1979) has forcefully argued that normalization constitutes one of the key microtechniques of modern power. In a similar spirit, anthropologists working on China have shown how the procedure of normalizing and naturalizing is used by the socialist party-state through the establishment of the officially sanctioned criteria of right and wrong conduct and thought (see, e.g., Anagnost 1995 and Mayfair Yang 1988). But normalizing certain practices, attitudes, and beliefs often requires a simultaneous process of abnormalizing other practices and values to create images of undesirable others to be suppressed and denounced. For example, Anagnost notes that in Chinese eugenics discourse it is China's ethnic minorities who are constructed as the internal "others" against what is inspired by the national narrative of progress, development, and modernity (Anagnost 1995: 31).[10]

In China, since a stable people-place relationship is largely regarded as a normal way of life and as a basis for social stability, migratory flows are considered destabilizing, abnormal, and even pathological. For example, the "shed people" (*pengmin*) in late-imperial China were largely considered by the state and by host communities to be an anomaly and a threat to social stability (Averill 1983; Leong 1997).[11] The same is true of rural migrants today. In particular, as urbanites experience increasing crime in a time of instability and uncertainty brought about by market reforms, their frustrations can be easily channeled toward migrant newcomers. Migrants' spatial mobility and perceived rootlessness are almost tantamount to being a potential criminal at large. The explanation for migrant crime presented by many city dwellers is that because migrants are not permanently attached to any urban community they do not have any moral responsibility for the places that they "pass through."

In sum, through homogenizing, dehistoricizing, dehumanizing, and abnormalizing, the migrant population is represented as a monolithic and formless entity consisting of unregulated, dangerous laborers who require stringent social control and surveillance.

THE CULTURAL SEMANTICS OF FLOATING

Further cultural implications of floating come from the domain of language itself. In Chinese, the word *liudong* (floating) has two different meanings: one is to be lively and unencumbered; the other is to be rootless, unstable, and dangerous. This double meaning opens the image of floaters to multiple interpretations. The dominant discourse tends to invoke and overamplify the negative meanings by emphasizing their relationship with related residual terms such as *liumin* (vagrants, homeless people), *liukou* (roving bandits), *liumang* (hooligans), *liucuan* (to flee), *liudu* (pernicious influence), *liuwang* or *liufang* (exiles), and *mangliu* (an unregulated flow of people), which is a transposition of the sounds in the derogatory term *liumang* (hooligans).

Perhaps it is due to the extraordinarily large agrarian population that a strong sense of territorial identity, or what Malkki (1992) calls the "metaphysics of sedentarism," has developed in official Chinese ideology (see also Granet 1975). Such earth-bound sentiments are clearly expressed in a widely accepted Confucianist saying, *antu zhongqian* (to be attached to one's native land and unwilling to leave it). Rootedness (not spatial mobility) is taken as the normal state of being in mainstream Confucianist culture. The idealized images of spatially bound social life constructed by Confucius and Taoist texts are often invoked today as a desirable moral way of life.[12] This emphasis on spatial immobility came to be reinforced through the *baojia* (household registration and surveillance) system in late-imperial urban China (Rowe 1979; Dutton 1992) and later mutated into the communist household registration system. This is not to say that there were no merchant activities, education-related spatial movements, or pilgrimages in imperial China—evidence of such movements is ample (see Skinner 1976; Watson 1975; Honig 1992; Rowe 1984). But the ability to move or relocate was by and large limited to a relatively small stratum of people and was most common in coastal regions.

In this cultural context, mobile people (*liumin*) tended to be associated with destructive images, such as *wu* (witches), *gui* (ghosts), *jianghu pianzi* (swindlers), and *youqi* (wandering beggars), which were all considered socially polluting and even dangerous to established communities (see Wolf 1978). For example, Kuhn (1990) shows that itinerant people and wanderers in late-imperial China were widely perceived as ghostlike "soul stealers" and were considered a potential threat to stable, rooted communities. In tracing the social roots of *liumin* in early-modern China, Chi (1996) notes that *liumin* were historically associated with landless and jobless peasants forced out of their homelands. Since these drifting, impoverished peasants often turned to banditry, they were regarded as a main source of instability. Mobile or displaced people were considered by the state to be unstable and dangerous social forces also because of their historical links to the formation of secret societies that challenged the established social order (Chesneaux 1972). Given the history of the cultural semantics of floating, calling migrants floaters calls up a host of derogatory meanings.

Regulating Migrant Subjects Through Everyday Practices

Although official and urban public discourse plays an important role in creating the floating population, everyday forms of regulatory power are also essential in getting migrants to conform to this subject position. Given the state's control over the media, the discursive strategies I have outlined above may seem to be homogeneous. But as we turn to look at actual regulation strategies at the local level, numerous problems and discrepancies become obvious.

REGISTRATION

The first step in the reregulation of migrants was mandatory registration, initiated in some cities as early as the mid-1980s. A new quasi-legal category was created to register migrants and to mark them as a distinct kind of person. This category is the floating population (*liudong renkou*), which is often used interchangeably with two other related terms in official documents: *wailai renkou* (population that arrives from outside) and *zhanzhu renkou* (temporary population).[13] Beginning in the early 1990s, migrants nationwide had to apply for a temporary resident card from the local police station if they intended to stay in the city for more than a month. In May 1995 the first complete national stipulation, "Application Procedures for Temporary Resident Cards," was enacted by the Public Security Ministry to demand that all migrants register with local authorities in order to maintain social order and stability. It required anyone sixteen years old or older who intended to stay somewhere other than his or her own *hukou* residence for more than a month to obtain a renewable temporary resident card (*zhanzhu zheng*) valid for six months or for a year at a time. In the same month, the Beijing city government established a special branch office to oversee the regulation of migrants.

Though many municipal governments became obsessed with registration in order to obtain a better demographic record of the migrant population and thus to improve regulation techniques, lower-level officials were more interested in collecting registration fees. To generate more revenue, many local governments established arbitrary fees for certificates and licenses. Although registering as temporary residents gives migrants a partial right to work and live in the cities, it does not grant them full citizens' rights such as access to state-sponsored food, housing, education, and health services.

Official efforts to get migrants to comply with registration rules frequently encounter resistance. Many migrants are reluctant to apply for the temporary resident registration card because doing so is time-consuming, costly, and provides them with no substantive benefits. For them, the registration rule is a pretext for government officials to tax them without delivering any promised services or legal protection. According to local authorities I interviewed in several areas in Beijing, less than half of the migrant population is registered. Many migrant workers regard the registration fee as too high. For relatively wealthy migrant entrepreneurs, the time rather than the money is their major concern. To apply for this card, one has to have a valid personal identification card, a letter from the local government of one's place of origin, a birth control certificate (which records the holder's fertility history and current contraceptive method), and a rental agreement from a local landlord. Since a temporary resident card is only valid within one district, a migrant who moves to another community has to apply for a new card.

Further, government practices are contradictory. Upper-level officials demand that all migrants register, but not all migrants can obtain a temporary resident card even if they are willing to apply for one. There are local hierarchies and criteria for determining who is a desirable or an undesirable migrant. For example, in one suburban Beijing community, migrants from Henan province, who are mostly engaged in garbage collection and recycling, have a reputation for being dirty, untrustworthy, and a source of instability. The local police thus refuse to issue them temporary resident cards based on the assumption that their presence makes permanent Beijing residents feel unsafe. In addition, applications from migrants without stable jobs or from those who have not yet rented housing from local landlords are usually denied. By not registering such migrants, local authorities hope to expel undesirable elements from their districts. But in reality, unregistered migrants often manage to stay in the area covertly. When discovered by the local police, they are fined or have to bribe the police in order to remain in the area. Some Henan migrants told me that even paying a fine three times a year (about fifty yuan each time) is less expensive than obtaining a temporary card. Some would rather pay the fines than apply for a card because they move several times a year.

FORMING AN ALL-SEEING GAZE?

The power of an all-seeing gaze created through the panoptic spatial arrangements in modern prisons can be adopted by other social regulatory systems (see Foucault 1972). In China the party-state attempts to create such a ubiquitous gaze to monitor the migrant population. It uses both formal state apparatuses and grassroots social networks in the form of "mutual societal surveillance" (*shehui jiandu*). A million sets of eyes are supposed to watch each other in everyday life. As this popular slogan puts it: "Everyone else polices me, while I police everyone else" (*renren guanwo, wo guan renren*). Because migrants are not attached to work units and thus cannot be easily located by officials, it is believed that such diffused social surveillance is an effective way to police migrants.

In suburban areas where migrants tend to congregate, government officials coerce local landlords to help monitor the activities of migrant renters. Rental households must hang a metal plate with a red sign saying *zu* (rented) on the front doors. This marking makes it easier for the police and neighborhood committees to make special checks of "problematic spots." Since the floating population is viewed as the biggest reproductive danger for the nation, in many areas urban landlords are also required to report unauthorized pregnancies among migrant tenants and force pregnant women to obtain abortions. Many landlords are reluctant to play this policing role because their lucrative rental businesses depend on the presence of migrants. But if they do not cooperate, they can be fined, reprimanded by local officials, or lose their rental licenses.

In some cities, random surveillance stations have been set up for anonymous reporting of birth control violations or criminal acts among the floating population. Patrol Teams for Examining the Floating Population's Birth Control (*Liudong Renkou Jihua Shengyu Xunjiandui*), composed of local cadres, have also been established in some places to monitor migrants' birth control practices. These experimental efforts, however, tend to be erratic and short-lived and are not as effective as coercing landlords to participate in daily surveillance.

TARGETING MIGRANT WOMEN'S BODIES

Because migrants are perceived to have high fertility, officials are concerned with "excessive birth" (*chaosheng*) among the migrant population and have intensified measures to monitor migrants' fertility practices.[14] All migrants (especially women) are required to obtain and carry a "marriage and fertility certificate" (*hunyuzheng*) issued by the local government in their place of origin. This certificate is usually required when migrants apply for temporary residence cards and work permits in the city. Migrant women who already have had one or two children are sometimes compelled by the urban authority to have an IUD implanted. To prevent migrants from breaking the birth control rule while away from home, some rural authorities demand cash deposits from the families of those who have migrated. Despite such efforts to control fertility, the official one-child-per-family rule is continually challenged by migrants. Violation of birth control contracts, however, may result in heavy fines or loss of temporary resident permits, sales licenses, or a place to live.[15]

For urban residents in China, birth control is usually implemented through work units and neighborhood committees, with a focus on the household as the unit of regulation. But since most migrants do not belong to any work unit, this mode of control does not work well for them. Further, a migrant household often consists of close family members, distant kin, village friends, small business owners, and their hired wage laborers, so focusing on the household is also impractical. For this reason, individual migrant women's bodies rather than migrant households have become the primary objects of fertility control.

POLICING PRIVATE AND PUBLIC SPACES

One of the obvious differences between being a floater and being a permanent urban resident is the degree to which the state intervenes in one's private space and activities in the public space. Based on a perception of the floating population as a high-crime group, police commonly conduct nighttime household inspections to regulate migrant activities. Nighttime inspections are unpredictable and further reinforce feelings of inferiority and insecurity among migrants. Although a migrant household is automatically subject to such inspections without a search warrant, the domestic space of permanent Beijing residents is usually free from such government intrusions today.[16]

Rural migrants are also the primary targets of street patrols. In Beijing, anyone who looks like a migrant is likely to be stopped by the police for an identification check.[17] They must answer questions about where they live, why they are in the city, and what they do for a living. Anyone without the proper card may be treated as a criminal suspect and taken to the police station for further questioning. A Wenzhou woman described to me what it was like to be constantly harassed by the police:

> I lost my identification card because my purse was stolen a couple of weeks ago. I became frightened about going out of my house at night because whenever the police see our Zhejiang people they check up on us. One day, I ran into the police and they asked me why I did not have an ID. I told them that it was stolen and that it will take several months to get a replacement card from my hometown government. They did not believe me and threatened to take me away. I begged them and eventually made a deal by paying them a 100 yuan fine. Most likely the money simply went into their own pockets because I did not get any receipt. But if I had been a Beijing resident, would they dare to treat me the same way?

In short, regulation contributes to rural migrants' sense of liminality and marginal status in urban society. This disciplinary power seeks to make migrants conform to a subject position as "secondary citizens" in the new national order of things.

Resisting Subjectification

Though floating (*liudong*) serves as a key symbol in the dominant discourse for stereotyping rural migrants as a highly unstable and chaotic social group, its meaning can be reworked by migrants for a different end. As Herzfeld points out, stereotypes tend to portray group characteristics as "fixed, simple, and unambiguous" and thus "disguise their own enormous capacity for multiple interpretation" (1992: 72–73). By seeming unambiguous and semantically stable, stereotypes are powerful justifications for prejudice and social exclusion. Although stereotypes tend to offer a single interpretation, they are not always seamless and can be contested or subverted by the dominated group under certain circumstances (see also Thomas 1992). In this section, I look at how a counterdiscourse on floating and urban belonging is created by Chinese migrant entrepreneurs by using Wenzhou migrants as a point of reference.

REVALORIZING FLOATING

In everyday conversation, Wenzhou migrants frequently present themselves as a people with a long history of mobility. Most can tell stories about how early and how far their ancestors and Wenzhou fellows traveled or migrated for business purposes all over China as well as to Europe, Southeast Asia, and North America (see Minghuan Li 1998). The story that they are most proud to tell is about Wenzhou sojourners in Paris who have established their own enclave based on family restaurants and garment manufacturing (see Xu 1993). It is common for Wenzhou people today to migrate to Russia and to Eastern and Western Europe as tradesmen. As one of them summed up, "wherever there are markets, there are Wenzhou people." The self-fashioning of floating as a way of life constitutes an important part of their identity. Such positive interpretations of spatial mobility are explained by one middle-aged Wenzhou trader as follows:

> In a new era to enliven a market economy, floating is inevitable. Willing to take risks, to eat bitterness, and to move from place to place for better economic opportunities is the core of the Wenzhou spirit. There is a popular saying: "Zhejiang people are like the sun. Wherever they go, they bring sunlight to brighten the place."[18] This means that we can bring prosperity wherever we go! By contrast, Beijing people are spoiled and lazy, and they lack creativity. Rather than going out to improve their situation, Beijingers would rather sit at home drinking plain water and eating steamed buns. Why? Because they do not want to take any risks or to eat bitterness. If our country really wants to develop a free-market economy, the entire nation should learn from our Wenzhou people rather than denouncing our innovative practices.

By linking spatial movement to a series of positive qualities such as vitality, bravery, flexibility, and being market-oriented, the Wenzhou trader subverts the dominant interpretation of floating, reasoning that spatial mobility is entirely compatible with the new economic trajectory promoted by the state. It is precisely the freedom of mobility and trade that have revitalized a declining socialist planned economy. Fears about migration and a free flow of labor reflect a rigid and conservative mentality that lags behind the national economic reforms. By pointing out the contradictions and inconsistencies of government policies and practices, migrants are able to use a liberal voice to criticize xenophobic urban attitudes toward their new spatial and economic practices.

Indeed, maximizing the use of consumer markets through migration is considered the secret of Wenzhou migrants' business success. For them, floating has become a necessary way of life and part of their mercantile-oriented identity. A Wenzhou woman once told me why she liked being an independent entrepreneur even though it required hard work: "Because I have freedom! With my own business, I do not have to go to work for other people on a fixed schedule or take orders daily from any officials or bosses." This sense of a self as mobile, flexible, and self-reliant is often juxtaposed with the static life of the majority of urbanites within the state-owned sectors. As another Wenzhou migrant perceived, "The biggest difference between us and them [Beijingers] is this: they rely on the state; we rely on ourselves. As a result, they are afraid of losing their benefits provided by the state and are tied to one place for the rest of their lives; but we have little to lose."

CREATING ALTERNATIVE MODES OF BELONGING

Many Chinese migrants, especially traders, have also developed a new vision of social space and belonging that transcends a single fixed locality. As Rouse (1995) has pointed out, in the discourse of (im)migration dominated by a bipolar framework, the experiences of migratory people are often conceived of in only two possible ways: circular and linear. In the first scenario, people retain their old identities, remain oriented toward their place of origin, and eventually return home. In the second, people abandon their homes and identities to settle in and become assimilated by the receiving society. Such bipolar assumptions of identity and social belonging are also the dominant way of thinking about the social trajectories of the floating population in contemporary China. Yet over the years, many migrants have developed a different sense of social space and identity, which is not based on a single geographic location as defined by the *hukou* system but is oriented toward two or more locales simultaneously. The following anecdote illustrates this multi-locale mode of thinking about self and community.

One day I was riding a minibus with several Wenzhou migrant entrepreneurs. For some reason, our conversation turned to the topic of "home."

One of them said to me: "I miss my home a lot. You just cannot imagine how beautiful and charming the landscape of my home province is. Walking along the misty West Lake in the morning and wandering in the jadelike green Yandang Mountains is like living in heaven. Although my village is small and remote, the hills are always green and the water is crystal clear [*shanqing shuixiu*]." I was touched by his homesickness and asked him why then he had decided to leave his hometown and stay in Beijing for so many years. He continued: "We left our homes not because we were poor and had to come to beg in the city as many Beijingers imagine. We left our homes because we wanted to make more money; and to make money we needed larger consumer markets. I can't help missing my hometown and I try to go back home once or twice a year; but this does not mean that I need to physically live there all the time. As private business people, we must be able to go wherever is best for business."

For this man, as well as for many other migrant entrepreneurs, migration (as a strategy for capital accumulation) and the creation of their urban settlements do not necessarily indicate a diminishing of their emotional and practical ties to their places of origin.[19] They are able to reconcile a local identity oriented toward their hometowns with a translocal identity based on spatial mobility. While moving to different places for entrepreneurial activities throughout their lifetimes, they also maintain close social and economic ties with their rural origins. For example, almost all rural migrants in China maintain the family plot of land allocated by the state. They also build new houses back home even though they are physically absent from the village for most of the year (see Figures 2 and 3). As they accumulate more savings, some of them use the money to establish small enterprises in their places of origin, and many donate money to rebuild ancestral halls, temples, and roads in their home villages (Mayfair Yang 1996).

In more recent years, improved transportation has reduced the time it takes to travel between locales, thus making it easier for migrants to maintain contact with their native places. The first airport in the Wenzhou region was opened in the early 1990s, and the railway connection was completed in the mid-1990s. Because of their increased economic power, many Wenzhou migrants can now afford to return home by air or train. During the Spring Festival, plane and train tickets are often completely sold out. As a response to the increasing need for long-distance transportation, migrants have established family-run travel agencies that offer chartered bus trips between Wenzhou and Beijing. During the special holiday period, villages and towns

2.   A nonmigrant peasant's house

in Wenzhou become unusually crowded as migrants return home to hold wedding banquets, build new houses, and visit relatives, friends, and ancestral tombs.

Further, improved telecommunications have made it even easier for migrants to maintain everyday social contacts with their friends and relatives in their places of origins. Most rural households in Wenzhou today have telephones. In the settlement in Beijing, it is common to see Wenzhou migrants carrying cellular phones and pagers because they are more easily obtained than residential phone service and also offer flexibility for conducting business. Public telephone booths run by private citizens can be found on almost every street corner in the Wenzhou migrant community.

In the context of Mexican migration to the United States, Rouse (1991, 1992) conceives of Mexican migrant communities spanning two or more locales as a transnational "migrant circuit." He argues that it is the entire circuit, rather than a single geographic place, that constitutes the primary social arena for the migrants. Although the Wenzhou migration I examine here does not cross international boundaries, this group does migrate transregionally. This sense of belonging in more than one social space is not uncommon among Chinese migrant entrepreneurs, and it challenges the

3.   The house of a newly rich migrant in Yueqing, Wenzhou

official conception of identity as "belonging," which means living in one's *hukou* residence.

CLAIMING URBAN MEMBERSHIP THROUGH CONSUMPTION

While maintaining close social ties with their rural origins, many migrant entrepreneurs and workers in China have also developed multiple socioeconomic involvements in the cities: through both the establishment of their private businesses and native-place-based settlements and through material consumption. Although rural migrants are officially defined as nonurban citizens and thus have no access to state-sponsored goods and services, the development of a market economy has opened up new access to consumer goods outside the state's redistribution regime. Because of their remarkable business success, migrant entrepreneurs generally enjoy a high degree of consumption power. As their economic capital has increased, they have also developed new ways of thinking about their relationships to the city.[20] An encounter I had with a young Wenzhou migrant woman illustrates the new conceptions that link wealth and consumption with identity formation.

Ruilan first left home with her elder brother for Xi'an at the age of fifteen and then went to Beijing with her brother's family five years later. When I met her, she was twenty-four years old. I was immediately struck by her sense of fashion: she wore a pair of nicely made leather boots that cost eight hundred yuan and carried a stylish black leather handbag that cost five hundred yuan. She made a point of telling me that the shoes and handbag were both from Saite, one of the most expensive shopping centers in Beijing. The total cost of these two items was more than twice the average monthly income of a Beijing household, which was five hundred yuan in 1995, according to a survey by the *Beijing Evening Daily*. Out of curiosity, I asked her: "Do you frequently spend money like this? How much do you usually spend a month?" Ruilan said: "Yes, this is nothing. I get five thousand yuan a month from my brother for helping out with his business. . . . He has a clothing stall in the Jingwen center, and business is very good. Sometimes, he can make 400,000 to 500,000 yuan a year." Over time, I came to realize that Ruilan was just one of many young Wenzhou migrants who see wealth and material consumption as an important way of gaining social status and cosmopolitan-based identity.

During my fieldwork, my conversations with young Wenzhou migrants frequently involved their perceptions of Beijing and the meaning of belonging to the city. What struck me most in their accounts was their correlation of urban belonging with economic status and the ability to consume goods and services in the city. Ruilan clearly articulated this view: "Let me put it this way: If you have a lot of money, Beijing is a place of great fun; you can do whatever you want and dream. But if you do not have money, it is a hell; and you can hardly survive." I asked whether she wanted to get a Beijing *hukou* so that she could stay in Beijing as long as she wanted. She continued:

> I do not need a Beijing *hukou* to stay in Beijing as long as I have money. Look at those arrogant Beijing *xiaojie* [ladies]—they work in state-owned units but make little money. They cannot even afford to go to expensive restaurants or to shop at Saite and Guomao [the International Trade Center Mall] as we do. How can they be so proud? Just for the piece of *hukou* paper? . . . Don't they realize that today's society belongs to those of us who have money? As long as we have money, Beijing is the place for us.

For many Wenzhou migrants like Ruilan, urban belonging in an era of rapid commodification and commercialization is no longer defined by one's *hukou* status. Rather, they redefine social status and reclaim urban membership through flexible consumption practices. Some Wenzhou migrants reason that since they contribute to the city significantly through production, trade, and consumption they are more entitled to be citizens of Beijing than the local people are. This notion of membership challenges the birth-ascribed *hukou* status by asserting achieved rights to a place through one's economic and consumption practices.

Why is material consumption such an important component in Wenzhou migrants' search for urban citizenship and rights to the city? First and most important, as members of the floating population, Wenzhou migrants are denied formal urban citizenship; thus they have to seek alternative ways of reinforcing their presence in the city by participating in urban social and economic life. Conspicuous consumption is one of the ways by which they make their presence a prominent element of the everyday urban social land-scape. By buying things, they make the city serve them and are thus assert-ing another kind of citizenship—consumer citizenship. But the emphasis on material consumption among Wenzhou migrants is also closely related to two characteristics of this group of people. First, these are predominantly young migrants (mostly fifteen to thirty-five years old) who came of age in an emerging mass consumer culture during the reform years. It is no won-der that they, like their peers of the same generation, easily turn to material consumption as a way to acquire urbanity and modernity. Second, this group of migrants is generally wealthier than others. The consumption power that the majority of Wenzhou migrants in Beijing enjoy is ultimately determined by their better position in the system of economic production. As small pri-vate business owners, Wenzhou migrants have the means to accumulate more wealth than other migrants and ordinary Beijing residents.[21]

Skinner (1958) and Oxfeld (1996) have both described a strong correla-tion between wealth and social status in overseas Chinese communities in Southeast Asia. They suggest that migrants tend to emphasize wealth as an indicator of status because most Chinese emigrated to improve their eco-nomic situations. This is also true in the Wenzhou migrant community, where wealth and consumption power are regarded as the primary compo-nents of social status. While "making money" (*zhuanqian*) and "doing busi-ness" (*jingshang*) have become popular mottoes for Chinese people in the reform era, this impulse is most clearly felt among migrant entrepreneurs because they are closest to the markets.

It is important to point out, however, that migrants' attempts to formu-late new modes of identity and social belonging do not mean that they can completely move beyond the shadow of the *hukou* in everyday life. Particularly when it comes to their children's future and education, the *hukou* barriers become obvious. Almost all migrant parents I spoke with said that their non-Beijing *hukou* status will negatively affect the lives of their children, who may well not want to stay in private business and may prefer to pursue professional or other careers in the city. Many of them believe that money alone cannot fully change their marginal position in society, but money and educational capital together will help their children achieve a better social status and encounter less urban discrimination.

Conclusion

The concept of a floating population was invented at a particular time in recent Chinese history and has been employed by the state as a unified social category in order to regulate and monitor migrants in the rapidly changing post-Mao socioeconomic order. In this process, both discursive forms of power, such as naming, categorizing, and representation, and nondiscursive forms of everyday regulatory state power served to define the social reality and position of migrants in the society. The proliferation of discourse on the floating population is by no means a historical accident; it is intrinsically linked to the changing modes of governmentality—a focus that is shifting from suppressing migration to regulating migrants more strenuously.

In viewing subject-making as a dialectical process of being-made and self-making, I have sought to illustrate that Chinese rural migrants do not just react passively to state domination; rather they try to make sense of their own experiences and develop new senses of self. There are official attempts to subjugate rural migrants to an inferior social position, but migrants often resist or partially subvert the official definition of their subject positions. Using Wenzhou migrants as an example, I have shown that although migrants may not be able to reject the category imposed on them, they are able to alter the meaning of that category by redefining floating as a positive way of life. By "reconsuming" categories that are denounced by the official discourse and through actual urban consumption, these migrants are able to craft a different sense of self and a sense of social belonging in more than one geographic place.

2.   Commercial Culture, Social Networks, and Migration Passages

Beginning in this chapter, my ethnographic lens zooms in on the lives and struggles of Wenzhou migrants and their community in Beijing. Although I focus on a single large migrant settlement, my analysis considers the broader geopolitics of Beijing and the rapidly changing political economy of late-socialist China. Before I delve into the reconfigurations of space, power, and social relations in this unofficial migrant community, it may be useful to trace the historical and cultural roots of the entrepreneurial spirit that has nourished Wenzhou migrants' spatial and commercial practices.

What cultural and economic conditions gave rise to an unceasing flow of migrants from rural Wenzhou to metropolitan Beijing? What kinds of social networks did Wenzhou migrants use to sustain such a large-scale long-distance migration? How did these migrants transform a once impoverished suburban area into a dynamic commercial center of the private garment business? Answers to these questions require one to heed both the historical-structural changes in the sending and receiving areas and the individual and family migration experiences through which macro-level forces were transformed into local practices.

Kinship ties and native-place networks played a significant role in sustaining the migratory flows and in the early formation of the Wenzhou migrant community in Beijing. These traditional social networks were not opposed to the development of a modern market economy; instead they provided the organizational framework for Chinese rural migrants' social life and private businesses. Further, Wenzhou migrants' current entrepreneurial activities were shaped and conditioned by their regional commercial culture and a pervasive anti-Confucianist "entrepreneurial ethic" (a term borrowed from Harrell 1985). Such practices in turn reshaped the distinct local mercantile culture and socioeconomic conditions of the region. Thus the Wenzhou migration was neither a result of migrants' free will nor a passive response to state policies. Their spatial mobility was conditioned by larger political and economic circumstances, but migrants also pushed the boundaries of the old system through their persistent and innovative capital accumulation strategies.[1]

My analysis of the Wenzhou migration draws from theoretical insights into the dialectical relationship between structure and practice, culture and history (see Bourdieu 1977; Giddens 1979; Mintz 1985; Roseberry 1989; Sahlins 1976). For example, working through the concept of "structuration," Giddens seeks to bridge human agency with structure by arguing that action and structure presuppose one another: all social practices are situated activities shaped by the structural conditions at a given time, and institutions are products of extended practices in time and space. In a similar spirit, Roseberry proposes to view culture (historically formed values and worldviews) as "at once socially constituted (it is a product of present and past activity) and socially constitutive (it is part of the meaningful context in which activity takes places)" (Roseberry 1991: 30). Since Chinese culture is internally differentiated by subgeographic regions and changes, it cannot be treated as a static, homogeneous system. Skinner (1976, 1977a), for example, divides China into eight large macroregions, each constituting an economic system and yet interconnecting with one another. These macroregions are not only different economic systems but also distinct social systems (see also Sangren 1987). I thus suggest that it is the distinct "cultural milieu" (Willis 1977) of the Wenzhou region that mediates between macro political-economic forces and micro migrant practices.

Commercial Culture and the Wenzhou Spirit

The majority of migrants in Zhejiangcun came from two areas under the jurisdiction of a prefecture-level city, Wenzhou, in Zhejiang province: Yueqing, a county-level city, and Yongjia, a rural county. In this book, I usually use Wenzhou as a shorthand to refer to the broader Wenzhou region, which includes Wenzhou city, two surrounding county-level cities, and six rural counties. Wenzhou, located in south Zhejiang province, is part of the southeast coast macroregion in the Chinese regional system (Skinner 1976). Because of its mountainous terrain cut by numerous rivers and valleys, a distinct regional dialect, and active bandit activities in the past, Wenzhou has a notorious reputation as an unruly place that is difficult for the state to reach (see Naquin and Rawski 1987; Parris 1993; Rankin 1986).[2] In the first three decades of communist rule, Wenzhou was the most impoverished and underdeveloped area in Zhejiang province. Local officials and scholars often attribute such backwardness to three factors: its rugged, mountainous land-scape, which hindered the development of ground transportation; its extremely low ratio of land to population, which was 0.37 *mu* per person in 1994 (Wenzhou Statistics Bureau 1995); and scarce capital investment by the central socialist state (see Li Haoran 1996; Lin 1992).[3] Taking up 38 percent of the province's land and 15 percent of its population, Wenzhou was largely ignored by the state for industrial and commercial developments partly because of its geographic proximity to Taiwan, which made it vulnerable to war damage.

Given its disadvantaged position in Mao's era, how did Wenzhou become one of most dynamic and innovative economic regions in reform-era China? Under what conditions did Wenzhou people use migration as a strategy for accumulating private capital? The following historical and regional account examines how a particular cultural milieu embodied in what I call the "Wenzhou spirit" helped to shape people's current practices. Much of the explanation of post-Mao migration has focused on a general, structural account of the changing national political economy, such as rural decollec-tivization and rapid urban economic growth (see Banister 1986; L. Cheng 1996; Hsieh 1993; Xiushi Yang 1996). Yet little attention has been paid to the local histories and cultures that shape migration flows in and out of a given region.[4]

PETTY TRADE AND MERCANTILE CONSCIOUSNESS

Wenzhou people tend to trace their spatial mobility and merchant activities to an early period of rapid commercialization. Wenzhou had been a pros-perous area with flourishing trade and petty commodity production as early as the Tang and Song dynasties. Although ground transportation was poor, water transportation was highly developed because of the region's numerous rivers and proximity to the sea. Wenzhou was also known as one of the ear-liest and best boat production bases in China. During the Tang dynasty (around A.D. 674), it became an important port city engaged in trade with Japan. In the Song dynasty (A.D. 999), Wenzhou was formally designated by the imperial court as an open port for foreign trade, and its commercial activities quickly extended to neighboring countries such as Korea and Cambodia, as well as to China's coastal areas, such as Guangdong and Fujian. The imperial court of the Southern Song dynasty subsequently established an institution known as the *shibowu* in this area to regulate overseas trade (see Zheng 1991; Zhou Houcai 1990). Successful sea trade further boosted fam-ily-based, small-commodity production including: tea, oranges, silk products, porcelain, leather, timber, medicines, and Buddhist texts and art objects that were traded both within China and elsewhere in East Asia. A famous Northern Song poet compared the port city of Wenzhou to "Little Hangzhou" because of its flourishing commercial activities (Li Haoran 1996: 2). Such dynamic trading and petty capitalist production nurtured a distinct mercantile cultural milieu in Wenzhou, which contrasts with the mainstream agrarian culture based on land fetishism.

However, fear of foreign invasion led the Ming and Qing states to implement the conservative *jinhai* (closing the sea) policy, which constrained commercial activities. Although sea trade and commodity production were seriously hampered by this new policy, some Wenzhou traders emigrated overseas to pursue their businesses at the turn of the twentieth century (Minghuan Li, n.d., 1998; Live 1998). Many of my informants thus claimed that this commercial tradition, mercantile consciousness, and spatial mobility were never lost among Wenzhou people.

Although petty commerce and commodity production were highly developed in Wenzhou, they were not confined to this region. Many parts of Chinese society (both urban and rural) in the eighteenth century were already highly commercialized (Naquin and Rawski 1987). Market participation brought both opportunities and anxiety to people whose lives were now under the influence of erratic market forces. What is interesting about Wenzhou is how local people today (including officials and scholars) make use of this part of history to serve their present economic practices. Conscious of the tradition of a Wenzhou commercial culture, they see their current capitalist-oriented economic activities as reflecting historical continuity rather than diverging from socialism. This vision of tradition is reinforced by the persistent influence of a well-known, unorthodox school of thought derived from this region.

The Yongjia school of thought (*Yongjia xuepai*) was promoted by two famous materialist thinkers, Ye Shi and Chenliang, from Yongjia county of Wenzhou in the Southern Song dynasty. Its influence was widely felt in the Wenzhou region, and later it became an iconoclastic ideology contesting mainstream Confucianism. Confucianism promoted a hierarchical order of occupations, which regarded only agriculture as *ben* (the "trunk," the fundamental) and denigrated trade and commerce as *mo* (the "branch," the incidental) (Ho 1962). According to this order, peasants are the true producers of value and the backbone of the nation, while merchants and craftsmen are perceived as cunning, secondary, and unstable.[5] Further, land is valorized and people's attachment to the land is highly revered. By contrast, the Yongjia school argued that the four kinds of commoners, namely *shi* (scholars), *nong* (farmers), *gong* (artisans and craftsmen), and *shang* (merchants/traders), should all be considered members of equally important *benye* (fundamental occupations). In so doing, it reclaimed a valuable position for previously belittled commercial and merchant activities in the Chinese order of things.

In examining the history of the capitalist development in Europe, Weber (1958) draws out an intimate relationship between the Protestant ethic and "the spirit of capitalism" as articulated in the pursuit of wealth by maximizing profits. In Calvinist theology, making money and accumulating wealth do not run counter to spirituality, but are a means of responding to the calling of God. In China the Yongjia school served as a counterpoint to Confucianism by glorifying merchant activities, private ownership, and profit-seeking. This subversive subculture initially grew out of the flourishing petty capitalist economy in Wenzhou and further created favorable psychological and social conditions for mercantile-oriented commercial activities. But at the same time, this entrepreneurial spirit cannot be treated as an unchanging, essentialized component of local Wenzhou culture or ethos that could simply be passed on to the next generation; rather it has been constantly created and reshaped through the practices of each new generation.

Let me further clarify my argument here. I am not suggesting that there is necessarily a direct historical link between the Yongjia school of thought that flourished many centuries ago and the current popular entrepreneurial culture in Wenzhou. My point is merely to demonstrate how history can be appropriated by people to meet their present ends. In the case of Wenzhou, my informants' citing of an ancient, unorthodox, local cultural tradition is one way they invoke and use history to validate and promote their contemporary conduct and values.

During the socialist period, especially the Great Leap Forward and the Cultural Revolution, Wenzhou's economy declined rapidly under leftist rule. Poverty became widespread. Peasants were tied to scarce land and could barely meet their basic survival needs. Traditional private handicrafts and trade were suppressed by the state because they were seen as "the tail of capitalism" or "profiteering."[6] Private businesses were labeled "underground factories," "underground stores," or "underground contract teams" and were condemned for eroding socialism and restoring capitalism. But even under those harsh political circumstances, a small number of Wenzhou peasants managed to resume covert small-scale family businesses as early as the 1970s, while some others emigrated as craftsmen and traders to other Chinese provinces (see Zheng 1991: 138–39; Parris 1993: 243). Many went to distant border areas such as Tibet, Xinjiang, and Mohe (in far northern China), and a small number were smuggled out of the country.[7] Since trade requires its practitioners to be flexible about where they live, Wenzhou people have developed their own relationship to place. They see themselves as a mobile people and regard migration as an important strategy for social mobility. Because Wenzhou sojourners are widespread within and outside China, they are informally called the Oriental Jews (*dongfang de youtairen*) or the Oriental Gypsies (*dongfang de jipusairen*). Unlike migrant workers who tend to see the city as a place to sell labor in exchange for cash, Wenzhou migrant entrepreneurs treat the city as a potential market, a highly competitive field for business ventures (Li Zhang 1998).

THE WENZHOU MODEL

A more recent influence on Wenzhou migrants' commercial engagement in Beijing can be traced back to a paradigm shift in the regional economy, which later came to be known as the Wenzhou model (*Wenzhou moshi*). This innovative economic model has four distinctive features. First, it consists of numerous private enterprises, small-scale cottage industries, and petty commerce in the Wenzhou region. To reduce the political risk of being accused of "doing capitalism," many private firms attached themselves to a state-owned enterprise to create what was called a *guahu* (hang-on household). De facto private entrepreneurs also registered their businesses as collectives with their neighborhood committee or village office. This was known as "wearing a red hat" (*dai hongmaozi*) (see Parris 1993; Tsai 1999). Second, this system is composed of large numbers of specialized wholesale petty commodity markets controlled by the Wenzhounese. For example, Qiaotou, once a small, quiet, mountain town in Wenzhou, has evolved into what is known as "the kingdom of buttons" or "the largest Oriental button market" in Asia. Buttons, a single small commodity, have profoundly transformed three poverty-stricken villages in Qiaotou into an affluent commercial zone. Third, this system is built on a network of tens of thousands of mobile Wenzhou traders throughout the country who facilitate smooth flows of raw materials and finished products from one place to another. Fourth, this system is made possible by various forms of nongovernmental financial arrangements created by people themselves to support private businesses (see Tsai 1999). These new economic practices grew out of the reviving unofficial economy permitted by local cadres in the 1970s and have spread rapidly in Wenzhou since the early 1980s, leading to some remarkable socioeconomic transformations in the region (see Yia-Ling Liu 1992; Parris 1993).

The term "Wenzhou model" first appeared in 1985 in an official newspaper, *Liberation Daily*. But not until 1986 did the term gain national attention, when it was officially announced as a new economic paradigm for China. Private economic development in Wenzhou was a highly politicized process that invoked controversial responses from different social groups. The crux of the debate was whether the Wenzhou model was socialist or capitalist. In the mid-1980s, the Wenzhou city government and the Zhejiang provincial government proposed that the central state use Wenzhou as an official site for experimenting with private economic development as a means of absorbing surplus rural laborers. This proposal was approved and carried out quickly, but it led to nationwide criticism and skepticism and heated debate in the 1980s over the nature of the Wenzhou model. Those who took a conservative view of the reforms spread criticism like this: "If one wants to see the restoration of capitalism in China today, go to Wenzhou," and, "If such experiments continue, it [Wenzhou] will soon mutate into what has happened on the other side of the Strait" [referring to capitalism in Taiwan] (Zhang Zhiren 1989: 1–2). It was not until the late 1980s that the Wenzhou model finally secured a legitimate position in China's political economy.[8] The Wenzhou model was then hailed by some scholars as "a remarkable historical transformation of Chinese peasantry to recast themselves as modern workers and merchants in an era of an advanced commodity economy" (Sun 1989: 153). By the early 1990s, there were some 800,000 Wenzhou people away from home for business-related reasons (Li Haoran 1996: 224).

My purpose in revisiting the Wenzhou model is to expose the interconnections among this economic paradigm shift, the commercial tradition, and out-migration in this region. Rather than relying on the state, Wenzhou people's economic innovations and early commitment to market forces have two significant social and political implications. First, pervasive engagement in private business nourished a strong sense of self-determination and autonomy among Wenzhou people. A laissez-faire kind of relationship has formed between individuals and the state in which local governments allow a considerable amount of freedom in private financial and commercial activities. This relationship reflects what Li Yining, a famous Chinese economist, has advocated as an ideal form of state-society dynamic: "a big society with a small government" (*dashehui xiao zhengfu*), in which the role of the state is minimized in order to allow citizens to engage in market activities. Second, the increase of economic power among rural entrepreneurs has also led to new forms of political and commercial alliances between officials and entrepreneurs, who exchange bureaucratic power for wealth. Both of these effects have had direct influence on the development of the Wenzhou migrant community in Beijing.

Migration Passages

Studies of current migration in China are mostly done by sociologists, economists, and political scientists, who tend to focus on the general patterns, structural causes, policy effects, and economic consequences based on quantitative survey data (see Banister 1986; Goldstein and Goldstein 1985; Xiushi Yang 1996; Davin 1999; Scharping 1997). Their research draws largely on three theoretical frameworks that seek to explain *why* migration takes place: the push-pull model, macro-analysis of structural and historical processes, and social networks theory (see Papademetriou 1989; Portes and Bach 1985; Wood 1981). Although these studies provide a valuable picture of the population movement trends, we know little about *how* people actually move and how structural forces affect migrants' everyday lives. The following ethnographic account aims to fill this gap by looking into the specific processes of Wenzhou migrants' spatial movement.

Previous scholarship on migration has focused on individual decision-making; and more recent studies have stressed the role of household and social networks in the process of migration (see Kam-Wing Chan 1994a; Chavez 1992; Kearney 1986; Mallee 1988; Davin 1999). This research demonstrates that migration is not just an individual effort but is often part of a family strategy for economic diversification. Personal networks facilitate migration by reducing the risk of long-distance migration; migration in turn reproduces and extends the networks. But the effects of social networks are not always harmonious. As Charles Tilly puts it, "they provide a setting for life at the destination, a basis for solidarity and mutual aid as well as division and conflict" (1990: 90). In focusing on family histories and social networks, we can discern how historical-structural forces and migrant practices dialectically inform and transform one another.

The stories of two ordinary Wenzhou families I will present indicate that migration was not a one-step effort but a long journey from place to place in search of better business opportunities. Family and native-place networking became the primary means by which Wenzhou migrants organized their merchandise production, trade, and social lives and played a significant role in channeling migration flows and sustaining their informal economy at the destination. But before moving to specific accounts of individual and family migration experiences, let me offer a brief discussion of two cultural principles related to the making of migrant social networks.

PLACE BONDS ('DIYUAN'), BLOOD BONDS ('XUEYUAN')

In *Earthbound China* (1985), Fei points out that people in traditional Chinese society were connected primarily through two ways: *xueyuan*, literally, consanguinity, or by blood; and *diyuan*, referring to people's attachment to a specific place, which was often their own or their ancestors' place of birth. He argues that in most traditional societies, these two concepts are inseparable because "*diyuan* is no more than the extension of *xueyuan*. . . . The idea of 'being born and dying in the same place' fixes the relationship between people and places" (1985: 72). For the same reason, *jiguan* (native place of origin), he argues, is simply "the spatial projection of blood connection" experienced by a society with growing spatial mobility, and it is a subjective negation of the actual spatial separation. Fei concludes that commerce and market activities are difficult in a *xueyuan* society because market exchanges require people to "bracket" their intimate kin relations and act as strangers.[9] He suggests that only under a new kind of relationship that ignores kinship bonds and is based on rational market relations can a modern market economy thrive.

While it is correct to emphasize the centrality of the place bond and the blood bond in Chinese society, it is problematic to oppose them to modern market development. Numerous studies have demonstrated that migrants commonly use kin and native-place ties to develop their businesses within and outside China (see Crissman 1967; Goodman 1995; Honig 1992; Oxfeld 1996; Rowe 1984; Sangren 1984; Skinner 1976; Bernard Wang 1987). For example, Goodman (1995) illustrates the powerful role of preexisting native-place ties in the formation of sojourning communities in Shanghai and in nationalist movements at the turn of the century. This ethnography will also attest that traditional social networks do not hamper a modern market economy; rather they provide the very social basis on which rural migrants organize their social and economic lives. This practice is inseparable from the larger Chinese entrepreneurial practices that stress familism and mutual benefit in other contexts (see Cohen 1976; Fried 1953; Gates 1987; Greenhalgh 1988; Naquin and Rawski 1987). While stressing the positive role of family and native-place networks, however, we must not obscure inequalities and exploitation within the household and the native-place group.[10]

Xueyuan and *diyuan* are fluid categories that vary with the social context. For example, family strategies for mobilizing social resources among Wenzhou migrants today go far beyond the narrowly defined notion of *xueyuan*. Affinal relatives are important elements of the kinship alliances for migrant families. Indeed, not only relatives in the patriline but also members of the wife's natal family have merged to form a sort of informal social and economic coalition in their urban settlement. In addition, fictive kinship relations created among friends and fellow villagers are also a popular way of extending one's social alliances. For instance, recognizing a powerful couple as the "dry mother" and "dry father" of one's own child can create a flexible kinship alliance between two otherwise unrelated families.

The boundaries of the native-place bond are even more complicated and unstable. There are many different ways of defining a common place of origin: by village, township, county, region, or province, depending on the context (see Crissman 1967; Skinner 1958). In Zhejiangcun, although people from the same county (*xian*) and township (*xiang*) were commonly taken as *laoxiang* or *tongxiang* (fellows from the same place), the boundaries sometimes contracted to the village or expanded to encompass the larger Wenzhou region and even Zhejiang province. The existence of a common identification among Wenzhou migrants on one level, however, did not always obscure internal social differentiations based on finer spatial demarcations.

EARLY MIGRATION JOURNEYS

Almost every Wenzhou migrant has a unique migration story. But their diverse experiences also strike some common chords: the centrality of kinship ties and native-place networks. Here, the experience of Ruihen and his family illustrates the early migration journeys many Wenzhou migrants endured. I was introduced to Ruihen by his younger sister at his clothing stall in Zhejiangcun. It was a hot day, and the trading building was crowded and noisy. That day, Ruihen was busy with his customers and had little time to talk to me. Later I learned that Friday and Saturday were usually his busiest days because most retailers buy goods in the early weekend in order to have them for sale in their stalls or shops on Sunday and Monday. The second time I picked a Tuesday and the marketplace was quieter. Ruihen was able to spend almost the entire afternoon talking with me, without much interruption.

Ruihen was born in a village of Hongqiao township. When I met him in 1995 he was twenty-eight and married, with two small children. At eighteen he had left home for the first time for Lhasa, Tibet, with a distant relative who had several years' experience running a private clothing business. He recalled that first journey vividly:

It was a very, very long way to go. In those days, we could not afford airplane tickets. In fact, I had never seen a train before, let alone an airplane. We were lucky to find a truck driver and offered him a small fee for a ride. He worked for a state enterprise and drove a freight truck, transporting vegetables and coal into Tibet. We were on the road during the day and slept in the truck at night. After seven days, we finally reached the periphery of the Tibetan plateau. Because of the very high altitude, it was chilly at night. The three of us had to get out of the truck and stay in a cheap small motel until dawn.

After a difficult journey, the three of them finally arrived in Lhasa, a remote, mysterious, underdeveloped city in the eyes of most Han Chinese. Ruihen was very excited and immediately telegraphed his parents in Wenzhou (telephones were still scarce) upon arrival. In those years, all sorts of terrifying stories circulated about Lhasa, and it remained unfamiliar to most Han Chinese. "I often heard people saying that there are many dark caves in Tibet and that no men can ever come out once they enter them. I knew several migrant workers from Sichuan who died there because of high blood pressure exacerbated by the lack of oxygen at an extraordinarily high altitude," said Ruihen.

For the majority of migrants, leaving home (*chumen*) was a significant event that marked the beginning of their "territorial passages" (Chavez 1992: 4). Leaving one's hometown for business began as early as age sixteen for many Wenzhou migrants. With that departure they crossed a line in the categorical order of people, entering something like what van Gennep (1960) describes as the "liminal stage" in ritual processes, or Victor Turner (1967) calls a state of being "betwixt and between." No longer peasants or permanent urban residents, rural migrants in China became floaters who did not have a clear structural position in society. *Chumen*, which meant going to a different world for work or businesses, was to them a synonym for "migration."

Life on the high Tibetan plateau was not easy for a Han Chinese. Language barriers and food differences were two basic problems. But Ruihen and his Wenzhou fellows gradually learned some simple Tibetan and were able to interact with the local people. The harsh weather made fresh

Pension.

vegetables and fruit scarce. Only a limited amount of rice and pickled pork was available on the black market at a high price. After growing up with rice and vegetables, Wenzhou migrants found it difficult to adapt to the local diet, which consisted largely of dairy products and preserved foods. There was no electricity either. So they had to use oil lamps for lighting and dried cow dung for cooking and heating fuel. Despite the loneliness and the harsh environment, Ruihen survived.

With the help of the elder relative who brought him to Tibet, and with several thousand yuan his parents had borrowed from friends and relatives, Ruihen was able to start a small clothing business. He began by making pants, which required less skill and initial capital than other garments. Although Ruihen had barely finished elementary school, he had learned some sewing skills at an early age. Sewing and tailoring were generally considered feminine work in China, but because Wenzhou had a long local handicraft tradition it was not uncommon for Wenzhou men to learn these skills. Soon Ruihen discovered that there was a small group of Wenzhou migrants in the clothing business in Lhasa. He quickly grew close to his *laoxiang*. Since he did not know how to make jackets well, he took his own cloth to another Wenzhou family and asked them to make jackets for him at the price of five yuan per piece. Then he matched the jackets with the pants he made to create a complete outfit. This was an early simple form of cooperation between households. Ruihen worked extremely hard and tried to handle production and sales by himself. At that time, it was difficult to find marketplaces where one could sell privately produced consumer goods. He recalled:

> I worked day and night with little time to sleep. Normally I could produce five to six pairs of pants at night and took them out for sale during the day. In those days, there was no designated marketplace like the stalls and counters we have now. So we just set up a small bench with a piece of cardboard on top in a large square at the center of the city. That was my "counter"! But the business went well. For the first year, I made a little over three thousand yuan, considered a lot of money in those days.

In those days, few Wenzhou migrants stayed in one place for a long time. Instead, they moved from place to place in search of better business opportunities. After paying off his debts and saving several thousand yuan, Ruihen decided to leave isolated Tibet and open his business in another city. He first considered the capital of Xinjiang and made a short trip to visit his *laoxiang* there. Upon learning that the clothing market in Xinjiang was not very good, he decided to head for Taiyuan, the provincial seat of Shanxi. He chose this city because his eldest brother had once worked in Taiyuan as a self-employed construction worker and had later established his own clothing business there. Ruihen thought that he could utilize his brother's networks to set up his own business. Up to that point, each of Ruihen's moves was connected to relatives or friends from his native village.

Ruihen and his uncle arrived in Taiyuan in 1986 along with several young female workers from their hometown. They planned to produce their own garments and sell them directly from their own counters. At that time, state commercial enterprises had just begun to lease counter space to independent entrepreneurs. So they were able to rent two small counters in a state-owned department store. Each was only 1.5 square meters but cost as much as three thousand yuan per year. Market competition was a merciless battlefield in which success was never guaranteed. After the first year, his more experienced and skilled uncle had earned thirty thousand yuan from his business, but Ruihen had lost more than ten thousand yuan. He explained to me how it happened:

> We both began by making women's coats. Although my uncle gave me some advice and help from time to time, our businesses were separate. I had never made coats before and did not really know how. The four girls I brought from home were not very experienced either. I thought we could just follow measurements and designs in fashion books. But the quality of the coats we produced turned out to be unsatisfactory. As a result, our products did not sell well. Most customers went for my uncle's and neighbor's. I had to sell our products at an extremely low price, something like thirty yuan each, half of the production cost, to prevent further losses from overstocking. That was a big blow for me, but I learned a lesson.

Despite this downturn, Ruihen did not give up. He spent several months learning how to make high-quality coats from his uncle and then taught his workers. He also went back home to borrow more money in order to keep his business going. Because he had had a relatively successful business in Tibet and had paid off the previous debt, he was able to convince some of the villagers to lend him more cash. In the second year, with an improved product, Ruihen made a profit of ten thousand yuan. His success continued for five years in Taiyuan, and by 1991 he had accumulated nearly eighty thousand yuan.

According to a survey of 120 Wenzhou migrants in Zhejiangcun, nearly 70 percent of them had been to at least one province other than Zhejiang

(Wang Chunguang 1995: 98). Of the migrants I interviewed, about 80 percent had been to two or more towns and cities before arriving in Beijing. They had also made numerous trips back to their home villages for financial support, labor recruitment, and other purposes. Therefore, the movement of many Chinese migrants is often not between two geographic points only, but from one point (the hometown) to many other places. As Logan has put it, "migration is not a one-step, final process which forever separates them [migrants] from their rural homeland but rather a continual exchange between city and country" (1981: 238).

It is worth noting here that most of the cities Wenzhou migrants had traveled to early in the reform era were located in less-developed peripheral areas like Tibet, Inner Mongolia, Xinjiang, and Yunnan. They chose those places in order to avoid the more stringent government controls present in the more centrally located cities. State migration policies in the early 1980s were still rigid. Staying and working in places other than one's *hukou* residential area without official authorization was illegal. As one Wenzhou migrant recalled: "In those days, we usually did not go to Beijing because it was not open to the outside world. Because Beijing is the national capital, the rules are strict and vigorously reinforced! We ordinary people did not dare to go there, let alone stay for an extended period of time." It was not until the late 1980s and early 1990s, with the strengthening of urban reforms and changes in government policies, that large numbers of migrants began to pour into Beijing.

Ruihen's experiences indicate that kinship and native-place networks were crucial for migrants in choosing their destinations, acquiring initial capital, setting up a business, recruiting workers, sharing information, and learning business skills. Let us look at labor recruitment more closely. Few Wenzhou migrants initiated their journeys alone. They usually departed from home with other relatives or friends from the same village. They chose a particular destination often because a relative or village member had already established some kind of social and economic base there. Those with migration experience were likely to bring relatives or friends from their home villages. This practice was called *dai*, which meant to take someone along and, more important, look after him or her. Usually a skilled senior relative would take a couple of junior relatives who were willing to work as helpers or apprentices. After a couple of years, when the junior members learned enough tailoring skills and had some business experience, they would set up their own independent businesses. Over time, an extended network of "chain migration" based on such practices formed among

Wenzhou migrants. This pattern was also common in other Chinese immigrant communities in Southeast Asia and North America (see Oxfeld 1996;
Paul Siu 1987; Skinner 1958; Bernard Wang 1987).[11]

There was a general principle of using "one's own people" (*zijiren*),
which normally included people in the following order of preference: direct
family members, relatives, fellow villagers, and people from the same township or county. Recruiting labor from one's own area not only reduced transportation costs, but also helped an entrepreneur form a reliable, stable, hard-
working labor force (see also Bernard Wang 1982, 1987). Given these social
ties, young workers were likely to become dependent on and loyal to their
employers and unlikely to run away. Their shared regional and cultural backgrounds also allowed employers to claim these workers as part of the household (at least on a rhetorical level) and avoid being criticized for crude labor
exploitation.[12]

Taking family members and relatives out of the rural villages had both
practical and symbolic purposes. It could reduce the internal production
cost, but it was also related to the notion of "face" and kinship responsibility. I once asked a Wenzhou man why, after residing in Beijing for more than
ten years, he continued to bring his relatives out of the village. He explained:

> Nobody wants to have poor relatives! If I had a poor brother, I would try to
> give him some money to help him out. My wife might be very unhappy
> about my giving our money to relatives on my side of the family. The same
> situation would be true for my wife if she had a poor relative. So the best way
> is that every relative gets rich and then no one will come to beg for money
> from you. Our Wenzhou people stress family bonds and mutual responsibil-
> ity. It is not good for a rich man to have poor relatives because people will
> laugh at you for being selfish and not willing to help out your own kin.

As more and more Wenzhou people established their own businesses,
workers became scarce. Thus, in the early 1990s, aside from employing
young people (mostly girls age fifteen to eighteen) from one's county, many
Wenzhou migrant households also began to hire workers from other
provinces, such as Hunan, Sichuan, and Hubei. Two distinct social classes
formed according to people's position in economic production and their
place of origin: Wenzhou migrants were the bosses because they owned the
means of production, and young workers from other regions were the wage
laborers.

Migrants raised the initial capital for starting a private garment manufacturing business predominantly through informal, private financial arrange-

ments. Kin-based networks were the most important source of private capital. According to Wang's survey of 171 Wenzhou migrants, 68 percent borrowed money from relatives, friends, or other private sources, 12 percent
took loans from state banks, and about 20 percent used their own personal
savings (Wang Chunguang 1995: 124). Wenzhou migrants rarely put savings
in the bank, but reinvested them in their own business or lent their money
out to earn interest.

It is important to note that this capital-raising strategy was not motivated
by the sense of *renqing* (human feeling, emotion) that bound together those
in rural society (Kipnis 1997; Yunxiang Yan 1996), but was largely based on
shrewd calculations of cost and return, even between family members. In
other words, there was little sentiment involved in lending money. This
instrumentally oriented financial practice brought extraordinarily high
returns: the annual interest rate on a private loan ranged between 25 and 30
percent. But lending money by word of mouth was potentially risky; if the
borrower's business failed the lending party might lose both the principal and
the interest. Kinship and *laoxiang* ties helped reduce the risk of money lending since the lender usually knew something about the business sense and
reliability of a family member.

INTO THE "FORBIDDEN CITY"

Beijing was once known for its conservatism and for being closed to outsiders, but gradually, as the post-Mao reforms took effect, the door to
Beijing was pushed open.[13] Although some Wenzhou migrant pioneers first
appeared in Nanyuan township during 1982 and 1983, it was not until 1985
that migrants began to congregate there in great numbers. The timing of this
influx was closely correlated with the progress of urban commercial reforms.
In the early 1980s, most Chinese cities were still stranded in a rigid, centrally
planned economy. Urban residents struggled to obtain the necessities of
everyday life—vegetables and meat, suitable clothing, child care, and repair
services. In Beijing there was an urgent need to develop the service sector
in order to resolve these basic problems.[14]

Outside the city, after several years of rural reforms, peasants were eager
to sell their own agricultural products directly in the city; others hoped to
open small businesses in Beijing, which had a potentially huge consumer
market. The initial response from the municipal government was to block
(*du*) the influx of rural migrant workers and tradesmen and drive out those
who were already there. But this policy did not effectively prevent migrants
from entering Beijing. Those who had already made it to the city proved

that their goods and services were in demand by the urban population. As a result, the government began allowing some peasants to sell their products in the city and to provide basic services. In 1981 the Beijing municipal government passed an ordinance establishing officially regulated marketplaces (*nongmao shichang*) where peasants could trade their agricultural products directly. On May 31, 1985, Beijing Mayor Chen Xitong said to some Hebei farmers: "On behalf of the Beijing people, I welcome and thank you all for coming to sell vegetables in Beijing and enriching the markets of the capital" (Shi 1993: 103). Two days later, the *Beijing Daily* reported Chen's speech, which was regarded by many as officially sanctioning a market economy and migration into Beijing. Indeed, many of my migrant informants quoted Chen's words to legitimate their stay in the city. As they put it, "we are invited by the government!"

Shortly after 1985, two more important policies were implemented in the spirit of "opening up and enlivening the economy" (*kaifang gaohuo*). The Beijing government encouraged peasant entrepreneurs to set up basic services such as restaurants, retail stores, and repair shops. In 1978 there had been 15,000 registered small private businesses in the service and trade sectors in Beijing; by 1988 the number had reached 111,000. In addition, several thousand small-scale, state-owned commercial enterprises were transformed into small units that could be leased (*zulin*) to individual entrepreneurs beginning in 1986. Two years later, some large and mid-sized state commercial enterprises began to adopt a similar system of contracting (*chengbao*) (Duan et al. 1989). These path-breaking new practices sought to salvage unprofitable state enterprises while encouraging individual entrepreneurs (both Beijing residents and migrants) to participate in the private sector. After a decade of development, Beijing is now imbued with flourishing petty capitalism; every street has become a marketplace. The door of the "forbidden city" was finally opened up.[15]

It was in this context that Ruihen and other Wenzhou migrants entered Beijing. He recalled, "I heard from my *laoxiang* that the garment market in Beijing is excellent because of the city's central geographic location and convenient transportation system. Not only do Beijing residents buy our products, so do small retailers from all over the country." He decided to follow in the footsteps of fellow villagers who had arrived in Beijing before him.

But why did Wenzhou migrants choose Nanyuan township as the base for developing their enclave? To answer this question, we must first familiarize ourselves with the social geography of Beijing. The administratively defined city of Beijing is a vast, sprawling, warrenlike metropolis divided into three parts: (1) the urban core (*chengqu*), consisting of four downtown districts where major political, commercial, and cultural activities take place; (2) the near suburbs (*jinjiaoqu*), also called the "urban-rural transitional belt," consisting of four districts that are the most rapidly urbanizing part of the city; and (3) the far suburbs (*yuanjiaoqu*), mostly covered by farming communities. The core districts consist of almost exclusively urban *hukou* holders, and the near suburbs are composed of both urban and rural *hukou* holders. The near suburbs are popular among migrants for two reasons. First, despite urbanization in these areas and the subsequent shrinking of farmland, most local farmers have retained their private houses. They enjoy more living space than urban households, and can rent their spare rooms to migrants. Second, because suburban areas are mostly considered the countryside, they are subject to less governmental regulation than the urban core. Therefore, suburban courtyard communities on the edge of core districts became host to clusters of the floating population. Nanyuan township, in which Wenzhou migrants live, is a typical rural-urban transitional zone.

When Wenzhou people first arrived in Beijing, not all of them settled in the Nanyuan area. Some stayed in other suburban neighborhoods such as Qinhuayuan and Wudaokou in the northern suburbs, and Dondaqiao and Jiuxianqiao in the eastern part of the city. But many eventually came to the Nanyuan area because of its excellent geographic location for commercial activities and housing availability. Nanyuan township is proudly called "the number one township in front of Tiananmen" for its proximity (only about five kilometers) to the heart of the city, Tiananmen Square, and to Qianmen, which has been the most vibrant, bustling, traditional downtown commercial district in Beijing since the 1930s. During the Ming and Qing dynasties, Nanyuan was designated as the royal family's hunting field and was the site of wealthy noble families' graveyards and flower gardens (see Fengtai Local History Office 1994). After the socialist revolution, the area was converted to agricultural production; as the supplier of vegetables to Beijing residents, it was not a priority district for commercial developments despite its proximity to downtown.[16] The arrival of Wenzhou migrant entrepreneurs quickly transformed this farming community.

According to local residents in Nanyuan, migration into this area began as early as 1981, when they occasionally noticed out-of-towners speaking a Zhejiang dialect. But it was not until the mid- and late 1980s that large numbers of Wenzhou migrants began a chain migration into Nanyuan township. A widely circulated story traces the origin of Zhejiangcun to December 1983, when two peasant brothers surnamed Lu from Yueqing County in

Wenzhou passed through Beijing on their way home from Baotou, Inner Mongolia. Having failed in business there, they put out their remaining products on the streets of downtown Beijing (near Qianmen and Wangfujing). To their surprise, the clothes sold quickly at a fairly good price, so they decided to stay. They rented a room from a local farmer in Haihutun village in Nanyuan for clothing production.[17] The business expanded rapidly, and many relatives and fellow villagers followed them to the area. Over the next ten years, based on kin and native-place networks, the migrant population in the area snowballed, reaching an estimated 100,000 in 1995.

Early Wenzhou migrant life in Beijing was characterized by hard work and struggle. It was common for several migrants to share a small room that served as a combined residence and production site. One migrant, Gugang, described to me what life was like when he first settled in Nanyuan:

> I left home when I was seventeen and went to join my uncle in his clothing business in Xinjiang. Later, I established my own clothing business and stayed there for two years. In 1983 we came to Nanyuan with a few *laoxiang* who had been here before. I rented a small room, smaller than ten square meters, from a local farmer's household in Ma village and began to produce clothing. I brought four girls from my hometown. While they were making clothes at home, I went into the city to sell our products. Transportation was a problem for those of us who needed to travel across the city daily. We all had to carry a big bundle of clothing while struggling with the crowd to try to squeeze into the crammed bus. Beijing people shoved their shoulders against us, cursing us *waidiren* for taking up their space with our bundles.

Some migrants managed to ride a bike with a big bundle of their clothing products tied on the back. It was physically exhausting and sometimes humiliating for migrants, who frequently encountered prejudice against them in the city. Their rural accents, clothing styles, and big bundles were all markers of their outsideness. As Gugang recalled, "We were afraid of Beijingers. They thought that they were the favored citizens of China just because they had been living in the capital city, so they could behave arrogantly toward us *waidiren*. They used to call us *shamao* ["silly hats," meaning fools] and looked down on us because we appeared earthy and clumsy to them."

Another problem facing migrants was the lack of legitimate marketplaces for trading. Agriculture and trade markets (*nongmao shichang*) had just begun to emerge, but there was not yet any special trading space for nonagricultural products. A few migrants and local urban entrepreneurs (*getihu*) put up temporary stalls on some out-of-the-way streets to avoid government surveillance. If caught, they were subject to fines, confiscation, and threats of deportation. Despite such risk and harassment, Wenzhou migrants continued to sell things in these "informal" markets by trying to stay one step ahead of city authorities and official crackdowns.

At the same time, in the mid-1980s, a small number of Wenzhou migrants began to rent retail counters in state-owned department stores. In order to rent a counter, which was considered a big favor, one had to have *guanxi* with department store managers. As nonlocal permanent residents, Wenzhou migrants usually did not know managers directly and thus had to establish relationships with state enterprise managers using patience, money, and friends' help. A successful businessman from Yueqing told me his brother's experience:

> People doing business must rely on relatives and friends. Especially in the beginning when you have just arrived at a new place, you do not know any important people who have power to give you favors. So you must ask friends who might be able to form an initial link for you, and then you can go ahead and send gifts. To give you an example: My younger brother wanted to rent a counter in the Longfu Department Store, but he did not know the manager. He went to the manager's home with gifts and was kicked out the first time. But he did not give up and went a second time, and a third time. . . . Only on the ninth time was the manager finally touched by his persistence and sincerity, and agreed to take the gift and lease a counter to him. We joke that this is like *"san gu mao lu."*[18]

As Beijing residents realized that the clothing sold by Wenzhou merchants was much cheaper and more diverse than what state stores offered, the demand for their products grew stronger. News about the demand in Beijing also spread back to their hometown, Wenzhou, pulling many villagers with capital and tailoring skills into Beijing in the late 1980s. For example, after staying in Beijing for two years, Gugang married a woman from his village and brought her to Beijing in 1985. She was in charge of household clothing production and domestic work, including taking care of their two young children; he was responsible for purchasing raw production materials and sales. Two years later, Gugang's younger brother and sister also came to Beijing to join his operation. After three years, they became independent and set up their own clothing businesses. Since then, Gugang has established a garment production factory (on a scale larger than a family-based workshop) with two close fellows from his township and simultaneously rented a stall to sell his own products directly. With his business expansion, Gugang brought his parents to Beijing to help with housework and childcare so that his wife could look after the stall. His family hired several young women to work in its expanded garment production. Over the next ten years, Gugang directly or indirectly brought forty to fifty relatives and fellow villagers to Zhejiangcun. Some of them later established their own clothing businesses and brought more friends and relatives with them. It was such traditional social networks that sustained the unceasing migration flow into Beijing.

The Formation of Zhejiangcun

The formation of Zhejiangcun was a process of transforming a local suburban area into a migrant space through demographic shifts, commercial developments, and the reorganization of social and spatial relationships over some fifteen years. This transformation took place in several phases. First, from 1980 to 1984 about a thousand Wenzhou migrants arrived in the Dahongmen-Nanyuan area and lived in local rural households. They had not yet formed an identifiable community, and there was little business cooperation between migrant households.

Second, from 1985 to 1990 was a period of rapid expansion, in which large numbers of Wenzhou migrants flowed into Nanyuan township. It was during this period that the settlement came to be known as *Zhejiangcun*. Some of the Wenzhou migrants came directly from their hometowns, but many came from other provinces (such as Inner Mongolia, Shanxi, Hebei, and the three northeastern provinces) where they had operated businesses for several years. The factors contributing to the large influx of Wenzhou migrant entrepreneurs included increased demand for clothing by urban consumers, newly established social networks, and relaxed migration policies. By 1989 there were already some thirty thousand Wenzhou migrants living and working in the area. Some Wenzhounese also opened profitable family-style restaurants, clinics, vegetable markets, and barbershops to meet the basic needs of a growing migrant population.

During this period, two important events—the prodemocracy student movement (in 1989) and the Asian Games (in 1990)—had a direct impact on the development of Zhejiangcun. To ensure political stability and keep social order in such special times, the city government mobilized several "cleanup" drives to force migrants out of Beijing. Zhejiangcun became a major target of these campaigns. Large numbers of Wenzhou migrants were pushed out of the settlement and displaced to the far suburbs and surrounding counties temporarily. But each time, only two or three months after the campaign, displaced migrants returned to the settlement to resume their economic activities.

Third, from the early 1990s to 1998 was a turbulent period with major developments as well as destruction. By 1995 nearly fifty large private compounds had been constructed by migrant housing bosses as residences and production sites for tens of thousands of Wenzhou migrant manufacturers and workers. A full range of community facilities also appeared, including child care, restaurants, beauty salons, clinics, repair shops, vegetable markets, privately owned pay phones, pedicabs, and long-distance bus transportation. Many self-organized wholesale markets (for example, Muxiyuan Light Industrial Products Wholesale Market, Haihuisi Industrial Product Trading Market, Henfa Clothing Wholesale Market, Tianhai Clothing Wholesale Market), composed of several thousand small stalls (*tanwei*), were created by Wenzhou migrant market bosses. These stalls were then leased to ordinary migrants. In 1992 and 1993, two permanent multi-story modern trade buildings (Longqiu and Jingwen) were also completed to house the businesses of several thousand stall keepers. The consumer goods sold here included clothing, leather products, cloth, shoes, socks, sheets, comforters, cookware, and other household items.

But just as this migrant community was developing and maturing, it was again moving into the political shadow, which eventually led to a devastating government campaign to demolish it in 1995. The demolition and the subsequent mass exodus and return of displaced migrants are documented and analyzed in the last two chapters of this book.

With the rapid growth of the migrant population, local Beijing residents became the minority in Zhejiangcun. A new economic dependency emerged between the locals and the migrants. Almost all local farmers became landlords by renting extra rooms to migrants, and rental income became the primary source of their livelihoods. As agricultural production rapidly disappeared, local farmers retreated from the productive economic realm. In their place, migrants became the most prominent social actors in the local economy and its social space. The Wenzhou migrants and their private wealth also reshaped the local power dynamics. The chapters that follow provide a detailed ethnographic account of these changing spatial and social processes.

3. The Privatization of Space

Obtaining temporary housing is one of the most difficult problems facing rural migrants in Chinese cities. In Zhejiangcun in the early years, nearly all migrants rented rooms from local farmers in the suburban neighborhoods. In the early 1990s, however, because of the rapid population increase, business expansion, and the heightened fear of robbery and extortion, Wenzhou migrants began constructing walled residential compounds. From 1992 to 1995, more than forty large-scale, privately owned housing compounds were constructed by a small group of migrants. These compounds became the homes of several thousand Wenzhou migrant families. At that point, Zhejiangcun began to look like a squatter settlement, which differentiated it from other migrant enclaves in Chinese cities.[1]

Wenzhou migrants' creation and control of their own housing space facilitated the development of group solidarity and identity. It was also in the contestation over space that intense sociopolitical conflicts and commercial alliances emerged among social groups and different state agencies. The aim of this chapter is twofold: to trace the production of a peculiar kind of migrant residential space, *dayuan* (which can be roughly translated as "big yard" or "big compound"); and to explore how this new spatial construction has played a significant role in reconfiguring power, social relationships, and collective identity in Zhejiangcun. My analysis of the migrant housing development highlights the commodification of both space and bureaucratic power by focusing on the clientelist ties formed between migrant bosses and local officials. In Zhejiangcun, such political-commercial patronage networks made it possible for Wenzhou migrants to bypass official rulings and appropriate part of the space and resources of the city for their own community development. Money became a new form of authority, which at times displaced official rulings and transformed the role of bureaucratic power.

Under the Roofs of Local Farmers

Strict city planning and regulations have prevented rural migrants from obtaining permanent housing or building on vacant land.[2] But migrants have managed to meet their housing needs in other ways (see Wang and Zuo 1996; Solinger 1999: 257–62). Most wage workers live in overcrowded factory dormitories or temporary housing provided by their employers, construction workers in on-site makeshift shelters, and maids (*baomu*) in their employers' houses. But a large number of migrants, especially those who run their own small businesses, depend on private rental accommodations.[3] This is also true of Wenzhou migrants in Beijing. Generally speaking, there are two kinds of housing ownership among the Beijing *hukou* holders. One is called *gongfang*, which means state-allocated housing, which is commonly allocated by one's work unit. The majority of housing in the city proper is this type, which cannot be used for private rental according to the official rules. The other is called *sifang*, privately owned housing, and is usually built by suburban farmers. *Sifang* in the rural-urban transitional zones are the main sources of migrant housing.

The relationship between local farmers and Wenzhou migrants has shifted greatly over time. When migrants first arrived in the Dahongmen and Nanyuan area to look for housing, they encountered a great deal of discrimination and rejection from local suburban residents. As outsiders who spoke a radically different dialect from Beijingers, Wenzhou migrants were perceived of as intruding strangers by local farmers. Many local households thus refused to rent rooms to migrants they considered untrustworthy, dangerous, and uncivilized. A migrant recalled his own early encounters with Beijing residents as follows: "When we first came here, Beijingers treated us like dogs. Many times when I knocked on their doors to ask if there was any space available for rent, they looked at me through the slightly open door as if I were a thief or beggar, then yelled at me: 'Hey! You outsider, get out of here.' I felt very offended, but was afraid of them at that time. After all, this place was theirs, and there was nothing we could do about it." Some migrants were eventually able to find a place to rent, but they could be kicked out by their landlords or forced to return to the countryside by the police at any time for unpredictable reasons. Migrants lived in the shadow of the law that defined them as illegal floaters.

The farmers' xenophobic mentality and reluctance to rent rooms to migrants also reflected the political and economic conditions in China at that time. In the early 1980s, nationwide economic reform was in its experimental stages. The Chinese economy was still dominated by rigid central planning, and free-market forces were very weak. Constrained by this rigid socialist economic mode, the majority of Beijing residents regarded engaging in private business (such as renting) as an unusual and dangerous practice that could subject them to social criticism and monetary penalties. Most farming households in Nanyuan township preferred to depend on vegetable farming and small township industries for income. Only a few daring and profit-minded farmers rented rooms to migrants for the side-income.

The suburban farmers' sense of insecurity and uncertainty was not unique but was inseparable from what Mayfair Yang (1994) has called "the culture of fear" nationwide in early reform-era China. This pervasive fear was a measure of the extent of state control over citizens' everyday conduct and thought. Like others in the country who remembered the Cultural Revolution and continued to distrust the new liberal economic policies, suburban farmers in Beijing then feared political persecution for unorthodox social and economic activities. Many people (both local residents and migrants) believed they were under constant surveillance by an invisible yet omnipresent gaze of the state whose political mood was unpredictable.

Local farmers gradually realized that renting was extremely lucrative, and government authorities did not explicitly prohibit it. By renting out one or two small rooms, a household could live a very comfortable life without working in the vegetable fields or taking a second job. For example, the monthly rent for an average-size room (ten square meters) ranged from forty to fifty yuan in 1985. This amount of money was significantly higher than what a local farmer could earn from agricultural work. As migrant newcomers' demand for housing increased each year, so did rents. By 1995 the monthly rent for an average room was three to five hundred yuan per month, depending on its location and condition. Even taking inflation into account, the increases in rent were remarkable. This income was about five times the monthly pension paid to a retired farmer by a local agricultural production team and was roughly equal to the average monthly income of a household in Beijing. As the local residents gradually overcame their political anxiety and were enticed by the money, renting eventually became the primary source of livelihood for local farmers. A Wenzhou migrant commented on this significant economic benefit to the local population:

> This entire area was really poor when I first came. From here to south of the Jingwen trade building, there were no inhabitants, but only in fertile lands covered by deep weeds. The annual incomes of most local people were just

three hundred yuan, provided that they worked very hard on their farmland. But look at how they live now! Renting a single room can bring them at least three hundred yuan per month. Those who have seven or eight extra rooms for rent can easily collect several thousand yuan a month without doing anything else. They are much better off now than before because of us.

In Mao's years, it was an unattainable dream for suburban farmers to get the urban *hukou* and permanent state jobs with stable salaries and attractive benefits (see Potter 1983; Walder 1984). But with renting so profitable, many suburban farmers in Beijing prefer to keep their rural *hukou* in order to retain the right to limited housing construction for family usage. In Beijing, each suburban farming family is usually entitled to a small piece of land assigned by the production brigade (*dadui*) for constructing its own house.[4] In recent years, however, land regulations in Beijing's suburbs have become extremely strict. Only when a male rural *hukou* holder who is a member of an agricultural production team gets married can he apply for a piece of land on which to build his new home (usually a small courtyard surrounded by two or three rooms). A person who changes his or her rural *hukou* to an urban one is not entitled to any land on which to build a house. Therefore, many urban residents now envy rural residents for their ability to transform part of their private housing space into an income-generating commodity.

At first, most local farmers rented out existing rooms in their houses. To make more money, some of them added two or three small rooms in the middle of their courtyards; and others put up narrow rooms against the outer courtyard walls, which made streets in the villages extremely narrow. By 1995 more than 90 percent of the families in this area rented two to four rooms per household. A few families even moved out of the community completely so as to rent their entire homes to the migrants. With the rent money, they could buy nicer modern apartments with better facilities in downtown Beijing. In the beginning, renting was done simply through an oral agreement by both parties, and no formal lease was involved. In June 1995 the Beijing municipal government passed a regulation requiring all landlords to apply for a "housing rental license" from local authorities and to sign formal leases with their renters. Landlords were also required to participate in the regulation of migrants by urging them to obtain temporary resident permits and by monitoring their fertility practices. But in reality, most landlords did not adhere to these regulations.

The changing social relationship between landlord families and Wenzhou migrant renters was articulated in their shifting spatial relationships. Tradi-

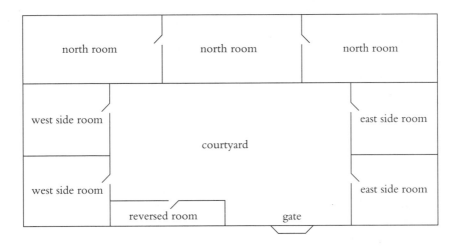

4. A typical suburban Beijing courtyard house

tional Beijing residential housing, called *siheyuan*, consists of a rectangular courtyard with rooms on all four sides (see Figure 4). Typical *siheyuan* built in the Qing dynasty are large, with splendid decorations and gardens. In the suburbs, courtyards are much simpler and smaller, varying from sixty to eighty square meters. The majority of courtyards in the villages of Nanyuan township are surrounded by two or three main rooms (*zhengfang*) on the north side, also called "north rooms"; two side rooms (*xiangfang*) on the east and west sides respectively; and a small room on the south side near the gate, also called the "reversed room" (*daozuofang*). The spatial layout of a *siheyuan* and its family members' locations in it are ritualized to reveal, structure, and maintain the familial hierarchy and power relations. *Zhengfang*, with windows facing south into the courtyard, are regarded as the most comfortable and respectable and are usually reserved for senior household members and the eldest, married son. These rooms are usually more spacious and receive more sunlight than other rooms. By contrast, *xiangfang* are lower, darker rooms, designated for unmarried daughters and junior sons. *Daozuofang* is the least desirable place in the house because it is small and dark and has no window. It is usually used for cooking or storage rather than living space. A gate is set at the southeastern side of the courtyard for good luck according to Chinese geomancy.

When Wenzhou migrants first arrived, it was common for the locals to rent out only *xiangfang* and *daozuofang* to migrants, while reserving the main rooms for themselves. Such spatial arrangements were symbolically important because they defined and demonstrated the hierarchical relationship between the locals as the masters or controllers of the space and migrant newcomers as subordinate sojourners. This arrangement was also advocated by local government officials who wished to maintain a vertical power structure. But the situation has changed significantly since 1990. Despite the fact that the cadres urged local farmers not to rent their *zhengfang* to migrants, many of them moved into the smaller and darker *xiangfang* and rented the larger rooms out to maximize their monetary gain. Rent for a large *zhengfang* was seven to eight hundred yuan a month in 1995, twice as much as that of a side room. It was hard to resist such income. Meanwhile, because of the one child-per-family policy, the average size of the younger-generation families has decreased significantly, making it possible for them to stay in smaller rooms while renting out the larger ones.

It is clear that this changing use of space and the subsequent reconfiguration of social relations between the locals and migrants are propelled by the local farmers' desire for money. The concern for profits has outweighed the concern for the old notion of face (*mianzi*), as this Beijing landlord explained:

> Several years ago, renting one's *zhengfang* was deemed improper and not allowed by the local authority. Village cadres told us that we locals must remain in *zhengfang* because we are the masters [*zhuren*] of this place; if we let them [migrants] stay in *zhengfang*, it will be hard to tell who are the real masters. Before, people cared about "face" and wanted to remain in *zhengfang* to maintain their host status. But now everyone wants to rent their largest rooms out even if it means that they have to move into the side rooms. . . . Why? Because making more money is more important than anything else now. After all, how much is "face" worth if one does not have money in the pocket?

This landlord's view reflects a new way of thinking about social status and authority among local residents. According to the Chinese regional stereotypes, Beijingers are known for putting face above material gains, as described by a southern migrant: "They would rather drink plain water and hide at home, but are not willing to take any hard, dirty work under the sun like us if they feel that they are losing face." Yet in the new era of commodification, the criterion for measuring one's social status or face has changed for many Beijing residents. There is a shift of values from the old symbolically based conception to a tangible, money-oriented interpretation of face. Further, we see a new attitude among local farmers toward local authority. As cadres' demands hamper their pursuit of personal economic gains, suburban residents are no longer afraid of defying official orders to defend their own interests.

In sum, local families and Wenzhou migrants developed a mutually dependent economic relationship. Without housing provided by rural Beijing households, it would be impossible for these migrants to set foot in the city. At the same time, if not for significant rent contributions by migrants, it would be very difficult for these local families to survive dramatic economic changes such as inflation and the loss of farmland due to urbanization. This form of socioeconomic interdependence, based on market demand and supply rather than bureaucratic arrangements, has reshaped the lives of both the locals and the migrants, leading to new configurations of social status and power in migrant congregating zones.

Dayuan: *A Space of Their Own*

The early 1990s brought significant changes to the spatial organization of migrant housing in Zhejiangcun. Large, self-protected housing compounds, inhabited exclusively by Wenzhou migrants and their workers, emerged one after another. While the earlier ones were relatively small, hosting about fifty households, the later ones were capable of accommodating two to three hundred households. The largest compound consisted of six thousand migrants in seven hundred households. Each compound tended to be occupied by families from the same county, township, or village. These housing compounds were locally called *dayuan*, meaning "big yard" or "big courtyard." This term signified a sense of spatial enclosure.

How and why did this form of large-scale, organized residential compound emerge at that particular time? The two main reasons are population growth and fear of crime. Although some Wenzhou migrants were able to rent larger rooms from the locals, their living conditions did not improve; in some cases living conditions even worsened because housing became scarcer and more expensive. The chain of migration brought more and more families to Zhejiangcun from Wenzhou, and they needed housing space. Meanwhile, the expansion of garment production among the existing migrant households required more live-in laborers and thus additional housing space. In many local neighborhoods, there were three times as many migrants as local permanent residents (see Beijing Municipal Government 1995b). The countless extra rooms added by local residents outside their houses made the villages extremely crowded. The wooden utility poles that lined the streets became engulfed by new housing additions, in some places blocking or narrowing the roads. Firemen complained that if a fire broke out it would be impossible to bring fire engines into the villages.

The average living and production space in a Wenzhou migrant household was less than three square meters per person. In especially crowded villages, it was common to find eight or ten people crammed in a room of less than twenty square meters. There was no privacy for family members and hired workers. A one-room apartment was usually crowded with bunk beds, sewing machines, raw materials, finished products, and cookware. The small public bathrooms that were originally built for the use of several hundred local families now had to meet the needs of several thousand families. And the high concentration of population caused housing prices to skyrocket.

As migrant private businesses developed rapidly, the distribution of wealth became uneven in Zhejiangcun, which created the conditions for robbery and extortion. Because the local police were corrupt and both unwilling and unable to maintain good public order, migrants had to seek help in other ways. The erratic distributions of narrow alleyways and isolated individual courtyards made it very difficult to organize a crime-watch among migrants. "Beijing landlords do not like us to bring friends over, so we have to reduce interactions with other families," one migrant told me. At night, there were only a few dim streetlights, and the darkness made it easy for criminals to evade capture. A young migrant woman told me that her family had moved several times because her home was twice broken into by masked robbers. She described one of the incidents:

> I do not know how they broke into the outer room of our house. As I was going to bed, I heard a noise. They [robbers] kicked the door and told me to open it. They said that they had a knife on one of my worker's necks and that if I did not open my door they would kill her. I was afraid that they would hurt somebody. So I opened my door, and they turned the knife to my neck, asking me where the money was. I told them that I had no cash at home. They did not believe me. They searched everywhere and took away all my gold earrings, necklaces, rings, and whatever they thought valuable. I tried to push the knife away with my hand. You see . . . that is how I got this big cut on my hand.

I asked her why she did not cry for help. She said that it was no use because her family lived in an isolated local courtyard and no one could have heard her. When she eventually ran to find friends and returned with them, the robbers had vanished in the darkness. This woman's experience was common among Wenzhou migrants. Indeed, many of them suffered similar frightening incidents and lived in constant fear of indoor robbery. They longed for a better-protected and more organized environment. The construction of private housing compounds was a direct response to overcrowding and crime.

The origin of *dayuan* can be traced back to 1991 when the Dongluoyuan village committee in Nanyuan township cleaned up a small piece of deserted land and built 240 poorly constructed houses for rent (see Xiang 1994–95). The houses were quickly rented out to Wenzhou migrants for 280 yuan each, and the village easily collected as much as seventy thousand yuan a month. Likewise, two other village committees built several rows of houses and rented them to Wenzhou migrants. In the beginning these were just houses arranged row by row in an open area. Later, the village committees put up walls around the houses and created the early *dayuan*. One village committee even moved its office into a housing compound in order to regulate migrant tenants more directly. Unlike those built later, the several early big yards were constructed and managed by local village heads.

In 1992 some wealthier Wenzhou migrants looking to profit from the real estate market themselves turned to the construction of housing compounds. These private migrant developers later came to be known as *dayuan laoban* (big yard bosses). The first and most difficult problem facing them was obtaining land. In Beijing, land use is strictly regulated by the government on multiple levels.[5] Even temporary use of land for construction by state-owned work units or villages for legitimate reasons has to be approved by the district or county government. Land use by Beijing *hukou* holders for private businesses is rarely granted. Migrants, considered "outsiders" in the city, are not even entitled to apply for temporary housing construction in the city. The only way to build housing is to go through informal channels by creating commercial alliances with local village heads in order to lease their land for construction. This is problematic because according to relevant rulings, any use of land by a suburban village for nonagricultural purposes has to be approved by the district or city government. Even though such collaborations could not be officially granted at that time, land-leasing deals were done covertly between village heads and migrant developers. Only the two or three largest compounds obtained some sort of approval letter from the district planning office, and this was because their developers had powerful clientelist connections with higher-level bureaucrats. Local village heads were willing to participate in such collaborations to compensate for the decline in income from agriculture in suburban areas.

A land-lease deal was considered "done" when the two parties signed a simple contract specifying the term of the lease and the amount of payments to be made by housing bosses. A common term was five to six years, with the possibility of renewal. The village could receive up to 10 percent of the total annual rent collected by the housing bosses. Village heads were not usually involved in the actual construction or management, but they were expected to help smooth the relationship between migrant bosses and those local officials in charge of allocating resources such as water and electricity.

The second issue was raising private funds for construction. For a smaller compound owned by a single family, the cost was normally less than 1 million yuan, so the money often came from the family's own savings (usually accumulated from its garment business) and cash borrowed from relatives and friends. But for a larger, mid-size housing compound, the initial construction cost could be anywhere between two and five million yuan. It was difficult for a single family to raise such a large sum for construction. Therefore, another popular way was to pool money together in a rudimentary form of shareholding (*gufenzhi*). This system was largely based on mutual trust and word of mouth among a small group of relatives and close friends from the same region. There was little legal paperwork involved, and most of the shareholders (*gudong*) were not registered with local authorities. They usually kept a simple signed agreement as a private record of their initial investment and entitlement to future profit-sharing. For them, personal trust built upon kinship and friendship was just as binding as formal legal agreements. Shareholders usually had co-ownership of a housing compound and retained some decision-making power. But the most important thing for them was their right to share the rent profits, 100 percent of which were usually distributed rather than reinvested.

The use of this shareholding system by Wenzhou migrant housing bosses was no doubt influenced by the popularity of shareholding cooperatives in their rural places of origin. In a study of the regional evolution of ownership forms in Wenzhou and Shanghai, Whiting (1999) has illustrated various local forms of property rights under the fuzzy and unstable shareholding cooperative regime (see also Lin and Chen 1999; Vermeer 1999). But there were some major differences between the quasi-shareholding arrangements formed in Zhejiangcun and shareholding cooperatives established in Wenzhou and elsewhere. One difference had to do with legal and official recognition. The majority of the shareholding enterprises in Wenzhou were formally registered and thus had legal recognition. By contrast, migrant compounds built by the housing bosses in Beijing were not recognized by city officials, and migrants' shareholding arrangements remained outside the legal regime of property rights. The informal contract signed by shareholders was merely evidence of investment and was not recognized outside their circle. A second difference was the motivation for adopting such a system. According to Whiting (1999), in Wenzhou people preferred cooperative shareholding enterprises because they provided political-legal protection as well as tax deductions and exemptions and bank loans. But the Wenzhou migrant housing developers in Zhejiangcun were not entitled to any such benefits. Their shareholding arrangements were primarily a way to pool family-based financial resources in order to produce profits down the road.

Since these compounds were unofficial constructions, they were not entitled to receive any city resources and services that were already in high demand by the officially recognized permanent residents. Housing bosses had to create informal clientelist ties with local officials, and pay high prices, to obtain water, electricity, trash collection, and other services. Most big yard bosses had been in Beijing for about ten years, much longer than their fellow migrants. Over time, many had developed personal contacts with local officials and cadres who covertly accommodated migrants' needs in exchange for cash, banquets, and material goods. The following two examples detail how such clientelist ties with local officials were established.

Housing compounds were in high demand. As soon as one was completed, it was fully occupied within a week. There was not a single unoccupied room in all the yards I visited. By 1995, about half of the Wenzhou migrant households (thirty to forty thousand people) had gradually moved into forty-eight big yards. This form of residence was popular not only because it provided larger and better housing space for individual families, but also because it offered localized protection against crime. Further, *dayuan*, which were inhabited exclusively by Wenzhou migrants with the same geographic origin and occupation, provided a convenient place for economic cooperation and business information exchange. Finally, along with this new spatial formation, a type of patron-client network based on three vertically positioned social groups (local officials, housing bosses, and ordinary migrants) also took shape. Housing bosses became at once "clients" in relation to officials above and "patrons" in relation to migrant renters below. They became a mediating social stratum that maintained local order and organized community life. Renters thus received protection from housing patrons who had more economic and social capital for influencing local affairs.

Let us now look at two examples of how migrant housing bosses mobilized private wealth and informal clientelist networks to create their own housing compounds despite the state monopoly on allocating space and other urban resources. Both cases show how the covert exchange of money and bureaucratic power between housing bosses and local officials played a crucial role in migrant housing development.

JIN 'LAOBAN' (BOSS JIN)

In Zhejiangcun there was one eye-catching housing compound surrounded by brick walls. It stood out like an old fortress on top of a knoll. This place belonged to a local village and once had been a vacant lot used for dumping excavated dirt from the construction of a nearby gymnasium. A Wenzhou migrant entrepreneur, Jin, noticed this place and had the idea of renting it for housing construction. He went to talk to the village heads several times and finally negotiated a lease. He promised to pay the village forty thousand yuan each year out of the total rent income. At that time (1994), there were already more than thirty-five *dayuan*, and the local township and district governments knew of their existence but simply ignored them. This was because almost all local villages depended on rental income, and many individual officials had been bought off by housing bosses.

In our conversation, Jin emphasized many times that the site they used was considered "waste land," not good for farming, and what they did was simply to turn virtually infertile land into housing space, to the benefit of both migrants and local villagers. Because appropriation of farm land for nonagricultural uses can result in severe punishment, by claiming that the land used for building houses was infertile, Jin hoped to change people's perception and thus reduce the potential punishment.

I later found out that Jin was not the sole owner of this *dayuan*. The ownership was split among five investors or shareholders, but he was the initiator and the manager of daily operations. The estimated construction cost was nearly three million yuan, an amount that exceeded the financial ability of an individual family even if they borrowed money. Just assembling the cash for his own share was not easy. Besides using all his family savings from their previous clothing businesses, Jin and his wife borrowed heavily from relatives and fellow villagers at home at the extremely high interest rate of 30 percent.

The construction was completed by a contract team composed of migrant workers from Hebei province. In Beijing, Hebei migrants dominated almost the entire construction sector because of their early established occupational networks and relatively cheap labor. The hired workers flattened the surface of the knoll with a bulldozer and turned it into a small plateau on which some 150 rooms were built. These single-room houses were very small (about fifteen square meters each), and were lined up in four parallel rows. A typical migrant household of five to eight people would live and work in each of these houses. There were walls surrounding the houses with two gates guarded by four security men. The guards were young Hebei and Anhui migrants between eighteen and twenty years old. They were paid very little (two to three hundred yuan per month) and had to stay in a small room near the gate all day long.

The monthly rent for each house in the compound was four to five hundred yuan. According to Jin's own calculation, the annual net income of rents from this entire compound was roughly 800,000 yuan, out of which a small portion was paid to lease the land from the local village. The rest went into the five shareholders' pockets. In about four years, the profit itself would pay the initial construction cost. Migrant housing bosses wanted to make big profits within a short period of time partly because they had already foreseen the danger of being wiped out by the government at any time given their unofficial status.

When I met Jin *Laoban* in 1995, he claimed that he jointly owned three other housing compounds. Other informants told me that he did not really own those compounds, but was only entitled to receive a small portion of the profit because he used his existing *guanxi* with village cadres and local officials to help other migrant developers negotiate land deals and gain access to water and electricity.

Some migrants in the community told me that Jin was a successful housing boss because of his extensive connections with local village heads and the township and district officials in three key divisions: the bureau of industry and commerce, the tax bureau, and the police. He paid frequent visits to these officials and cadres, drinking, smoking, and eating with them in restaurants or bars at his own expense. He believed that a good *guanxi* relationship needed constant cultivation and care, and he did his best to maintain good personal ties with officialdom. He once made an analogy between making *guanxi* with officials and establishing a relationship with a deity: one cannot expect to get help from the Buddha if one does not go to burn incense and show devotion on a regular basis. Local officials benefited not only from free banquets and entertainment, but also from higher prices charged for resources provided to migrant bosses. For example, officials in charge could set the electricity price for migrant housing compounds at two or three times the normal price charged to local residents. The excess usually went into the pockets of these officials. But in a market where demand far exceeded supply, deals like this were still considered a favor to migrants who otherwise would have no access to city resources.

WU 'LAOBAN' (BOSS WU)

I first met Wu at a small food stand outside his *dayuan*. As we ate, we had a long conversation about his migration experience and housing business. Wu *Laoban* was a stocky man in his forties. He came to Beijing with his wife in 1985 from a village in Furong township, Wenzhou. The Wus operated a family-based clothing production shop for several years before turning to the housing business. His *dayuan*, built in 1992, was one of the earlier ones and was considered relatively small, with only fifty households. The construction cost 800,000 yuan, and the Wu family was the sole investor and owner, though they had borrowed heavily from relatives and friends.

A few days later, he showed me around his housing compound. Like other big yards, this compound was also made of cheap bricks, and the houses in it were laid out in three long rows resembling military barracks. The members of the fifty households were almost all from Yongjia county and specialized in leather jacket production. To save money, each family rented one room for both living and production. As we walked around the compound, he introduced me to several families. At one point, Wu said to me with emotion: "You know, for me, this *dayuan* is like a large extended family. I know everyone here. Since I have put all my heart and blood [*xinxue*, a Chinese expression] in it, I must take good care of it." Then he told me how, during the month of construction, he and his wife alone oversaw all the details day and night, practically without sleeping. As soon as the compound was finished, they moved into one of the rooms and began to manage the units and handle disputes among the renters. In a sense, they acted as the heads of a large household.

Wu *Laoban* was proud of his local reputation as someone with *benshi* (the ability to get things done) even though he only had a few years' formal education. As he claimed, "I have stayed in Beijing for a long time, nearly ten years. Almost everyone here knows me. If you do not believe me, just mention the words 'Wu *Laoban*' to people in this area, they all know who I am." He stressed that being a housing compound boss was not easy because one must have *benshi* to deal with interfamilial disputes and various local officials. For example, not everyone was able to get a land-leasing contract even if he had the money for housing construction. Only those who had the right kind of *guanxi* with village cadres could make such deals. If one did not buy off key officials in charge of water and electricity, the *dayuan* could not function at all. Like other housing bosses, Wu also knew members of the local police station well, and gave them cigarettes, liquor, and expensive leather products from time to time. These goods were usually given as "gifts," but he joked that they were informal "taxes." He described one instance of "gift-giving" as follows:

> One day a local policeman in charge of our area [*pianjing*] asked me to bring him to several leather production households in my *dayuan*. He said that he wanted to buy a good-quality leather jacket with a fox fur collar. A piece like that normally costs over a thousand yuan. After seeing several families' products, he finally picked one, but then he said that he did not bring enough money and asked whether I could lend him some money. I knew from the start that he could not afford it because his salary was less than eight hundred yuan a month. It was obvious that he expected me to give it to him for free. So I let him take the jacket as a "gift." You know, if I had not done so, he would have found excuses later to give my *dayuan* a lot of trouble.

Although Wu underscored his close connections with local officials, he never referred to them as his friends, but only as *shouren* (familiar acquaintances), because this kind of relationship was primarily based on mutual economic benefit with little emotional bond. All these activities, including handing over money directly, providing banquets, and offering expensive leather jackets to officials, were called *yingchou*, meaning gift-giving in exchange for favors from the receiving party. The receiver of the gifts became a future contact (*guanxihu*) from whom the giver could solicit more favors later. Wu disliked this form of crude *guanxi* and hated greedy local officials, but he also admitted that such connections were essential for the existence of his housing compound: "We are *waidiren*, not the natives of this place. If you do not use the power of money, nothing can be done . . . but if you have a lot of money, you can even order the devil to push the mill for you" (*youqian nengshi guituimo*, a traditional Chinese expression).

In sum, even though Wenzhou migrants were represented as ignorant, law-breaking peasants who did not know how to live an urban life, the above cases show that their building of illegal migrant housing was not a result of their ignorance; rather it was a practical choice made to improve their living and production conditions. Further, such informal privatization of space was made possible through the collaboration of local cadres drawn into clientelist networks by migrant bosses. Indeed, almost all big yards that appeared between 1992 and 1995 were joint endeavors by migrants and local village heads. The pursuit of money served as a bridge between differently positioned social groups in a common economic framework. As one of my informants put it, "We have money but need a place to live. They [local residents] have land and need money. So we help each other out. And it is a good match." Such informal economic alliances were generally supported by local villagers. Even though some of them initially feared that the increased housing availability would bring rental prices down, such concerns gradually disappeared because the demand for housing remained so high.

Wenzhou migrants' practices indicate the power of private wealth in transforming modes of state power on the local level in the economic reform era. Although Wenzhou migrants did not have normative rights to land and city resources, they were able to meet their ends through bribes, payoffs, and personal ties with officials. In this context, money brought migrants access to urban space and resources monopolized by the state. Thus bribery and corruption can also be understood as forms of popular resistance to the state monopoly on economic and social life (Mayfair Yang 1994).

Such thriving clientelist ties do not necessarily work against state power or automatically challenge state authority. Rather, state agencies now tend to rely on commercial ties to strengthen themselves financially and become more deeply intertwined with the world of private entrepreneurs (see Pieke 1995; Solinger 1992). Indeed, several studies of the relationship between urban private entrepreneurs and the post-Mao Chinese state have convincingly demonstrated that clientelist ties do not necessarily chip away the power of the socialist state; rather clientelist networks have become one of the most important elements of the new pattern of state-society dynamics (see, e.g., Pearson 1997; Wank 1999). Even though clientelism has long existed in both rural and urban politics in the socialist era (see Oi 1989; Walder 1986), the rapid post-Mao commodification and commercialization have further intensified and diversified clientelist practices. Private wealth is becoming a powerful mediator that bonds structurally different social groups together and thus blurs the boundaries between society and state.

Spatial Inscription of Marginality and Liminality

In his study of the symbolic meanings of the Kabyle household, Bourdieu (1990) provides a classical analysis of how social relationships and people's conceptions of the world are shaped by and inscribed in the spatial organization of the domestic realm. In a similar spirit, Davis's (1992) reading of the social space of Los Angeles suggests that architectural forms and city planning do not exist outside of the social; instead spatial organizations are laden with sociopolitical meanings and play a salient role in structuring class relations and class consciousness. Using a semiotic analysis to unpack the social meanings of the built environment, Davis discerns how architectural styles and the spatial layout of buildings, streets, and public spaces help maintain power relations and social domination. Drawing on what Davis calls "archi-semiotics," the following pages offer some of my readings of the location of Wenzhou migrant *dayuan* and their modest construction style.

Zhejiangcun is divided into two distinct parts: an open market area and relatively hidden residential and production sites. The majority of clothing traders and buyers visit the marketplaces but rarely enter migrant residential areas. Only the more experienced, returning buyers venture into the villages to look for better bargains directly from the manufacturing households. Because almost all migrant housing compounds are surrounded by farmhouses and away from main streets, nonlocals are unlikely to see them. To find the housing compounds, one must wander through many small, twisted alleyways, deep in the villages, where pedicabs can barely squeeze by. Several of the largest compounds were built in even more remote parts of the community in order to reduce their social visibility.

Further, architecturally, houses in *dayuan* are built to blend in with the existing local farmhouses. All are *pingfang* (single-story dwellings rather than multi-story buildings), And the materials used for construction (such as cheap bricks and asbestos roofs) were not so different from those of surrounding farmhouses. Unless one pays special attention to them, it is hard to differentiate migrant houses from local farmers' houses. The only obvious differences are the walls and gates that separate houses in the compounds from the surrounding buildings. Many migrants confirmed that such hidden locations and modest structures were indeed intended to elude the gaze of city officials and residents, who would regard them as eyesores (see Figures 5 and 6).

The poor quality and extremely simple construction of these housing compounds also inscribes a clear sense of liminality shared by Wenzhou migrants. When I asked several compound owners why they did not build two- or three-story buildings to maximize the use of space, they cited another important reason for choosing low-cost, semipermanent constructions rather than permanent *loufang* structures: the potential financial loss if they were forced to leave the city. As a big yard boss explained:

> You never know when state policies will change. If the government decides to kick us out of the city, they will start with tearing down our houses. If we

5.   The entrance to a Wenzhou migrant big yard

invest in more expensive multiple-level buildings, the loss would be unimaginable. *Pingfang* are cheaper. If we have to give them up when the situation tightens up, the loss will be smaller.

After carefully calculating the cost and return, most housing bosses decided to minimize the initial construction costs to obtain quick returns. The principal investments for most *dayuan* could be earned back in about two years. The rent thereafter would be pure profit. But no one even knew for sure whether these unofficial constructions would be allowed to stand for two years. In short, the location and construction style of *dayuan* can be read as the concrete materialization and externalization of Wenzhou migrants' marginalized, liminal, and unstable social status as "strangers" in the city.

The Formation of Space as a Social Process

In his analysis of the formation of the proletarian class, Marx called attention to the intimate connections between the spatial organization of modern large factory production (the shared shop floor) and the emergence of collective activities and class consciousness among industrial workers (see Marx

6.   A crowded alleyway in a big yard

1978). This insight is useful in understanding how spatial changes in Chinese migrants' residential arrangements (from scattered living space to more organized and concentrated housing compounds) influenced their social dynamics and the formation of a collective identity: "Space and the political organization of space express social relationships but also react back upon them" (Soja 1989: 81).

When Wenzhou migrants first arrived in Beijing and lived scattered among local farmers' houses, they were largely unorganized and could be described as "a plate of loose sand" (*yipan sansha*, a traditional Chinese expression). This kind of residential pattern reinforced a sense of being subjugated to other people (*ji ren li xia*) because migrants did not have a space of their own. By contrast, *dayuan* provided shared physical space, which allowed Wenzhou migrants to envisage themselves as a collectivity for mobilizing group action. "Self-service, self-regulation, and self-perfection," a principle articulated by the dwellers of the largest compound, expressed the migrants' increasing determination to achieve self-control. Beijingers call this *zhadui*, a word that denotes a group of people with similar backgrounds sticking together, like a tight bundle of sticks. *Zhadui* is powerful because it brings scattered individuals together in a common spatial and social framework.

The emergence of migrant housing compounds caused a number of important changes in migrant social interactions and collective consciousness. Whereas local farmers' houses tend to be closed to the outside, and the spatial separation impeded the formation of social solidarity among migrants, migrants in housing compounds could interact freely. One migrant woman described life in a farm household: "When we were scattered in Beijingers' homes, the landlords did not like us to *chuanmen* [socialize with each another by visiting from door to door]. Some of them did not even allow us to bring friends over. If we chatted or laughed aloud in the evening, they would come to interfere with us." In contrast, *dayuan* enabled migrants to avoid social surveillance by landlords and form informal social gatherings without worrying about upsetting local residents.

A sense of group solidarity developed among the dwellers within *dayuan*. Since migrants felt safer living in the compound, they simply left their doors open all day long. Neighbors, friends, and customers could visit at any time. The open layout of the houses with shared alleyways also encouraged frequent social interactions between families. I myself benefited from this openness and social dynamic during my fieldwork. Although there was certainly business competition between families, the residents of a compound shared similar economic activities, rhythm of life, and place of origin, and offered each other mutual help. For many migrants, the *dayuan* provided an almost familylike environment, despite that fact that they were under the control of the housing bosses.

The growing group solidarity was best expressed in residents' collective efforts to fight crime. Before moving into *dayuan*, victims of robbery and extortion had no place to report the incidents because the police did not take their cases seriously. Some migrants were unwilling to report for fear of revenge. Given this situation, some compounds adopted strategies to motivate residents to report crime and link individual misfortunes with the collective interests. For instance, many compound bosses collected a small fee from renters to hire round-the-clock private security guards (see Figure 7). In some compounds, a family who was robbed and reported the crime to the housing boss or the security team received reimbursement from a fund contributed to by all the households. A victim who did not report a crime not only received no compensation but also was punished with a heavy fine. The idea was to motivate residents to participate in community watches and combat crime collectively. Robberies in most housing compounds indeed decreased significantly.

Living together in the compounds also reshaped migrants' interactions

7.   Security guards employed by Wenzhou housing bosses

with local government officials. For example, rather than going to individual migrant households to collect taxes and fees, local officials could work through the housing bosses. Officials with close private ties with the bosses might charge the migrant families less and in turn receive less resistance from the migrants. It was in the best interests of housing bosses to mediate conflicts between officials and tenants, whom they relied on for bureaucratic protection and rental income. But for local social organizations with little bureaucratic power, collecting fees from migrants in *dayuan* became almost impossible. Local neighborhood committees (*juweihui*) wanted to collect a small fee for cleaning up the public areas and removing trash in the villages (*weishengfei*). But the majority of compounds refused to pay the fee because the relevant agencies never delivered the promised services. And members of *juweihui* eventually gave up because they were afraid of direct conflict with migrants in *dayuan*. In short, living in self-organized housing compounds made migrant collective action possible.

Finally, even though migrant big yards appeared to be closed and cut off from the outside world, in fact they were quite open and dynamic. Members of different yards frequently visited each other, and their interaction promised a more sophisticated economic cooperation and division of labor. As garment manufacturing and trade among Wenzhou migrants became more and more specialized, households doing the same kind of work tended to live in the same compound. For example, individual traders used to buy clothing from many scattered manufacturing households in this area, which was both time-consuming and costly. Later, traders could procure the goods they needed by visiting only two or three compounds that specialized in those products.

Despite their advantages, *dayuan* were not entirely harmonious places. Multiple layers of social and economic tension existed—for example, among households that competed for business. New forms of social dependency and exploitation also emerged between housing bosses and ordinary renters, and between Wenzhou business owners and their wage workers. In addition, conflicts between *dayuan* occurred when housing bosses competed for more personal influence in a given locale. While *dayuan* helped consolidate a sense of collective identity among Wenzhou migrants, it also deepened the social differences between local Beijing residents and migrants who now had a space of their own. The anxiety and negative attitude toward *dayuan* by some local residents reflected their uneasy position in the shifting local power structure. As one Wenzhou migrant summarized, "Before it was our Wenzhou migrants who feared the local Beijing residents because we were unorganized 'outsiders.' Now we not only outnumber them but also have got our own space to live. It is they who are intimidated by us now." The following two chapters look at how these emerging social differentiations and shifting power relations are at work both within and outside migrant households.

4.   The Privatization of Power

As the migrants developed their own residential and market spaces, a small number of Wenzhou migrant leaders emerged within Zhejiangcun. Migrant leadership is central to understanding local control and the relationship between the state and emerging social spaces under late socialism. Because Zhejiangcun was created by rural migrants, for many years urban officials were unwilling and unable to intervene in this place imbued with strong regionalism and internal solidarity. Thus a nonbureaucratic migrant leadership began to emerge, assuming the role of organizing and policing the local economic and social life while mediating the troubled relationship between migrants and the city government.

This chapter explores the social construction of power through the formation of the migrant leadership and its critical role in reordering social and spatial relationships in this unofficial community. This alternative form of popular authority, however, was not articulated in any formal organizations or institutions. Instead, local bosses built up their power through informal networks and evaded official rulings through clientelist ties with local state agents. The social bases of this popular leadership provide crucial insights into the local power dynamics of migrant communities and into the larger implications for state-society rearticulations in China. In this chapter I trace the specific ways in which popular migrant leaders mobilized social, economic, and personal resources to develop their power, influence, and legitimacy in Zhejiangcun. I argue that the power of migrant leaders was based primarily on the control of two different kinds of social spaces—the combined production/residential space and the marketplace. Further, migrant leaders mobilized kinship and native-place networks, personal loyalty, and clientelist connections to consolidate their power.

I begin with a brief look at the curious absence of contemporary migrant organizations and the historical proliferation of native-place-based migrant associations in China. These circumstances suggest alternative ways of looking at migrant leadership beyond formal organizations. The bulk of the chapter is then devoted to an ethnographic account of the attributes, functions, and social bases of three kinds of migrant leaders, namely housing bosses, market bosses, and public activists.

Local Order and the Politics of Popular Organizations

How to maintain local order and balance the relationship between central state control and local autonomy has been a key concern for students of Chinese society. It has been widely established that a distinct social formation based on landed elites, known as the gentry (*shenshi*), played a vital role in mediating the competing political and economic interests of the central government and local communities in historical China (see Esherick and Rankin 1990; Chang 1955; Ch'u 1962; Fei 1953; Ho 1962; Huang 1985; Wakeman 1975). While incorporated into the imperial political order, the gentry were also deeply rooted in their communities, through which they gained power by controlling land, irrigation systems, and ritual events in the community. With increased commercial activities and expanded market forces in the Qing period, powerful families who acquired both money and prestige combined merchant activities with the gentry's lifestyle to create a new local leadership class known as the "gentry-merchants" (*shenshang*) (see Mann 1987). In the republican period, the gentry-merchant coalition faced serious challenges as local bosses began to dominate the rural landscape by forming alliances with the military regimes and cultivating patron-client relationships with ordinary peasants (Helen Siu 1989).

Under state socialism, landed elites and private merchants were eradicated by the Mao regime. In the absence of this mediating social group, what made local control possible in the socialist context? Shue (1988) suggests that it was a pervasive cadre-network system that played a similar dual role in reconciling the central-local tension in the countryside. Although rural cadres were designated state agents, they often faced a dilemma—how to meet state demands as well as serve the interests of their own communities (see Oi 1989; Friedman et al 1991; Chan et al 1984). In the cities, where the *hukou* system caused spatial mobility to decline significantly, social control was made possible through work units (*danwei*) and neighborhood committees (*juweihui*).[1] As members of a work unit, most urban residents were placed under the direct control of the work-unit authority. Residential communities were largely organized according to state-owned work units, which combined work and residence in a common space, surrounded by walls.

Unofficial migrant communities that have sprung up in the post-Mao cities do not fit neatly into the existing social and spatial order because they do not belong to any work unit, and neither are they considered a "real" part of urban society. The questions that puzzle many scholars are how local order is maintained, and what kinds of social structures have formed in these nonstate-defined communities. Numerous studies have shown that native-place associations (*tongxiang hui*), occupational guilds, trade coalitions, sur-name associations, funeral societies, and other kinds of migrant organizations played a powerful historical role in constructing place-based identities and communities among Chinese sojourners both within and outside China (Crissman 1967; Goodman 1995; Ho, n.d.; Mann 1987; Rowe 1984; Sangren 1984; Skinner 1958, 1977b). Popular organizations provided a structural basis for the migrant leadership to mediate local affairs and intergroup relation-ships. For example, in his study of leadership and power in the Chinese immigrant community in Thailand, Skinner (1958) shows how local leaders consolidated their power through voluntary organizations and gained power to allocate social and financial resources in the community. Migrant associ-ations based on traditional Chinese cultural principles—descent, locality, occupation, and brotherhood—were generally welcomed by state authorities in the host areas for the indirect control the state maintained over the migrant communities.

The communist takeover in 1949 marked a new turn for the fate of pop-ular organizations in China. In particular, territory-based associations were regarded as a threat to, and thus suppressed by, a centralized state that elim-inated local centers of power. Other kinds of popular organizations (*minjian zuzhi* and *banghui*) were either eradicated or brought under direct state con-trol to prevent them from developing into oppositional political forces (Wang Ju et al. 1993; Wang Ying et al. 1993). Such state anxiety about pop-ular organizations must be understood in light of the fact that popular organ-izations of various kinds had been the wellsprings of peasant uprisings to overthrow the established political order, and that the Chinese Communist Party itself also consolidated its power by working through popular organi-zations such as workers' unions, peasant associations, and women's associa-tions.[2] Officials are afraid that popular organizations today may become oppositional centers of power against the socialist regime.

Only in the post-Mao reform period have popular organizations and associations reemerged in China, with a strong "semiofficial and semipopu-lar" (*banguan banmin*) characteristic (see White 1993). They are required to register with local authorities, and their activities are constantly monitored by the government. Some associations seek the participation of government officials in order to secure a certain political patronage. In short, in China there are no civic organizations or public spheres that exist entirely outside the gaze of the state.

Despite the resurgence of popular organizations, curiously, almost no comparable entities have formed among the floating population. The only exception is the case of the Ruian Merchant Chamber in Beijing, which was created by a small group of eyeglass merchants from Ruian in Zhejiang province. Although this chamber receives some official support from the Ruian local government, it is not recognized by the Beijing authorities and is thus deemed illegal (see Yuan et al. 1996). After I began my fieldwork in Zhejiangcun, I realized not only that formal registered organizations did not exist among Wenzhou migrants, but also that migrants were extremely reluctant to speak about popular organizations at all because the phrase *zuzhi* (organization) was politically charged. Popular migrant organizations could easily be labeled "criminal gangs," "the underworld," and "secret societies." Only after building a rapport with Wenzhou migrants was I able to bring up the sensitive issue of organization. The following excerpt from my conversation with a prominent Wenzhou migrant leader describes the adverse situation:

> LZ: Did you ever think about forming a migrant association like a *tongxiang hui*? It was very common in the past for mutual help among sojourners.
>
> Zhen: We have thought about that idea, for example putting together something like a chamber of commerce among our Wenzhou migrants. . . . But we know it would not be approved by the authorities.
>
> LZ: Why not? There are many popular organizations in China today.
>
> Zhen: Yes, but when it comes to our place, things are different. In recent years, Zhejiangcun has been seen as an eyesore by some officials and Beijingers. So they wanted to disperse us or expel us from Beijing. Establishing our own association would be viewed as a subversive act. Who dares to touch this sensitive issue and become a political target?

In this context proposing any sort of self-organization to the government would have been tantamount to political suicide. I gradually learned that the formation of the Wenzhou migrant leadership had taken a different route on less visible terrain. In order to see the subtle power relations in this community, one must look beyond formal social institutions and into what

Comaroff and Comaroff (1987) have called "the texture of the everyday." Although this leadership was not articulated in an explicit organizational form, it was inherently political because it provided an alternative to the standard state-society dynamic within the migrant population.

Migrant Leadership and Local Power Dynamics

In a study of the organizational conditions within Beijing's floating population, Yuan et al. (1996) summarized three types of recently emerged local authorities among migrants: "opportunity-supply authority," based on the control of work, market, and social resources; "crisis-handling authority," based on personal connections with the local government and one's ability to get things done; and "collective-image integration authority," based on public services to enhance the collective image of a migrant group. They point out that these three kinds of migrant authority are all based on *situations* rather than institutions, but they do not provide further analysis of the social bases of these alternative forms of authority. My own research on Zhejiangcun indicates that since the power of migrant leaders was not based on formal political institutions, it was invested in diffused social networks such as kinship ties, native-place networks, and clientelist *guanxi* connections with local bureaucrats. Kinship and place-based ties provided a mode for organizing personal relationships as well as for structuring political relationships between groups (see Fortes and Evans-Pritchard 1958). More important, the power of migrant bosses was inseparable from their control over two kinds of communal spaces: the household and the marketplace.

HOUSING BOSSES

In the process of building and managing migrant housing compounds, the social stratum called big yard bosses (*dayuan laoban*) became the de facto local leaders in Zhejiangcun. Housing bosses generally had been in Beijing longer than other migrants and thus had accumulated considerable wealth, social ability (*benshi*), and local prestige (*mingqi*). They were not just landlords who collected rents; they also acted as patrons or household heads for migrants in their compounds. To illustrate how housing bosses came to power and their role in mediating conflicts and disputes, I here provide an ethnographic portrait of Zhen, a prominent big yard boss, focusing on the culturally specific production of power through spatial control, traditional social networks, and personal attributes and experiences.

I was introduced to Zhen *Laoban* by a mutual friend from Wenzhou.

When we arrived at his house, Zhen was rushing through his late lunch and looked exhausted. Because many families had just arrived in his newly completed compound, he was busy collecting rent and making sure that water and electricity were available to each household.[3] Zhen was in his early forties and was a tall and husky man with dark, thick eyebrows. He wore a Western-style suit with a tie and a thick gold bracelet on one of his wrists, a typical local symbol of wealth. His hair was carefully combed and oiled, almost as shiny as his black leather shoes. Zhen stood out among Wenzhou migrants because of his unusual height and charisma.

From the outside, his house did not appear to be different from others in the compound. But inside, the differences were obvious. Unlike other households that usually had only one room for sleeping and working, his family enjoyed three rooms and a modern bathroom and kitchen. The living room had nice furniture and a display cabinet full of imported liquors and several expensive Chinese distilled sorghum liquors. I later learned that these liquors were mostly given by people who needed his help and were generally consumed at personal gatherings with other local bosses or Beijing officials. This living room was more than a domestic realm; it was an important site where major decisions about the compound and political negotiations with the government took place.

Zhen was the second of nine children in a middle-income family. His parents owned a corner store in a small town called Yueqing, and the business was prosperous. After five years of elementary school education, he drifted without stable work for many years. For a while, relying on his physical strength, he made a living by transporting people on the back seat of his bicycle. This was considered low-end, strenuous physical work (*liqihuo*), similar to pulling a rickshaw. But Zhen had enjoyed the mobile nature of this work, through which he formed social bonds with other drifters in society (*zai shehuishang hun de ren*). They became "iron brothers" (*tiegemen*) who pledged personal loyalty (*yiqi*) to each other. In several fights, Zhen earned a reputation as a local tough. Later, during a harsh state campaign to crack down on pornography in 1983, he was sentenced to three years in prison for watching pornographic videos at home. From the years in prison, he said, he learned how the police system worked and how to deal with it.

Zhen and his wife came to Beijing in 1986 and began a small clothing retail business. His wife told me how they decided to come to Beijing:

> I remember one day I was doing laundry outside and heard from someone that it was very easy to make money by selling clothes in Beijing. I thought

to myself, why don't we try it too? I am not less capable than anybody else. I had an uncle who used to go to Beijing often for his hardware business. He told me that one of my cousins was already in Beijing renting clothing counters and that he might be able to help us. My husband and I borrowed money from relatives and friends and came to Beijing. We rented a small room from a family in downtown. My cousin helped us rent four counters in Wanfujing [the most prosperous downtown area at that time] for three thousand yuan each month.

After making a net profit of eight thousand yuan in their first year (a large amount of money at the time), they set up a family-based garment manufacturing shop and moved into a local farmer's courtyard in Nanyuan township, which later came to be known as Zhejiangcun. As the business grew, they turned to the more profitable leather jacket production, which generated annual earnings of 100,000 yuan. At the peak of production, the Zhen family employed more than twenty workers and owned their own store. In the following several years, Zhen accumulated more wealth and spent 200,000 yuan to build a new townhouse in his hometown. This house served more as an emblem for his success than as a residence. With his growing economic capital and expanding kinship and native-place networks, Zhen also acquired more prestige (*mingqi*) and influence (*shili*) among Wenzhou migrants.

As the development of migrant housing compounds became popular, Zhen decided to turn to this risky yet profitable business. Zhen and his kinsmen first formed a private garment corporation and used its title to negotiate a land-lease contract with local cadres. Through their extensive personal connections and large bribes, he formed a commercial alliance with a powerful local enterprise run by the Nanyuan township government.[4] According to the contract signed between the two parties in August 1994, the enterprise would provide Zhen with fifty-two *mu* (nearly four hectares) of land on the less-populated southern edge of Nanyuan. The term was set for seven years and could be renewed later. The enterprise was also responsible for obtaining necessary documents from the local government and for arranging water, electricity, and sewage services with the relevant bureaus. As a return, the local enterprise would receive 300,000 yuan for the first year and collect 30 percent of the annual income from the Wenzhou developers thereafter. Meanwhile, using a shareholder system, Zhen raised nearly ten million yuan from some twenty shareholders, most of whom were relatives from his lineage and his wife's natal family.

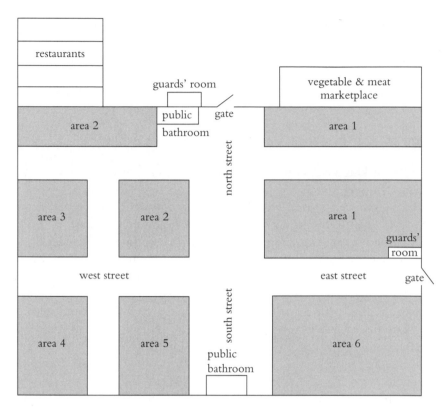

8.   Jinou, the largest Wenzhou migrant housing compound

Zhen's housing compound, Jinou (meaning "the golden Ou river"), was completed in July 1995 and named after a famous river in Wenzhou. This was the largest and best-organized compound, which accommodated about six thousand migrants. The living conditions of Jinou immediately struck me as tidy, orderly, and pleasant. The main streets were wide and clean with newly planted small trees on both sides (see Figures 8 and 9). There was a variety of family-run services such as a day-care center, beauty salons, grocery stores, telephones, restaurants, video stores, clinics, and entertainment centers for youngsters. In response to migrants' demands, the local state-owned postal office established a branch office within Jinou and provided basic banking services as well. All these facilities and services made this compound attractive to migrants in the area. Since Jinou would inevitably draw the attention of city officials and the media, its residents tried to keep it tidy

9. The main street inside the Jinou housing compound

and well organized. As a shareholder said, "We hope to use it as a window through which more and more Beijingers can better understand what Zhejiangcun is like and that this place is not all about crime and disorder as presented in the propaganda. We are conscientious, law-abiding, hard-working citizens."

Although migrant big yards were owned and controlled by different bosses, Jinou evolved into a centralized place for the Wenzhou migrant leadership. As the boss of the largest housing compound, Zhen's local influence expanded rapidly. He further consolidated his power through the self-appointed Jinou Dayuan Regulation Committee. This committee led by Zhen was a covert form of semistructured, autonomous migrant leadership in Zhejiangcun. To reduce the political risk of being alienated from the urban social order, the committee adopted popular terms promoted by the state to describe its goal: "to enhance the construction of spiritual civilization (*jingshen wenming*) of the capital by building Jinou as a qualified, civilized big yard." The committee created a popular slogan—"self-development, self-discipline, and self-perfection" (*ziwo fazhan, ziwo guanli, ziwo wanshan*)—to express their determination to maintain good communal order by themselves. This notion of self-regulation and self-improvement had a strong neo-Confucianist flavor and was originally advocated by the state to recast its citizens through self-indoctrination in the socialist ideology. Wenzhou

migrants reshaped its meaning to justify their new spatial and social formations outside state command as a form of self-development.

Zhen consolidated his leadership power in the following ways. First, as a
prominent local patron, he protected the interests of his renters by establishing a security system to prevent robbery and theft. Twenty private security
guards were placed on twenty-four-hour shifts. Second, he and other housing committee members became the mediators in settling various disputes
and conflicts within the compound, including domestic quarrels, inter-
household conflicts, and labor disputes between employers and workers.
Third, Zhen mediated the relationship between local state agents and ordinary migrants. Periodically the district tax bureau, the bureau of industry and
commerce, and the police sent officials to collect fees and dues from migrant
households. These unwelcome officials often provoked conflicts between
government agents and migrants. Housing bosses usually worked with both
sides to reduce the friction: on the one hand, they bought off the bureaucrats
through gifts and banquets in exchange for special favors such as lowering
fees and taxes; on the other hand, they tried to persuade renters to comply
with some routine official taxation in order to avoid deeper governmental
hostility. In many ways, a housing boss was like the head of a household.

MARKET BOSSES

Market bosses were local migrant leaders who gained power by controlling
the newly emerged private marketplaces. While upper-level governments
regarded migrant housing compounds as an anomaly in the urban order of
things, they largely tolerated and even encouraged the development of
migrant marketplaces. This is because thriving marketplaces are generally
viewed as a positive sign of commercialization and modernization. By contrast, family-based production involving the use of wage laborers is associated with the crude class exploitation found in cottage industries during the
early stage of primitive capital accumulation in the West.

By 1995 a number of large and middle-sized marketplaces were established in Zhejiangcun.[5] There were four types. One type consisted of several
hundred small individual shops on the two major local streets. Some were
privately owned, and others were established by the local subdistrict government and leased to migrants. A second type included nearly one thousand makeshift stalls in two enclosed areas. They were put up and managed
by a small group of market bosses. A third kind was a permanent, modern,
multistory building, Longqiu. It was owned by a few Wenzhou bosses and
contained several hundred stalls. The fourth type was a permanent market

10.   Semipermanent garment stalls on the street in Zhejiangcun

building, Jingwen, owned and regulated by the district-level bureau of industry and commerce, although Wenzhou migrants had paid much of the cost of construction (see Figures 10 and 11).

Like other market bosses, Hu, the owner of Longqiu, consolidated his power by maneuvering among government agencies, migrant stall keepers, and customers. At the entrance area into Zhejiangcun, the first thing that caught one's eye was a large two-story building with shining blue glass walls. This was the Beijing-Longqiu Commercial and Trade Center, a major garment trading market run by Wenzhou migrants. Local people just called it "Longqiu" ("dragon pond"), named for a famous scenic site in the Yandang Mountains in Wenzhou. Every day, from dawn to dusk, thousands of customers went in and out of this building to buy and sell clothing products. It held about seventeen hundred stalls, and the products sold there included leather jackets, seasonal clothing, shoes, and household items such as sheets, school bags, and kitchenwares. Its owner and manager, Hu, in his midthirties, came from a small town in Wenzhou. He had left home for the first time when he was sixteen, to work as a helper in his uncle's business in Hangzhou. A few years later he came to Beijing with two senior relatives. "When I first came to Beijing, life was harsh and unstable. I often had to run

11.   Migrant merchants in front of the large, permanent garment trade building, Jingwen

from one street to another to sell clothes and avoid the police. I did not know how to speak Mandarin at that time and was afraid of the locals." Later Hu married a woman from his village. They were able to set up a small clothing production shop and rented counters to sell garments in two large state-owned department stores in downtown Beijing. Like other Wenzhou migrant bosses, Hu relied on his extended kinship network to help him procure the social resources he needed for his business expansion. After about ten years' capital accumulation, he decided to develop a large-scale clothing market.

Longqiu was formally registered as a subsidiary of a state-owned Beijing seafood products company, which provided temporary land-use rights and served as a camouflage. The initial construction cost, about thirty million yuan, came from nine migrant shareholders who borrowed money at high interest rates. Hu and another shareholder eventually bought all the shares and forced the seven smaller shareholders out. Since this market building was funded exclusively by private individuals rather than government agencies, migrant bosses had strong control over it. But this did not mean that private marketplaces operated without state control. Market bosses had to constantly negotiate with greedy government officials over the issuing of business licenses and the collection of "regulation fees" and taxes.

Market bosses also sought political backing (*kaoshan*) from powerful upper-level bureaucrats. For example, Hu managed to obtain for his market the autograph of an influential national figure in China—Wang Guangying, the brother-in-law of the PRC's first president and himself a wealthy entrepreneur and highly positioned bureaucrat. Wang's autograph was prominently displayed in big golden characters on the roof of the Longqiu market as a political talisman. This connection to high bureaucratic power was believed to be the main reason Longqiu was not removed during the 1995 government cleanup campaign.

Unlike housing bosses who were deeply involved in policing everyday migrant life and public order, market bosses were only interested in maintaining market order and mediating the relationship between stall keepers and customers. Market bosses frequently faced the dilemma of deciding whose interests they should represent and protect. On the one hand, they wanted to protect the interests of migrant stall keepers so that they would continue to support the market; on the other, they needed to appear impartial in settling disputes so that customers would return. One day while I was visiting, a female customer with a Hebei accent rushed into Hu's office in tears. She claimed that she had bought a blouse in the building, but when she discovered that it was defective and tried to return it, the seller refused her request and initiated a fight with her. Hu was embarrassed that this incident occurred in my presence, worrying that I might report it to the newspapers. He asked his assistant to take the weeping customer downstairs and promised to resolve the problem immediately. Incidents like this happened almost daily. If a market boss favored the stall keepers, customers might complain to the local industry-commerce bureau, which could threaten to shut down the market. But if a boss stood up for customers, stall keepers would regard him as a traitor to his Wenzhou kinsmen.

Market bosses tended to adopt a metropolitan-oriented attitude and view themselves as independent "industrial and commercial entrepreneurs" (*gongshangyezhe*), not just petty migrant entrepreneurs (*getihu*). Their ties with the migrant community were not as close as those of housing bosses, and their power tended to be limited to the market sphere. Hu's family lived in a semi-secluded, upscale elite Beijing community inhabited mostly by movie stars and wealthy entrepreneurs. He drove to Zhejiangcun every day in his expensive Mercedes and kept his address secret to avoid potential robbery and extortion. The Hu family also paid more than ten thousand yuan in annual fees for his two children to go to a good Beijing elementary school, hoping that they could attend college someday and become socially accepted by the mainstream urban society.

THE SOCIAL BASIS OF POWER

The above account describes how control over the use and organization of social space constituted a key source of power for both housing and market bosses. Their ability to create and regulate private housing and market spaces was essential for the development of their popular authority. Next, I elaborate on three sets of social networks embedded in their spatial control, which enabled migrant leaders to create a "cultural nexus of power" (Duara 1988).

Extended Kinship Networks

Anthropologists working in Africa and other regions have demonstrated the importance of lineage in the formation of political systems in stateless societies (see, e.g., Fortes and Evans-Prichard 1958). Several decades ago, Maurice Freedman (1958) also developed a sophisticated analysis of the complex relationship between lineage organization (*zu*) and political, social, and economic control in southeastern China. Likewise in Zhejiangcun, the extended kinship system (if not the more strictly defined lineage or clan organization) provided the very social basis for local bosses' consolidation of power. Fried points out that the *zu* system (what he translates as "clan" in English) is much stronger in the south than in central and northern China (1953: 34). For Wenzhou migrants who originally came from the southeast but have lived in urban Beijing for an extended period, the situation is more complicated and has undergone some changes. Though the concept of *zu* is still an important one for some Wenzhou migrants, I found that, in practice, social coalition, local influence, and economic cooperation today are based primarily on loosely defined bilateral and extended kinship ties.

Before migration, married women in rural Wenzhou usually did not maintain strong economic connections with their natal families. But after migrating to the cities, daily social contacts and economic cooperation between the wife's natal family and the husband's family increased rapidly. In other words, migrant kinship networks extended beyond the patriline to include the wife's natal kin as well. This expanded kinship also expanded individual families' communal resources, which could be used to form business partnerships and help relatives survive intense market competition.

Both Zhen and his wife came from large families. He had nine siblings, and she had four. Most of their siblings also married into other large fami-

lies and thereby formed an extensive web of kinship ties. By 1995 the majority of their relatives on both sides (more than one hundred) had left rural
Wenzhou and settled in Zhejiangcun to run their own garment businesses.
Zhen's brothers became partners in several business projects. Later, the relatives of Zhen's wife became involved in the development of the large housing compound. These more inclusive kin ties provided a social nexus for
Zhen's far-reaching influence (*shili*). As his influence expanded, even distant
relatives and friends identified themselves with him in order to receive the
protection of his name, which further reinforced the power of the Zhen
family.

Extended kinship networks are the most important elements in the fabric of this migrant community. Marriage strategies help create social and
commercial alliances in the new urban sojourning setting. When people
make their marriage choices, besides wealth and common native place,[6] they
often consider the size of the extended family and the scale of the family
business on the other side. One woman from a wealthy household explained
to me why this is so: "If you join a big family with recognizable local
influence, it is easier for you and your relatives to do business, and your family is more likely to be better protected against robbery and blackmail."
Further, extended kinship networks are established not only through blood
ties and marriage alliances but also through fictive kinship relations, especially among close friends. But as far as I know, the practice of establishing
informal fictive kinship relationships is more common in the stratum of local
bosses and their close followers.

Despite their indisputable centrality, kinship ties alone are not sufficient
for building up the power and authority of local bosses in Zhejiangcun.
Migrant leaders must also mobilize extra-kin relationships such as *bang* and
clientelist ties with officialdom to consolidate their positions.

Bang

A *bang* is an informal social grouping based on sworn brotherhood, personal
loyalty, extended kinship networks, and shared locality. Although the core of
a *bang* may be built on kinship ties, the group often cuts across lineage and
incorporates migrants from the same place but with different economic
backgrounds.[7] Without government protection against crime, it was common for Wenzhou migrants to align or identify themselves with the patronage of a prominent local boss. Most such groupings were informal and did
not require any formal membership or ceremony, although some of the participants took an oath of fictive brotherhood.[8] *Bang* provided ordinary

migrant families with some local protection and a form of casual social organization. For example, if a migrant family had a strong relationship with a powerful patron, its business was relatively safe from robbery. Ordinary families who did not have such connections had to pay extortionists' demands and keep quiet about it to avoid future revenge. A young migrant explained to me how such patron–client relationships worked: "Say we want to extort fifty thousand yuan from you because you have just made a lot of money. Now, if you are on good terms with a patron, he might persuade us to take only five thousand yuan. If his *shili* and *mingqi* were very strong, we would accept his proposal. Otherwise, he would lose face and give us trouble later."

Unlike bureaucratic power that relied largely on impersonal rules, legal codes, and official appointments (see Weber 1981; Herzfeld 1992), the power and prestige of migrant leaders was inseparable from personal traits such as valor and fearlessness. "Not being afraid of death" was seen as a core component of masculinity and central to the construction of power in this social setting. A patron must be willing to risk his life for his follower, and the very risk and potential danger were what earned him respect and power. One local patron painted a vivid picture of how he had faced potential death in order to restore moral order for his people as well as demonstrate his patronage power:

> *Patron:*   One day a group of youngsters demanded money from a family I
> knew well. When I showed up to talk to them, they left without
> taking a penny. But the next day while I was eating at a local
> restaurant, they suddenly came up to me and put a knife to my
> neck. They questioned why I had interfered with their "busi-
> ness." I said to them: "If you want to kill me, you'd better do
> it quickly. Otherwise, your heads will be on the ground soon."
> Just at that moment, my brother passed by and saw us. He
> immediately ran to get our people, and we beat them to the
> ground until they begged us to spare their lives.
>
> *LZ:*   What if they had really decided to kill you before your people
> arrived?
>
> *Patron:*   No, they would not have, because they still wanted to stay in
> that area. If they had killed me, it would have been difficult for
> them to remain there. That was how I knew they would not
> actually kill me. They only wanted to scare me and slash my
> power so that I would not interfere with their businesses later.

Too often in social science accounts, power is viewed as something dis-embodied. But the production of power in Zhejiangcun was inseparable from the embodiment of masculinity. Women were excluded from acquiring formal leadership status in local politics. All big yard bosses were men, and their power and prestige were largely contingent upon locally recognized "prowess" (Boretz 1996) or masculine ability to get things done. Prowess was more than abstract valor or ability; it conveyed a sense of charisma based on the special gifts of the body and spirit. Masculine persona as embodied through one's body image and manner was essential for demonstrating one's *benshi*. Zhen's height and physical strength as well as his ability to fight (*dajia*) were all regarded as concrete expressions of his masculinity—the basis of prowess. It was the combination of this near mythical, latent masculine prowess and his benevolent appearance in public that gave him an aura of power.[9]

While taking risks for his followers, a migrant patron also depended on them for popular support. He usually had a group of youngsters who enjoyed cigarettes, drinks, and meals at his expense. These young men could easily be mobilized to fight when conflicts with other groups erupted. They also prevented the patron's business from being sabotaged by rivals. As a Wenzhou migrant told me: "Those who have large private businesses all have their own people [meaning hired thugs] in hand. Otherwise, local toughs will destroy their businesses and take their fortunes away, especially since the police are not much help and are themselves connected with hooligans."

In sum, the emergence of migrant *bang* was an alternative way of establishing order and control at a place where local protection was not offered by the government. Such informal groupings, however, were not entirely innocent or as benevolent as they claimed. The leaders could use their power to exploit other ordinary migrants. Further, because of conflicting interests among *bang*, at times they also sought violence against others to strengthen their own power. Nevertheless, migrant *bang* were different from those who lived solely on robbery, extortion, and drug trafficking. Lumping this form of migrant grouping together with the "underworld," as the official discourse did, could only obscure rather than illuminate the complex role of migrant leadership.

Clientelist Ties with Officialdom

Clientelist ties were derived from asymmetric personal connections (*guanxi*) with the police, village cadres, and officials who had direct control over land use, resources, and regulations. Such ties were central for local bosses, who needed to demonstrate their ability to get things done for their clients. For example, since migrants were not considered real or full members of the urban community, they were frequently treated as criminals by the police. A common duty for a local boss was to act as a middleman with the police in order to get troubled migrants out of jail. One day I ran into Zhen *Laoban* outside the local police station and asked him what brought him there. He said:

> Last night the police raided my friends' houses to check their temporary resident permits. They took away identification cards from some of them whose permits had already expired. The police also threatened to expel them from the city. But the problem is this: the police station in the area suddenly stopped issuing or renewing permits to us recently; at the same time they insisted on checking our permits and accused us of being illegal floaters. I think that they intentionally create this situation. I know some people in the police station. So I went to get my friends' cards back.

He said this as if it was an effortless task. But I knew how difficult it was for an ordinary person to ask favors from the police, let alone ask for the return of seized identification cards. It was obvious that Zhen had special connections with the police. As one migrant described, "Zhen knows the local police so well that he can walk in and out of the police station frequently and easily as if it were his own home!"

Building *guanxi* with officials requires some tactical maneuvering. Some officials are unwilling to accept cash for fear that they will be charged with corruption, so one has to find more subtle ways to cater to their special needs. One migrant patron explained how he maintained *guanxi* with Beijing officials who helped him obtain a permanent Beijing *hukou*:

> You see, they have power, and I have money. So I often bring them to expensive banquets and karaoke or dancing bars. . . . I tell you these officials are more interested in sex than other people, but they are worried about being recognized by the public or friends while seeking "forbidden" pleasure. So I take them to those hidden places with fewer people and present my business card to the manager to cover up those officials' real identities.

Even though this migrant boss frequently interacted with Beijing officials, he did not consider them his true friends: "Such relationships are fragile and temporary because we are only 'friends' in the business sphere. There is nothing common among us except for our interest in making money. So we can easily become strangers tomorrow when we no longer need each other."

Besides establishing clientelist ties with Beijing officials, housing and market bosses also created ties with their regional government officials. For example, Zhen recruited a Wenzhou official appointed at the Beijing liaison offices to be a shareholder in his compound.[10] This was a special "empty share," which meant that the holder did not have to provide any investment money but was entitled to receive part of the profit later, a sum that could reach ten times his salary. By accepting this favor, this director became personally tied to the fate of the compound and would do anything he could within his power to protect it.

In addition, the migrant bosses contributed to the public welfare of their hometowns to gain government support and societal recognition in their place of origin. In 1994, Zhejiang province suffered severe damage from one of the worst floods in its history. The local and provincial governments solicited emergency funding from the general population. Many Wenzhou migrants in Beijing donated money. Zhen himself generously contributed 100,000 yuan and thus earned recognition for his considerable economic power and praise for his collectively oriented spirit. His philanthropic act was cited as a good example of what the official ideology promoted: getting rich is glorious, but getting rich without forgetting others in poverty is truly laudable. The Zhejiang provincial government awarded Zhen an honorary cup. This cup, displayed on a shelf in his dining room, was more than a statement of his humanitarian act; it was also a symbol of his political capital.

Clientelist networks created by migrants can be seen as a special form of *guanxi*, a social phenomenon that has been widely explored by anthropologists and sociologists in both rural and urban Chinese contexts (see Mayfair Yang 1994; Yunxiang Yan 1996; Kipnis 1997; Wank 1999). Although some anthroplogical studies have highlighted the vertical, asymmetric power relations between ordinary people and officialdom, they tend to emphasize the production of horizontal *guanxi* networks among the people. By contrast, my account here focuses on the vertically integrated clientelist ties among ordinary migrants, migrant bosses, and officials. This type of *guanxi* contains little affective sentiment or *renqing*, but is built on mutual economic benefits calculated on the principle of market exchange. The absence of emotional ties in the clientelist networks formed in Zhejiangcun is conditioned by the asymmetric structural positions between officials with formal bureaucratic power and migrant entrepreneurs with newly acquired private wealth.

Transactions based on bureaucratic power or the exchange of money and favors between officials and private entrepreneurs are certainly not unique to migrant communities. Clientelist ties have become the operational principle for private business in the reform era (see Pieke 1995; Solinger 1992). In particular, according to Wank, patron-client networks with local state agents have become a vital means of maximizing security and profit for private trading firms (Wank 1999). Through the commodification of local bureaucratic power, private entrepreneurs increase their bargaining power with and influence on local state agents, but at the same time local state agents are able to penetrate more deeply into the private business sphere and gain access to new economic resources. Historically, a similar process called *guanshang heliu* (cooperation between officials and merchants) was most prominent in the nineteenth century China (see Ma 1995). Even if private entrepreneurs have gained considerable economic power, they have sought cooperation and commercial alliances with state officials to secure their positions.

THE LOVING HEART SOCIETY

The group I call "public activists" sought control over the largest trading center in Zhejiangcun in a different way. With the rapid growth of garment trading markets, some Wenzhou migrants began to envision the market not only as a site for commodity exchange but also as a new public domain through which their collective voices and concerns could be articulated. Public activists gained power and legitimacy through their association with the "Loving Heart Society" (*aixin she*).

The original "Loving Heart Society" was founded in late 1993 by students at Peking University, who called for the return of loving hearts that they believed had been lost in a society dominated and cursed by money and commodities. By engaging in voluntary activities that benefited the general public, these students wished to demonstrate that, even in a market-based society, love, conscience, kindness, and altruism were still alive and indispensable. Because this movement adopted a fresh, depoliticized, and humanistic language, it quickly attracted media attention and created far-reaching influence across China (see *Guangming Daily*, October 22, 1994; *People's Daily*, December 28, 1993, November 7, 1994; *China Daily*, February 1994; *China Youth Daily*, December 9,1993).

One winter day in 1994, a successful Wenzhou migrant, Jiang, who had had a Christian upbringing, saw a television report on the Loving Heart activities.[11] He was attracted by their ideas because they were compatible with the Christian notion of universal love, and yet the group was also acceptable to government officials. He asked himself: "Why don't we also do something like this to reconstruct the market order, enhance our market reputation, and improve the image of Zhejiangcun?" After sharing his idea with a few stall owners in the Jingwen market, Jiang contacted the Communist Youth League office at Peking University. The office responded warmly and immediately sent a special "social work team" to help Wenzhou migrants establish their own Loving Heart Society.

The politics of this migrant society needs to be understood in the context of power struggles within the newly formed Jingwen market. Jingwen (meaning Beijing-Wenzhou), was the largest garment wholesale market in Zhejiangcun, with 1,754 stalls on five floors. It was constructed through the joint effort of the Fengtai district and the Wenzhou city governments. The sixty million yuan construction cost was raised from mixed sources: Wenzhou migrants, bank loans taken by the Fengtai bureau of industry and commerce, and regulation fees previously collected from Wenzhou migrants. Although Jingwen was funded in a semiofficial and semipopular way (*banguan banmin*), the Fengtai district government claimed full ownership. Migrants who had invested enough could reserve a stall space and receive a rental discount for the first several years.

As soon as Jingwen was opened in late 1994, control of the market became a highly contested issue. The district bureau established a branch office in the building to regulate migrants' activities. The appointed cadres controlled the allocation of the stalls and decided what kinds of activities would be allowed in the market building. As a result, they received favors and gifts from those who hoped to get a better stall location and those who wanted to utilize areas (such as fire emergency paths) for additional sales space. Most stall renters despised the assigned cadres and wanted to form their own leadership to represent their interests and coordinate business relations. The local government, however, did not want to give up its control. It feared that migrant leaders might establish "an oppositional force to government control, which could mobilize protests against us," as one of the cadres working in Jingwen told me. Hence, several appeals by migrants to form their own leadership were rejected by the local government.

The Jingwen Loving Heart Society (JLHS), organized by several prominent Wenzhou migrants, first appeared as a small team of volunteers who devoted themselves to public service (*zuo haoshi*) in order to improve the environment of the market. For example, they provided free drinking water to customers, cleaned up the floors, set up "civil codes" (*wenmin gongyue*) for proper business conduct, and offered special services to military personnel, disabled people, and the elderly. Each member donated several hundred yuan to install air conditioners in the building to make the place more comfortable in the summer. These activities initially appeared apolitical and thus were welcomed by government authorities. The JLHS invited the director of the government branch office to serve as their "consultant," a ritual commonly practiced by most popular organizations in China to obtain official backing.

The media and press also became interested in the JLHS's activities. Many television stations and reporters came to interview Jiang, who was a core member of the JLHS. Jiang was enthusiastic about media attention, viewing it as a source of power that could be used to restrain the domination of the cadres. He also used his relationship with prestigious Peking University to attract Beijing celebrities' attention and support. "But local officials and cadres did not like our contact with the media and tried to suppress our activities because they were afraid that their dirty business and corruption would be exposed to the public," said Jiang. As time went by, the JLHS's intention to develop its own power and participate in market regulation became obvious. Cadres began to feel threatened by the migrant activists. They grew hostile toward the JLHS's activities and stressed repeatedly that "the JLHS is only supposed to provide good public services, and should not interfere with administration and regulation matters" (Li Yanhong 1995: 41). In particular, after the JLHS mobilized popular resistance against an increase in stall fees in 1995, it lost all official support. As the power struggles between migrants and officials intensified, the district government ordered the dismantling of the JLHS.

The failure of the JLHS was also a result of its gradual loss of popular support. While Jiang was becoming a celebrity in the media, many Wenzhou migrants grew suspicious of his motives. An incident in April 1995 further exacerbated tensions between the JLHS and its constituencies. A public security guard in the market beat up a stall owner badly, closed down his stall, and fined him. This guard was a member of the security team sent by the local police to keep market order. Outraged stall owners viewed this incident as an expression of the local government's disrespect toward Wenzhou migrants and wanted the JLHS to demand justice from the local government. The social work team from Beijing University also believed that this was a crucial moment for the JLHS to regain popular trust and drafted a letter to the district police on behalf of the JLHS, pressing for an official apology and for a dialogue with the government. But none of the JLHS leaders was willing to submit it for fear that it would jeopardize their own business and personal safety. As one leader explained: "Ultimately, it is we who will be punished! Whoever sticks out will be out of luck." Therefore they chose to keep silent, and silence cost them popular support.

In sum, public activists pursued a different way of building up power and legitimacy. Since they were not the owners of the market, they could claim no spatial and financial control over that place. Instead, they had to convince stall keepers that their public activities could indeed benefit the great majority. Although the JLHS originally claimed to represent and serve the stall keepers' interests, its position constantly oscillated under pressure from the local government and the migrants. When the public activists tried to develop their power by appropriating outside influences such as the media and a well-known university, they were alienated from both local official support and migrant support. Officials saw the exposure to the media as a threat to their corrupt practices; ordinary migrants viewed the use of the media as a way for the leaders to pursue personal fame, which ran against their stated goal of serving the public interest.

In recent years, much has been written on the emergence and power of voluntary associations in post-Mao China and other postsocialist countries (see White 1993; Calhoun 1994; Brook and Frolic 1997; Hann and Dunn 1996). Scholars have entertained the idea that such associations can play an important role in the development of civil society. Here I do not wish to delve into the debate over whether civil society exists or existed in China. Rather I would point out that the fate of the Loving Heart Society founded by Wenzhou migrants suggests that visible civic associations cannot serve as a plausible or long-lasting basis for the development of nonstate power precisely because they can be easily identified, monitored, and suppressed by the state authorities. Civic power within the migrant population is more likely to derive from traditional forms of social networks such as kinship ties, *bang* coalitions, and clientelist ties that are less visible to outsiders.

Conclusion

Migrant leadership provides an opportunity to examine the less visible, more diffused social networks and everyday practices in post-Mao China. In this chapter I have illustrated how Wenzhou migrant leaders developed a spatialized and embodied form of power (*shili*) by controlling key social spaces and mobilizing traditional social networks and clientelist ties, creating a style of leadership that was at once archaic and modern. In this context, housing bosses, market bosses, and public service activists all played somewhat dualistic leader roles as power brokers mediating between the migrant community and the political authority in the larger society.[12]

Without official status, attempts by the migrant leadership to mediate local affairs and social spaces could only be achieved through the informal aid of lower-level bureaucrats who were willing to trade their political power and control of public resources for personal economic gain. Such cooperation, however, was officially deemed "corruption." Popular migrant leadership based on traditional social ties, brotherhood, locality, and *guanxi* with local cadres was stigmatized by the state as a competing social force that would jeopardize state control.

Regulating the floating population and migrant enclaves has long been cited as the most difficult task facing the post-Mao regime. Although the Chinese state managed to penetrate local Chinese society by creating a grassroots cadre system in the relatively stable population of the past, it has not managed to recreate such a mediating social stratum to regulate the much more mobile, fluid, and culturally diverse migrant population of today. My analysis suggests that the tension between the floating population and state control is partially due to the lack of an officially recognized social stratum that can work between the migrant masses and the state. Historically, leading merchants and traders during the Qing period were often appropriated by the state to participate in what Mann (1987) calls "liturgical governance" to maintain local order. Helen Siu (1989) also shows that local bosses during the republican period acted as political brokers between formal state institutions and the rural populace (see also Billingsley 1981).

During my fieldwork in the 1990s, popular migrant leadership actually functioned as such a mediating force, offering better protection to migrants than that provided by official authorities. As individual entrepreneurs who had gained the most from economic reform, they did not want a fundamental restructuring of the national order, but only the partial reordering of the power dynamics in their local space, from which they hoped to benefit directly. But this popular leadership was criminalized and alienated by upper-level governments and thus could not fully develop its mediating role between unofficial migrant communities and the state.

5.   Reconfigurations of Gender, Work, and Household

A significant social change has taken place among Wenzhou migrants in the domain of gender and domestic relations, which is intimately related to the reorganization of their production and household space. Western studies of the floating population, however, have paid little attention to this important social realm. Only in the late 1990s did some feminist-inspired scholars begin to address gender issues in the migrant population (see, e.g., Lee 1998; Pun, forthcoming; Davin 1999; Fan and Huang 1998). In particular, Lee and Pun provide rich ethnographic accounts of the relationship between gender politics and labor discipline as experienced by female migrant factory workers in southern China.

Meanwhile, one problematic notion in the Chinese official and intellectual discourse is the assumption that by participating in commercial activities rural migrant women will earn their own incomes and eventually attain independence and social equality with men. Yet numerous studies in other cultural contexts have convincingly shown that economic development is not necessarily a liberating force for all women (see Fernández-Kelly 1981; Ong 1987, 1991; Sen and Grown 1987). For example, Ong shows that rural Malay women who were drawn into the capitalist production of transnational corporations may be under less direct familial patriarchal control, but are subject to new forms of gender hierarchy and industrial modes of control in the workplace. In the Chinese context, Lee's comparative (1998) study of women workers in two factories owned by Hong Kong capitalists also demonstrates that rural women who travel from inland areas to work in the economically booming south are routinely subject to overt, harsh labor discipline (see also Pun, forthcoming). She identifies two distinct regimes of production with contrasting disciplinary styles—"localistic despotism" and "familial hegemony"—each of which serves to control "maiden workers" and "matron workers" in the factory.

Existing studies of migration and gender politics in China tend to focus on women in the larger factory setting; in contrast, this chapter examines the explicit and implicit gender exploitation and class domination experienced by Wenzhou women and young wage laborers in relatively small, household-based garment manufacturing. I question the simplistic economic determinism that says women's increased participation in production and commerce automatically leads to their empowerment. A better understanding of gender politics in Zhejiangcun requires a fuller account of the mutually constitutive social, cultural, and economic factors. My analysis focuses on the interplay of three elements: control over family business, manipulation of spatial boundaries, and value transformation in women's work. Rather than formulating a model to identify an ultimate causal factor, my goal here is to illustrate how these factors inform one another in a dialectical manner to shape gender and work among Wenzhou migrants. In particular, I highlight the culturally formed spatial boundaries in order to arrive at an integrated analysis of gender politics that takes into account ideological constructs and socioeconomic changes (see also di Leonardo 1991).

In classical studies of gender, feminist anthropologists have tackled the problem of female subordination from different theoretical perspectives (Rubin 1975; Sacks 1974; Ortner 1974; Rosaldo 1974). What is particularly interesting to me about these approaches is the connection between social space and the formation of gender inequality. For instance, Ortner traces female-inferiority ideology back to the concept that men are related to the "cultural" realm and women are associated with the "natural" realm. Rosaldo's theory of women's subordinate position is built more explicitly on the separation of socially constructed dual domains (the domestic and the public) in which human activities occur. Both of them suggest that gender and power are inevitably shaped by culturally and historically formed social spaces. Yet the dual spheres (workplace/home, nature/culture, and public/private), derived from a Levi-Straussian (1969) binary framework, assume fixed boundaries between social spaces. There is also a tendency to seek universal explanations for women's lower status worldwide, while ignoring how the meanings of social space are culturally constructed and shift over time.

More recent feminist anthropologists have moved beyond universal dichotomies to examine gender inequality in locally and historically specific terms (see di Leonardo 1991; Moore 1988; Rosaldo 1980). In other words, they historicize, contextualize, and de-reify gender exploitation. Building on their insights, my analysis of gender politics among Chinese migrants seeks to explore how spatial boundaries between household, workshop, and market are socially constructed and used over time rather than taken for granted.

By focusing on space, I do not mean to suggest that it is the sole force shaping gender relations. By taking into account the interplay among gender, space, and work, I hope to provide an alternative way of thinking about gender and power beyond the economically determinist view that remains powerful in China. As Moore (1988) has argued, it is not work per se but what is conceived as "work" and the social value assigned to it in a given cultural context that shapes women's domestic and societal status.

"Household" as a Flexible Social Field

In this examination of the different gender dynamics in Zhejiangcun, I use "household" as the social field of analysis. Anthropologists have conventionally distinguished "family" from "household" based on their different referents: kinship for the family, and propinquity (or common residence) for the household (see Yanagisako 1979). While the family is a more strictly defined corporate kin group, the household may consist of a coresidential group that includes kin and nonkin. Anthropologists have also offered rich analyses of the Chinese *jia* (family) or *hu* (household) (Fei 1974; Lang 1946; Naquin and Rawski 1987; Wolf and Huang 1980; and Watson 1975). Although there are differences in these researchers' conceptions, a common set of understandings can be drawn from them. The *jia*, which usually shares both a stove and financial resources, is a social unit of common residence for production, consumption, and socialization. It is viewed as a harmonious, egalitarian, and self-bounded domestic group and a natural unit. By contrast, the *hu* may include a broader group of people who do not necessarily share a common stove or budget. Despite such differences, both the *jia* and the *hu* are treated as natural and bounded social entities located in a single fixed geographic locale.

Cohen's (1970) study of the developmental process in the Chinese domestic group began to call our attention to the temporal and more flexible spatial dimensions of the *jia*. As a dynamic social process and a multifunctional social site, the *jia* can appear in a "dispersed" form with its members scattered among several geographic locations, and its form can change over time. The notion of a "dispersed family" is particularly useful for understanding Wenzhou migrant households today, as I explain later. It suggests that a shared residence in a physically bounded space should no longer be regarded as the only proper form of the *jia* or the *hu*.

Today, with rapid economic, social, and spatial changes, it becomes even less meaningful to talk about "the Chinese family" or "the Chinese household" in an undifferentiated way. What constitutes a "family" or "household" and its relationship to other social spaces needs to be reexamined and reimagined according to specific social and historical contexts. Hence, a better understanding of the spatially extended migrant households requires a social imagination that envisages the household beyond a rigid coresidence bounded in physical space. Further, a Chinese *jia* is far from being a harmonious unit; instead, it is a power-laden social arena where patriarchal order and gender domination are made possible and contested (see Judd 1994).[1]

In light of recent socioeconomic changes, three distinct features of Wenzhou migrant households are worth noting. First, the majority of households, commonly composed of three generations, are not necessarily located in a single geographic place. Instead, they may be dispersed among two (or more) localities (such as their rural origin and the urban settlement). Though in different locations, the residents are viewed as members of one household. Members travel between the locations and fulfill kin obligations at both sites. Second, Wenzhou migrant households are not just places of residence and consumption, but also the primary sites for economic production and trade. The two conceptually separate realms—household and workplace—are combined in a shared physical space. The spatial boundaries between workplace, market, and home are thus blurred. Third, although hired workers may be nonkin, they share a residence with their employer's family and are regarded as "family members" in everyday rhetoric and government demographic surveys.[2] Keeping these three features in mind, we will now look at gender relations were transformed in different household situations.

Middle- and Lower-Income Households

Most of the migrant households in Zhejiangcun are lower- and middle-income households (*zhong-xiao hu*) with annual incomes between 100,000 and 500,000 yuan. Working wives in these households usually enjoy some power in family decision-making and some control of their own lives and the family business. But even if these working wives are highly active in economic production, the value of their work remains largely underestimated, and their domestic and social status is lower than men's. The questions I wish to explore here are: How is the value of women's work transformed and appropriated by men in this context? What is the relationship between the value of work and social domination? I argue that the transformation of work into a socially recognized value is closely related to the cultural conception of space in which work is performed. This value transformation serves as a critical component of gender exploitation and is central to the production of the patriarchal order.

In Zhejiangcun, garment manufacturing usually takes place within migrants' households. Usually, all family members participate in the production even if they hire wage workers for extra help. The production process involves four major integrated parts: (1) purchasing and preparing raw materials (such as leather, cloth, and buttons); (2) information-gathering regarding popular clothing designs and patterns; (3) tailoring and sewing; and (4) transporting the finished products to the market for sale. There is a distinct gender division of labor in migrant cottage industries: men perform the work outside the home; women work inside the home. In most cases, women are the primary producers, dominating the third stage, which is crucial to the entire production process. Working wives are responsible for coordinating production and for managing relationships among family members and workers. Unmarried daughters (if any) and young workers often spend more than fifteen hours per day in front of the sewing machines or tailing board. But it is the husband who is normally considered the boss (*laoban*) of the household business. His main task is to obtain raw materials from other places and make arrangements with wholesale dealers. Not tied to the workshop, he enjoys great spatial mobility. He may help out with production during the peak of a business season but usually does not do the actual cutting and sewing.

Despite women's key role in garment production and in labor and social relations, their work is deemed less productive and secondary in Zhejiangcun. To understand how and why women's work is devalued, I suggest that we look at the spatial organization of production within the household. In Zhejiangcun, because housing space is so limited, garment manufacturing is commonly performed in the residential quarters (see Figure 12). The space of an average Wenzhou migrant household (usually a single room of roughly ten to twenty square meters) is efficiently utilized for multiple purposes. The rectangular space is vertically divided into two parts by an overhanging wooden platform that provides an extra sleeping area, usually reserved for junior family members. Production takes up nearly 80 percent of the room; several semiautomatic sewing machines sit in the middle of the room. A large cutting board is set against one wall. Underneath the board is a small, dark space usually used as a sleeping area for nonkin workers. Cooking is done outside the house, and there is no specific dining area in the house. A folding table is set up for each meal. Sometimes workers simply eat in front of the sewing

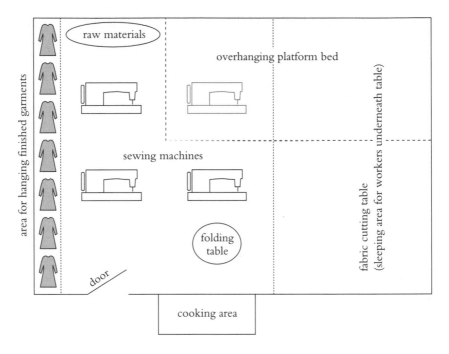

12.   A typical migrant household, used for both garment production and living

machines. In short, this multifunctional space is shared by the employer's family members and nonkin workers for both living and production.

The absence of spatial boundaries between work and residence has created what I call the "domestication of production" in the gender division of labor. Because labor-intensive work performed by women at home is easily deemed "natural," feminine, and private, and because their work is publicly invisible and can be conceived of as an extension of "domestic" chores, it is assigned less social value than men's work. And domestic work has been traditionally seen as less productive than publicly visible paid work (see Sacks 1974; Mann 1996).

In fact, neither domestic work nor private economic activities are called "work" (*gongzuo*) by Wenzhou migrants. *Gongzuo* is a term reserved for formal urban jobs associated with state work units (*danwei*) (see also Henderson et al. 1996). Domestic work, which takes place primarily at home and does not generate cash income, is called *jiawuhuo* (domestic chores). Other forms of economic activity are called *zuoshengyi* (doing business), presumably involving profit-making production and trade. *Jiawuhuo* and *zuoshengyi* are not simply different kinds of activities but are gendered activities that have different values: the former is "women's work" and the latter is "men's work." Clothing production that is performed in the household is feminized, privatized, and therefore devalued despite its labor-intensive nature and its importance to the business enterprise.

When Wenzhou men spoke about labor division and productivity, they often ignored or downplayed their wives' and daughters' roles as the primary producers. For example, a Wenzhou businessman once explained to me the division of labor in his household like this: "It is our custom for men to do business outside the home, while women just cook and take care of kids and chores at home." But when I pressed him further by asking who was in charge of production when he traveled to purchase materials, he said: "my wife." Then he quickly added: "Her chores [*huo*] are light. She stays at home helping out and looking after things when needed." How do we reconcile these contradictory pictures of his wife's role? I suggest that what he told me first is the normative ideology of what men and women are supposed to do. But what they practice in the migration context differs greatly from the social norms. Yet I do not believe that the patriarchal ideology this man articulated is a false reflection of reality. Rather, the ideology itself helps shape his very conception of women's work.

A related process is the social transformation of "outside" space into "inside" space. For families who specialize in garment sales, their stalls and shops in the marketplaces are the most important social site for daily activities. In most cases, working wives and daughters are in charge of these shops; better-off households may hire non-Wenzhounese migrant women to look after the sales. Although physically separate from their living quarters, stalls are treated as an extended part of the household. The trading space is thus domesticated, and so women's work performed in this space is also considered informal and less valuable than men's.

By contrast, men's work (purchasing raw materials outside the community) is more highly valued because it is performed outside the home and requires frequent travel. Since staying away from home is a cultural taboo for women, work that has to be performed in distant areas is reserved for men. This is how a Wenzhou businessman explained the division of labor: "Women are generally too cowardly [*danxiao*] to venture out alone. Moreover, it is not good for them to stay in hotels alone. But for men, it is not a problem. If I cannot go back home at night, I can just stay in a hotel as long as I need. But women cannot act like this." The social limitation on women's spatial movement was clearly articulated by a working wife: "If we women were to go on a trip to buy materials and stay outside, they [men] would think we are 'bad women' [*huai nuren*, meaning loose] and come to bother us because women are not supposed to go to that kind of place." Work that requires staying away overnight is regarded as a hardship and thus a masculine activity that women are unable to accomplish. The reasons for the perceived inability of women to work away from home are cultural rather than physical, but the perception is related to the common view of women as biologically inferior.

I would like to elaborate on another important, but often neglected, role of working wives in maintaining social relations necessary to production. Marxist analysis reminds us that to ensure the continuation of capitalist production, besides the supply of labor power, capital, and technology, the relations of production must be constantly renewed (Engels [1891] 1972). In Zhejiangcun, there are about forty thousand non–Wenzhounese rural migrants (mostly young girls, but also some young boys) working as cheap laborers for Wenzhou employers. Although these workers live with their boss's families in the same domestic space, there is a clear class difference between workers and employers and a sense of distrust between them. Further, after over thirty years of socialist collectivism in China, the use of laborers by private entrepreneurs is still seen by some as a form of exploitation and thus subject to social criticism.[3] Wenzhou migrant cottage industries have been likened to crude capitalist labor exploitation. Therefore, Wenzhou business owners are cautious about how to present their relationship with wage workers. One of the strategies is to present workers as part of one's own family, and wives play the primary role in creating a family-like atmosphere. "Being like a family" helps shade class exploitation, improve work proficiency, and create a relatively stable work force; at the same time, workers develop a sense of loyalty to the employer's family. For example, two Henan girls who were unhappy about their boss's condescending attitude told me why they decided to continue working for him:

> We have been working for this *laoban* for over a month, but he treated us coldly and never even asked our names once. We feel insulted and just want to drag during work. . . . I think that if we all eat and live together, they should treat us like a family. That way, we will be willing to work hard and sacrifice for them. But the *laobanniang* [the wife of the boss] is better to us. She cooks for us and talks to us in a nice way, not looking down upon us. . . . If not for her, we would have quit a long time ago.

When workers have personal problems or need a small amount of advance pay, they usually speak to the *laobanniang*, who acts as the family manager. Working girls who are away from home for the first time can become homesick or frightened about sexual harassment in their new, isolated environment. The social bond created between workers and the *laobanniang* secures workers' loyalty to the boss's family and thus ensures the continuity of the business.

In recent years, new places of consumption such as karaoke bars, dance halls, and hotels have become popular among middle-class Wenzhou entrepreneurs. Working wives tend to criticize men who go to those places, arguing that such leisure consumption is time-consuming and money-wasting. But they are primarily concerned about prostitution and extramarital relationships. Although middle-class businessmen cannot afford to visit these places often, many of them admire the wealthy men who can afford to do so. And it is not uncommon for them to seek out prostitutes on a long business trip. They justify their behavior as a "natural male tendency" and argue that it is not immoral if one keeps it within a certain limit. A common attitude is that as long as extramarital relations do not directly interfere with family life, they are not a problem. Such sexual practices are also seen as a way of demonstrating one's economic power and manhood among private entrepreneurs. These attitudes do not sit well with working wives, who question the changes brought by migration and reforms. Listen to the frustration voiced by one of them:

> I really feel that today's society is different from that before. Years ago, men in our hometown were innocent and honest. They wanted to get married and live a stable life. Marriage meant growing old together until your hair turned white [*baitou daolao*]. But now things have completely changed. Now everyone rushes into cities to do business. There are more chances for people to interact with strangers and experience different things, such as drugs and prostitution. In such a flashy world [*huahua shijie*], men change quickly as soon as they get money in their pockets.

The "flashy world" is an image widely invoked by migrant women to describe their perceptions of urban space as a playful yet decadent place dominated by money and commodities. Although this woman's idealized representation of the traditional rural life cannot be taken at face value, her juxtaposition of life before and now is a way of delegitimating undesirable practices by men that have undermined women's position in a new social and economic order.

Wealthy Households

Wealthy Wenzhou migrant households (about 10 percent of this migrant group) are locally called *dahu* (big households) and have an annual income above 500,000 yuan. "Big" here does not refer to the size of the household but to its economic and social status. The head of such a household is called a big boss (*da laoban*) and is always a man. To give readers a sense of *dahu* women's situations, I begin with a short anecdote and analyze the processes that led to this position.

One hot summer afternoon I was having a late lunch with the wives of three *da laoban* in a family-run, Wenzhou-style restaurant after their five-hour mahjong game. While waiting for the rice noodles, our conversation turned to their domestic situations. One of them, Yang, dressed in flashy clothes and gold jewelry, became quite emotional as she began to talk about the predicament facing her and her friends:

> We cannot do anything outside. We would like to do some business, but our husbands [*laogong*] would not allow that. Many people envy us for our comfortable lives, but they do not know that we are really no different from captives. Staying at home is like staying in prison because you cannot do anything but housework. My husband doesn't allow me to go out to do any business. But he himself goes out all the time, holding banquets and seeing other women. . . . So we are wives, but not like wives; we are not nannies but are treated like nannies.

From her voice, I sensed an emptiness and a yearning for personal autonomy. The words "captive" and "prison" describe vividly how these *dahu* women felt about their declining domestic status. What struck me most about Yang's complaint was that she linked her feeling of disempowerment directly to her lack of access to the world outside her home. Being able to go out means having geographic mobility, but more important, it means having social and economic involvements.

Big households did not start out "big" but have evolved over time. Members of *dahu* generally migrated to Beijing in the early 1980s, about ten years earlier than many other Wenzhou migrants. The timing was crucial for their capital accumulation because private business competition then was not as intense as it is now. Many migrants started with small-scale garment production or clothing retailing and then turned to real-estate-based businesses. In the early sojourning years, the wives were the primary producers in the family business. They operated the sewing machines, supervised young workers, and sold products on the street with their husbands. In those days, life was difficult and exhausting, but working wives felt closer to their husbands and had more decision-making power in family matters.

As some of these households accumulated more wealth than others, they gradually moved out of labor-intensive garment production and turned to market and housing development. Women in these families were subsequently pushed out of the business realm and gradually became confined to the domestic space. Further, as men began to use their homes for business negotiations (*tanshengyi*), the domestic space was also divided into gendered zones. Women's space inside a household was limited to the back rooms when men were present. Consider the spatial division of Lin's home, for example. Lin's husband is a prominent local migrant leader. Their house had six rooms, including a living room, two bedrooms, a dining room, a children's piano room, and a kitchen/bathroom. Several times when I visited the family, Lin's husband and his entrepreneur friends were smoking and chatting in the living room, which was regarded as a men's place for business talks, and thus an improper space for women. Male guests usually did not bring their wives. If they did, or if female visitors came, the women retreated to the dining room or the kitchen. Only when there were no men around would women occupy the living room.

In recent years, karaoke bars, restaurants, and hotels have also assumed a central role in the lives of wealthy migrant men. These places serve as the site for business negotiations as well as sex trafficking. I call this phenomenon the "bar culture of doing business." In the Wenzhou migrant culture, bars and hotels are marked as a space for male consumers only. If women are present in those places, especially if alone, they are immediately assumed to be prostitutes or women of questionable virtue. *Dahu* women especially are excluded from these places because their good reputation (*mingsheng*) is important for maintaining their husbands' status and influence. According to a popular saying, "If a man cannot discipline his wife, what else can he do better?" Such limitations on women's spatial mobility by wealthy men are both a form of sexual control and a way of eliminating women's participation in business activities.

Concerns about women's spatial mobility were clearly reflected in Wenzhou migrants' comments on my presence in their community as an unaccompanied woman. Throughout my fieldwork, I was frequently asked how my husband could possibly allow me to run around alone and talk to male strangers. My spatial mobility and daily interaction with men were viewed as a transgressive act, and irritated some *laoban* because their wives cited me to support their desires to engage in activities outside the home.

The declining social space available to *dahu* women and their husbands' new consumption activities have directly influenced the balance of power in the family. Because these women are more and more dependent on their husbands financially and socially, they have less leverage to make claims and demands in the household. More important, women's diminishing access to public spaces makes it harder for them to develop their own business and social skills and obtain support from social networks. One wealthy boss told me that he cannot bring his wife with him to business-related banquets and ceremonies because "she does not know how to act and what to say." During an opening ceremony at this man's "entertainment city," he and his brother both showed up in their red Mercedes-Benzes, not with their wives but with two pretty younger women from Beijing. One of them was a college student majoring in music, whose karaoke singing won applause and thus a great deal of face (*mianzi*) for him. In sum, women's failure to meet their husbands' social expectations (if true), which is a consequence of being excluded from public spaces in the first place, is now used to justify keeping *dahu* wives out of the social domain.

The Predicament of Working Girls

Wage-earning workers in Wenzhou migrant households are the lowest economic and social stratum in Zhejiangcun. Most are teenagers from poor rural areas in Guangxi, Anhui, Hubei, Henan, Sichuan, and Hunan provinces and are considered outsiders by their Wenzhou employers (see Figures 13 and 14). These young migrant workers have undergone a process of proletarianization while they are detached from the means of production (namely land) and only have their labor for sale. Their urban experiences as cheap manual laborers working in isolated household production can be summarized by focusing on the following three themes.

SHRINKING SOCIAL SPACE AND INCREASING SOCIAL ISOLATION

Wage workers in Zhejiangcun usually live with their employer's family and are confined to the workshop. Many have never been outside the community since the day of arrival. Their daily activities usually take place within a diameter of one kilometer from their living quarters. Except for sleeping and eating, their time is spent almost entirely in front of the sewing machines.

13.   A young Guangxi migrant worker operating a sewing machine in a Wenzhou migrant household

14.   A young Henan migrant worker operating an embroidery machine in a Wenzhou migrant household

Their social isolation makes young workers vulnerable to potential physical violence and sexual assault by the employer's family members.

Several factors contribute to the shrinking social space of young migrant workers. Working girls have little control of their own time and space. They must get approval from the boss each time they want to leave the house. During the busy production season, they are not allowed to leave the sewing machine except to use the bathroom. The area around public bathrooms thus became a place for workers to take a break, stretch out, and socialize with friends. In addition, most workers' wages are very low, yet goods and services are expensive in Beijing. One girl told to me, "If you go out to do something, you have to pay a lot of money for transportation, food, drink, and park entrance fees for sightseeing. We simply cannot afford it. So why bother going out?!" Other workers told me that it is not so easy to make money in the city, and they feel guilty spending any of their *xuehanqian* (money earned with blood and sweat). Many young workers are also afraid of getting lost in Beijing among the baffling street signs and advertisements, so they do not explore the city outside the enclave.

SHIFTING FORMS OF CONTROL

In their studies of Malay factory women and Mexican maquiladora women, Ong (1987) and Fernández-Kelly (1983) argue that although working women might be free of traditional male domination at home, they face a modern, institutionalized male domination at the workplace. Among the Chinese migrants I reached a similar conclusion, but with an interesting twist: the labor discipline in Wenzhou migrants' garment industry exerts parentlike controls that conceal gender and class exploitation.

Like primitive capital accumulation historically, the unbelievable economic growth in the Wenzhou garment industry is built on maximum extraction of surplus value from workers (see Mintz 1985). It is achieved using young female workers who work long hours for low wages. Wenzhou bosses prefer to hire young unmarried women not only because they are cheaper than male labor but also because they are seen as docile (*tinghua*), adept at sewing, and able to endure long-term, repetitive manual work.[4]

Young workers are subject to strict labor discipline. They are even told when to get up and when to go to bed. There are no breaks except for a short lunch and dinner, each limited to fifteen or twenty minutes. Any delay will draw a scolding or *lianse* (unhappy expression) from the boss's family members. Most working girls develop serious back problems from working such long hours at the sewing machines. Some said that at night they could barely keep their eyes open and occasionally fell asleep at their machines.

Employers justify the labor discipline and control by a patriarchal figure (not necessarily a male) by saying that because working girls are junior members of the household their activities should be directed and scrutinized by the household head. (Cf. Constable 1997 on the controls Hong Kong employers place on Filipina domestic workers.) Most Wenzhou bosses pay their workers in one lump sum at the end of a year. A *laobanniang* explained this practice as protecting young workers' interests: "This is because they [working girls and boys] are too young and do not know how to keep money well. If we pay them once a month, they will spend it all. This way [once a year] they can take all the salary back home before the Spring Festival." Workers, however, would prefer a monthly salary because the form of payment is directly related to the question of control and autonomy: "If we are treated unfairly or want to leave the boss before the end of the year, we are very likely to lose all the unpaid salary." In the worst situations, a boss can hold workers' identification cards and clothes, or labor bonds, making it impossible for them to leave.[5] If a household fails to make a profit, workers may not receive their wages at all, despite their year-long hard work. Isolated workers have no place to turn for legal help because, as one of them put it, "we are the unregistered aliens [*waidiren*], the target of government regulation; if we seek outside help, they can catch and punish us."

The "family" ideology appropriated by Wenzhou bosses is a double-edged sword. While allowing bosses to exercise domination over working girls and boys' time and activities, it can also be used by workers as a weapon to criticize and resist unreasonable treatment by bosses. Young workers routinely demand a small prepayment of their salaries (around 15 to 20 percent) each month to purchase clothes and personal items as a strategy for reducing the possible loss of wages. If an employer refuses to pay them, they argue that if they are not treated like family members they cannot be expected to work hard and remain loyal to their employers. Sometimes the bosses indeed give in to workers' demands.

THE DILEMMA OF RETURNING HOME

The majority of female migrant workers hope to use their earnings to help build new houses for their natal families, obtain a better dowry, or support their brothers' education. Some also view migration as an opportunity to experience the outside world (*jianshimian*). When they left their home villages, many thought that they would quickly make some money and then return home permanently. But things usually do not work out as expected. Their dream of a free and independent working life ends almost at the moment working girls enter the Wenzhou households.

After a time, working girls themselves also begin to change. Influenced by the urban consumer culture, some young workers began to spend part of their savings on clothes, shoes, and makeup, rather than turning all their money over to their parents. Some decide not to return to the rural life; others decide that their previously arranged fiancés no longer match their new expectations of an ideal spouse. The media's idealized image of urban life and modern romantic love reshape young migrant workers' ideas about marriage and courtship. When they find new boyfriends among fellow migrant workers, they want to call off existing engagements, which often causes familial and interfamilial disputes in their home villages. Canceling the engagement (*tuiqin*) used to be a social taboo, but is now accepted by more and more villagers, according to my informants. Still, most working girls are reluctant to reject their rural lives completely because of their uncertainty about their future in the city; but they also do not want to marry yet.

Therefore, a common tactic is to delay marriage by extending their migration time in the city despite the harsh working environment. Their physical distance from family members in the village makes this form of resistance possible.

Coping Tactics and Everyday Resistance

Although migrant women are subject to different forms of gender and class domination, they are not passive victims. As social agents, they make pragmatic choices and employ strategies to improve their own situations and resist gender oppression according to the specific circumstances.[6] In the remaining part of this chapter, I discuss several everyday coping and resistance tactics of Wenzhou women and assess their effectiveness and cost.

INFORMAL BUSINESS INVOLVEMENTS

"To control the throat of fate" (*zhuazhu mingyun de yanhou*) is a Chinese expression meaning to take control of one's own life. Some *dahu* women do this by engaging in relatively open and persistent struggles for control through indirect business involvements. Unsatisfied with being "captives" in their own houses, these women find ways to manipulate the male-dominated business sphere and local politics even though they cannot formally own shares in a business or be business leaders. I illustrate this point by describing what happened in one local leader's household.

Zhen and his wife, Lin, came to Beijing together in 1985. They began by renting four small clothing counters in Wangfujing, Beijing's busiest commercial district. At that time, Lin played a major role in most business negotiations because she spoke better Mandarin than her husband. Zhen was not opposed to her participation in business activities because he depended on it. A few years later, they established their own family business producing leather jackets. Lin was in charge of the production process, including quality control, teaching sewing skills, and overseeing ten employees; Zhen took care of things such as purchasing raw materials and finding wholesale buyers. As their business prospered, they accumulated a large amount of capital. During those early years, Lin had a prominent role in major family decisions. But as the Zhen family became a wealthy leading household in Zhejiangcun, things changed.

In 1994, Zhen decided to cease clothing production and turn to the development of migrant housing. Lin suggested that they should keep the garment business going because it was safer and lucrative; housing development, on the other hand, was risky since the family did not have Beijing resident status. Zhen did not listen to her but plunged into the housing project. He sold their newly built house in their hometown for 200,000 yuan and raised 50 million yuan for construction from some twenty shareholders. He completed construction of a large migrant housing compound in 1995, only to have it demolished by the government five months later.

Before the demolition, Lin had persuaded her husband to let her open a leather clothes retail shop. The business was successful and generated 500,000 yuan in the first year, part of which they invested in the housing compound. By then Zhen had already begun to feel insecure about Lin because of her increased daily interaction with other businessmen. He regarded such interactions as damaging to her reputation and consequently to his status as a local boss. After several conflicts, Lin was forced to close down this profitable shop. But instead of giving up, she changed her strategy. She opened a large children's day-care center, supervising several teachers, cooks, and workers. Because this kind of business sphere was viewed as domestic and therefore less threatening to the established gender boundaries, her husband did not interfere with it. The center became an important income source and a temporary residence for the family after the housing compound was torn down. Lin's business and mobility outside the home allowed her to develop social skills and draw support from friends.

Yet such attempts also have costs and can result in domestic violence, especially when gender is linked with other politics. During the government's campaign to clean up Zhejiangcun, local officials put constant pressure on Zhen because he was the most powerful local leader. To avoid direct confrontations, Zhen often left home early in the morning and asked his wife to stay at home to meet them. The idea was that since Lin was a woman the officials could not do much about her. Also, Lin could use her "honey tongue" with the officials, hoping to gain their sympathy for the Wenzhou migrants' plight. One police officer, a member of the leadership of the campaign, was indeed friendly and felt bad about the harsh situation facing migrants. At about this time, the son of Lin's good friend was arrested by the police for drug use. Because the Zhen family had extensive connections (*guanxi*) with the local government, the mother asked Lin for help. When Zhen found out that Lin had asked the friendly police officer for help, he became enraged and beat her up severely. She had a light concussion and was treated in the hospital for two weeks.

This domestic incident was clearly related to Zhen's sexual jealousy; but he also wanted to restore his leadership image, which had been damaged by the state campaign. He used political concerns to justify his violent behavior: "This so-and-so [the police officer], he tore down my big yard. We are enemies. How could she go to beg him for help?" An act of wife-beating was thus symbolically transformed into punishment of a traitor to the migrant community.

Lin had considered leaving home and her husband to start her own business in another province. But her concern for her young children held her back. In the meantime, Zhen was pressured by family members on both sides to save the marriage. As a local leader whose power is largely built upon extended kinship networks, divorce would diminish his influence. Zhen later apologized to Lin and promised to treat her better. Lin stayed but persuaded him to let her open a clothing sales stall in the family's name but under her supervision. He finally agreed.

THE USE OF "VIRTUE"

Women with less education and fewer social skills tend to use indirect leverage in domestic politics. They avoid open confrontation for fear of losing property, young children, and face in the event of divorce. Among Wenzhou migrants, how much alimony a wife receives in a divorce depends on the mercy of her husband. She normally cannot afford to hire a lawyer to defend her rights. In most circumstances, the custody of the children is given to men because it is assumed that women have little means of supporting themselves, let alone children. Further, it is also difficult for divorced women with children to remarry. Given these considerations, some women feel that direct confrontation can only invite more problems and ruin the marriage. For example, Mei's husband was a prominent local businessman who spent little time at home. She knew that he had had an affair but did not confront him about it directly. Her explanation for the choice is as follows:

> If your husband goes out to play with other women, it is no use to know it. Once you find out, the result is quarreling. The more you quarrel, the worse your relationship gets. You see, if he thinks you do not know about it, he may want to be cautious about what he does, so he might not do something too extreme. But if you tear his face away, what else does he care about?

In most people's eyes, Mei was an ideal virtuous wife—pretty, quiet, and never interfering with her husband's business. She took good care of the house and the children. But maintaining the image of a virtuous wife is not simply a gesture of total submission. Women also use "virtuousness" (*xianhui*) to win sympathy and support from kin and friends. The logic is that if she is virtuous and fulfills her wifely duties, the husband has no excuse to abandon her or treat her badly. Therefore, public opinion puts strong social pressure on the husband to set limits on his behavior.

Migrant women like Mei often attribute their deteriorating domestic status to "excessive money" and "bad women." They see money as a form of alienating devil eating away at human hearts and morality. They migrate to the city in the hope of becoming wealthy and living a happy life, but just as they become prosperous their status actually declines. Likewise, women feel that prostitution threatens their marriages and is beyond their personal control. National antiprostitution drives have been ineffective in the economic reform era, and prostitution has become a prevalent social problem in China. Middle-class Wenzhou wives view rampant prostitution as an inevitable result of the national policy of "opening up" (*kaifang*). Hence, some hope to use their "virtue" and social pressure to hold their husbands back rather than pushing them out.

Women in these circumstances frequently visit each other and their relatives to obtain emotional and pragmatic support. Talking is an important way for them to make sense of their situations and share resistance and coping tactics. In a sense, talking opens up a discursive space for women whose spatial mobility is limited.

WOMEN'S NETWORKS

Although no accurate statistical data are available, many informants told me that divorce in Zhejiangcun has become more common, though it is still considered a social stigma. Most divorces are initiated by men who have had extramarital affairs. Occasionally women may also petition for divorce when their husbands insist on keeping a mistress. Divorce is a traumatic experience for women both economically and psychologically. The sudden financial loss and emotional damage can lead to depression and feelings of shame and helplessness. When one young woman in Zhejiangcun discovered that her husband had kept a mistress for years and had two children by her, and that he did not intend to change this situation, she had a mental breakdown and was put into a psychiatric hospital. Suicide and mental illness among migrant women due to failed marriages are side effects of migration as migrants adjust to a different way of life in a highly commodified urban environment.[7]

While suffering from the breakdown of the family, some Wenzhou migrant women have also learned how to fight back by forming mutual support groups rather than remaining permanently trapped in a tormented life.

These groups consist of women who have been abandoned by their husbands, those who can no longer tolerate their husbands' affairs and have launched divorce proceedings, and those who chose to delay remarrying after divorce. These women encourage and help each other to start their own small clothing businesses as a means of self-support. Some cross the gender boundaries by going to places marked as taboo for female consumers, such as karaoke bars and dance halls. Some women also seek legal help through their networking groups. Several even asked me to find them a good lawyer because they thought that I, as an educated person, must have connections in the legal sphere. Since most women do not have the money to pay legal fees up front, they offer a lawyer a high commission, such as 10 to 15 percent percent of the settlement. Thus networking allows women to seek self-empowerment beyond the boundary of the household.

Conclusion

Gender relations in Zhejiangcun vary greatly by household and class status. The gender equality of wealthy migrant women has largely decreased as their households have accumulated more private wealth. As they are gradually pushed out of what is culturally defined as the productive sphere and public space, women in wealthy households become trapped at home with less control over their own lives than before. In lower- and middle-income households, wives are the primary producers in the cottage industry and have more family decision-making power than those in wealthy households. But their work, though indispensable, is largely devalued because it is performed at home. Finally, young workers with little spatial mobility are subject to both class and gender exploitation by their employers.

My analysis further suggests that linking gender exploitation to spatial, social, and economic control can reveal how these multiple factors intersect to reshape the lives of Wenzhou migrant women. The existing power relations reinforce men's superior position in social spaces; in turn, the social boundaries and meanings of these spaces reshape power relations within the family. Women's participation in and contribution to economic production and trade are important in helping them gain power and enhance their social status (see Boserup 1970). But it is certainly not the only determining factor. More recent anthropological accounts have pointed out that women's economic activities cannot be automatically translated into socially recognized values (Judd 1994; Munn 1986; Sangren 1996). In Zhejiangcun, gender domination and the value of women's work are closely linked to the construction of gendered spaces (household, workshop, marketplace, bar and hotel, etc.) and to the cultural perceptions of what is proper or improper, domestic or wild, pure or dangerous, productive or unproductive.

Post-Mao labor migration marks a giant step toward economic liberalization, but it is not socially liberating for all migrant women. Men and women do not benefit equally from economic reform and state modernization projects. Under certain circumstances, a liberal market economy can create new forms of gender oppression. Progress toward gender equality is contingent upon not only women's economic participation but also a transformation of societal values and beliefs that revalorizes work performed by men and women and envisages more flexible social spaces that migrant women in diverse social positions can freely embrace. By only looking at how poor rural households can achieve prosperity through migration, we might fail to note that some women are further disempowered and subject to new forms of gender exploitation during the process of "getting rich."

6. Contesting Crime and Order

A by-product of the rigid socialist rule of Mao's regime was extremely low crime rates and hence a sense of security among urbanites. As China moves toward a market-based economy, however, people's sense of security has eroded. With worsening crime, many urban residents have turned their apartments into small fortresses protected by metal bars and security doors. In 1996 the state undertook a nationwide campaign to crack down on crime, which was perceived to be endangering political stability and public order.[1] To demonstrate the unfailing power of the state, even in an era dominated by money and commodities, major newspapers created a special daily column to report solved criminal cases.

In official discourse, urban crime represents the "evil nature" of free-wheeling market capitalism. Yet the "market" is too abstract to blame directly. In everyday life it is the "floating population," the embodiment of the instability and changes brought by the market, that has become a primary target for criminalization. By "criminalization," I refer to the process through which all migrants are seen as potential criminals by the urban public simply because of their spatial mobility, rural backgrounds, and nonresident status in the city. And migrant enclaves are imagined as hotbeds of crime and disorder and thus as a source of uncertainty, insecurity, and instability.

In this context, migrant congregating zones in general, and Wenzhou migrant housing compounds in particular, stand as dangerous sites in the popular imagination of Beijing officials and residents. Why are rural migrants accused of being responsible for the surging crime in the city? What cultural mechanism makes possible the criminalizing procedure? What is the origin of crime? As I was to learn through my fieldwork, there is no single answer to these questions. What constitutes order, what kind of space is considered safe or unsafe, and what leads to rising crime rates are all highly contentious issues. Different social groups hold different views about social order and the origin of crime. While examining the politics of the social representation of migrant crime, I focus on "multiple visions of a passing historical moment, on variability, and on contestation" (Moore 1993: 4). More important, I argue that the dominant discourse that represents migrant communities as dirty, chaotic, and dangerous is itself a form of social ordering and part of the official effort to turn "out-of-place" migrants into controllable subjects. At the heart of this discursive contestation is the production of knowledge and power that are central to the state's strategies to reregulate migrants in the city (see Foucault 1972).

Although the migrants and their social spaces may have been criminalized unfairly, that does not mean that there is no crime in migrant enclaves. Yet crime in this community should not be seen as an isolated social phenomenon. Crime is perpetuated in migrant communities not because of some fundamental cultural traits of the migrants, but because of the problems inherent in the existing social and legal system. As I will show, the majority of Wenzhou migrants are victims rather than predators. But this important fact is often obscured by the dominant urban discourse that uniformly displaces criminality on the socially marginalized migrant population.[2]

Crime and Representation

Since the mid-1980s, discourse about the criminality of the floating population has proliferated nationally. Official reports, mass media, popular reportage literature (*baogao wenxue*), and social science research on the floating population have attempted to document, understand, and interpret migrant crime and criminality. In the 1980s and 1990s the floating population was presented predominantly as an urban social problem rather than a source of cheap labor and services needed by a growing market economy. Social representations function as "signifying practices" (Hall 1985), which define the reality of migrant enclaves and justify stringent regulation of migrants by the state. In this section, I first juxtapose the dominant urban discourse on migrant crime and a cultural logic of migrant criminality with the views of some Chinese scholars and local Beijing farmers who have daily contact with migrants. I then present the counterdiscourse provided by Wenzhou migrants, which subverts the dominant explanation of the origin of crime.

THE DOMINANT REPRESENTATIONS

In Beijing, official discourse and urban public discourse have many similarities and also some subtle differences. Both tend to regard migrant congregating zones and big yards as the crystallization of "urban cancer" or "filth and mire" brought about by a market economy (Hao 1992). The popular perception that links migrants to crime and instability draws from and is reflected in the media. Official reports have a tendency to magnify one aspect of migrant settlements as the overall reality. For example, one report by several city officials characterized Zhejiangcun as *zang* (dirty), *luan* (chaotic), and *cha* (miserable): "Although they [migrants] have some positive influences in enlivening markets and making local people's lives convenient, they have also created a number of problems, such as overcrowding, traffic jams, poor hygiene, and disorder, and in addition have engaged in crime and other law-breaking activities. All of these problems have seriously impaired the regulation of the local government" (*Beijing Evening Daily*, November 28, 1995). Another article by four officials of the Beijing Municipal Planning Committee claimed, "In recent years the number of crime and law-breaking cases among the incoming floating population has increased. . . . Especially in the congregating zones of the floating population, gambling, prostitution, drug use, and drug trafficking have emerged in an endless stream, creating many new problems for government control of social order and security in Beijing" (Ji et al. 1995: 80).

Unlike official reports, newspapers and magazines are especially interested in spicy, exaggerated anecdotes about crime, drugs, and prostitution associated with the floating population in order to attract readers and earn greater profits.[3] For instance, the *Beijing Evening Daily*, a widely read newspaper, has created a special column entitled "People and Law" (*ren yu fa*) to report crime and illegal activities related to the outsiders (*waidiren*), presumably migrants.[4] Urban residents regard these social reports as a "window on society" (*shehui zhi chuang*) through which they can detect social problems in the city in order to better protect their own personal safety. The images and information produced by the press are the raw materials that the urban public uses to shape its knowledge, imagination, and action toward the migrant population.

Rumors of gunfights, gang violence, and conflicts with the police in migrant communities circulate widely among Beijing residents. Most of these stories are recreated and distorted as they are passed from one person to another. I was warned many times by friends and strangers not to enter Zhejiangcun because, as one of them said, "you will never be able to come out of that dark cave." Taxi drivers are the informal social messengers in the city; one told me about Zhejiangcun: "I heard that Zhejiang people have formed their own little independent kingdom, with their own police, handcuffs, guns, and rules. Outsiders are not allowed to enter the tightly guarded, walled big yards. They run the place in their own ways. Some policemen who tried to step in were murdered."

Like a stream without a source, these images and anecdotes circulate in the city, eventually running together to become elaborate urban myths that shape the popular urban imagination about migrants and their communities. Through repetition, circulation, and expansion, these fantasies, desires, and facts merge to construct the "reality" of the migrant communities. No longer ideological, such representations become part of the "common sense," a naturalized form of ideology, the validity of which people cease to question (cf. Gramsci 1971; Comaroff and Comaroff 1991; Hall 1985). This is not to say that the official and urban public responses and perceptions are all fantasies and paranoia without any social basis. Rather, my point is that crime and illegal activities attributed to the floating population are often exaggerated, statistically manipulated, and taken out of the broader context of changes occurring in Chinese society.

Let us consider three factors here. First, the resurgence of urban crime is a nationwide phenomenon in the post–Mao society; it is not confined to the migrant population. Representations that focus solely on migrant crime divert public attention from other covert, serious crimes committed by officials and local residents. Because of their long-established social networks and connections with urban authority, the locals are less likely to be monitored, exposed, reported, and punished than migrant newcomers who are used as the scapegoats for emerging urban ills. Government officials tend to publicize the crimes migrants commit because those officials cannot be expected to prevent crimes by unofficial residents of their districts. Second, statistics on migrant crime in official reports are largely inflated. For example, criminals who have escaped from jails are usually lumped together as "outsiders." Perpetrators of crimes who escape from the scene are also assumed to be floaters, either by their nonlocal accents or by their dress and demeanor. Third, since crime statistics are not available to the public, numbers cited in the media are not verifiable. Contrary to most newspaper reports, I learned in a personal interview with a local police officer of the Fengtai district that according to police arrest records, Zhejiang migrants do not constitute a high-crime group. Rather, because of the high concentration of wealth among them and the little government protection they receive, they are more often the victims of robbery and drug trafficking.

THE CULTURAL LOGIC OF "MIGRANT CRIMINALITY"

The criminalization of marginalized or displaced groups is by no means unique to Chinese society. In fact, displaced people who cross spatial and social boundaries tend to be regarded as a source of danger and social pollution because they are seen as "out of place" (see Douglas 1966). Therefore, being out of place is often equated with social disorder and uncontrolled destructive power. In many cultural contexts, scholars have illustrated similar processes in which displaced and marginalized groups—refugees, immigrants, blacks, gays, and the homeless poor—are criminalized and pathologized (see Castles and Kosack 1985; Chavez 1992; Foucault 1978; Gilroy 1991; Malkki 1995; Santiago-Irizarry 1996). For example, Malkki has rightly critiqued a powerful sedentarism in thinking about identity and territoriality by which "refugees' loss of bodily connection to their national homelands came to be treated as a loss of moral bearings" (1992: 32). Like the case of refugees, Chinese peasant migrants' spatial mobility and perceived rootlessness are also frequently interpreted in urban public discourse as the result of a lack of moral and social responsibility. The floating population is seen as a diseased social body, polluting urban life because it does not occupy an accepted structural position in the existing societal order.

What is really problematic in the dominant discourse on crime in China is how migrant criminality (*liudong renkou fanzui*) is interpreted. Crime is viewed as a central expression of migrants' spatial mobility, displaced rurality, and craze for money. According to this cultural logic, rural migrants are seen as not morally accountable to urban communities owing to their mobility. Some urbanites explain the problematic relationship between migrants and the urban community by citing an old Chinese saying: "A rabbit never eats the grass around its own nest" (*tuzi buchi wobiancao*). It means that it is natural for people to protect their immediate interests or environment. The implication is that since migrants are not true members of any urban community, they are most likely to take advantage of it by committing crimes. This logic is reflected in the words of an urban resident:

> We locals do not commit crime. Crime in this city is mostly done by the outsiders. They want to bring money and gifts back to show off in front of their folks during the Spring Festival. When they cannot earn money, they naturally go for robbery and stealing. Since they do not live in the city permanently, they do not care about *mianzi* [face] and are not afraid of being captured.

According to this reasoning, rootlessness naturally leads to crime because it removes migrants' moral constraints and concern about saving face since they are strangers in the city. "Nobody wants to do dirty things in his or her own locality because there are friends and acquaintances around. But at places other than one's hometown, face is not much of a concern," a taxi driver explained.

Spatial mobility and displacement are also associated with political instability and disorder. The underlying logic is that since mobile people do not
have long-term investments in any given urban locality, they tend to be
oblivious to the established order and rules and thus difficult to discipline. A
key political term, *dongluan*, links spatial mobility to chaos and disorder. The
state's concern with the impact of the floating population on political stability has roots in the past: "Historically, those who lost the means of production and basis for livelihood tended to become floating people [*liumin*]. They
were the most unstable, destructive, and explosive social elements in Chinese
history. . . . This kind of social force, mainly derived from rural surplus labor
and unemployment, has reappeared today and become the major source of
crime in China" (Ba and Ma 1989: 65). It has also been shown that the
pengmin (shed people, mostly Hakka migrants) in late-imperial China were
perceived of as a threat to the established social order (Leong 1997).

In addition, mobile peasants are viewed as a form of social pollution and
a source of illegalities. In official discourse, the peasantry and the countryside are predominantly regarded as lagging behind in the nation's march to
modernity (Cohen 1993). Negative descriptions of the peasantry, such as
cengci di or *suzhi di* (low class, low quality), *yumei* (primitive or unenlight-
ened), *wuzhi* (ignorant), and *luohou* (backward), are also used to describe the
floating population. These qualities, presumably derived from the deeply
rooted "dark and poor dispositions" (*liegenxing*) of the peasantry, are considered incompatible with the official vision of Chinese modernity and civility.
This is a typical official narrative about rural migrants: "These people's *suzhi*
is generally lower. Their sole purpose in leaving home is to make a living in
the city. Thus, money and wealth are their most direct and basic needs. . . .
Those of low *cengci* tend to take advantage of their mobility to engage in illegal and criminal activities" (Zhang and Wang 1991: 32). In some accounts,
poor environmental conditions in migrant communities are also taken as an
expression of migrants' low *suzhi* (Ji et al. 1995: 80).

It seems to me that the concept of *suzhi* can be better understood in light
of the notion of "habitus" (Bourdieu 1977). Like "habitus," *suzhi* refers to
one's disposition, ability, and way of acting, which are determined by one's
upbringing and thus cannot be easily changed. But *suzhi* is a fluid and vague
concept that means different things to different people, and its meanings can
be manipulated by people to serve their own interests. For instance, the
floating population is stigmatized by urbanites as a social group of poor *suzhi*
mainly because of migrants' lack of formal education and their association
with rural cultural values and way of life. In fact, many migrant entrepre-

neurs are shrewd, capable, and successful business people with economic capital and consumption power. Judging from this perspective, one can say that their *suzhi* is very high, but migrants' business skills are often not counted as a criterion for measuring *suzhi* in the dominant urban public discourse. Instead, their ability to accumulate private wealth upsets (and sometimes replaces) the old social hierarchy based on *hukou* status. In this context, complaints about migrants' low *suzhi* seem to reveal some urban residents' own insecurity and jealousy over being symbolically displaced by successful migrants and failing to assume a prominent place in the new post-Mao economic order. Wenzhou migrants in Beijing are well aware of the urban perception of them as a low-*suzhi* social group; but they contest this stereotype by succeeding in business and adapting to a modern market economy. Even though it is usually urbanites who use *suzhi* to talk about migrants, some Wenzhou merchants have also appropriated the same language of *suzhi* to describe Beijing people as low *suzhi* because they are afraid of hard work, are rude to *waidiren*, and have poor business skills.

Finally, the dominant discourse construes crime as a result of migrants' greed, presumably unleashed by market-oriented city experiences that promise too many unfulfilled dreams. Migrant workers are frequently depicted as ignorant, poverty-stricken, and envious of the urban affluence they lack. For example, one article claims, "Peasant workers who have left their homeland cannot help but be driven by money—the crazy beast. They sell their lives and souls to the 'devil' of money" (Zhang and Han 1993). Another city official concludes: "The contrast between city and countryside is too difficult for peasants in the cities to adjust to; and this huge contrast of material wealth produces an imbalance in their minds . . . leading to the path of reaping without sowing" (*bulao er huo*, implying illegal ways of getting money) (*Beijing Evening Daily*, March 24, 1996).

The above interpretation of migrant criminality functions as what Gilroy (1991) calls "cultural absolutism" in that the problem of urban crime is mapped onto a particular marginal group and is explained by its essentialized "culture." In so doing, the origin of crime is not sought in broader social and structural transformations, but rather is indiscriminately attributed to migrants' inferior *suzhi*. Stereotyping migrants as a homogeneous low-*suzhi* group locked in an unchangeable rural culture juxtaposes them with the presumably modern, sophisticated, cosmopolitan culture of Beijing. This cultural distance between the city and the countryside is then used to justify the argument that rural migrants are not suitable for urban life and ought to return to their origins eventually (see Huang and Ning 1987).

ALTERNATIVE VOICES

Although Chinese social science generally echoes official representations, there is a group of scholars of the younger generation who hold a very different view toward migrants in the cities. These scholars have conducted research themselves in migrant communities and seek to revalorize migrant communities and their economic practices based on their personal observations. Such alternative voices are best articulated by two young researchers, Wang Chunguang and Xiang Biao (see Wang 1995; Xiang 1994). While addressing the problem of crime and disorder in Zhejiangcun, both of them argue that crime should not be exaggerated to encompass the entire social existence of these migrants. Crime is committed by a small section of the migrants and should not be attributed to the entire migrant population. Wang identifies the origin of crime and disorder within the maladjusted social structure in the reform period, such as the legacies of the statist system that impede market competition, the undermining of the efforts to build a legal system by corruption, and local protectionism that perpetuates unfair treatment of migrants. Xiang says that migrant compounds created a better way to maintain local order and mediate the relationship between state control and migrants' self-regulation, and that Wenzhou migrants as a whole are "a politically stable social group" (1994–95). This liberal discourse, although still marginalized, has begun to reshape the popular imagination of the floating population.

Suburban Beijing farmers who have personal interactions with migrants also tend to hold positive attitudes toward migrants in their communities. For them, the economic prosperity brought by migrants is far more significant than the side effects, which they believe are exaggerated by the media. The picture they provide differs from the one held by the general Beijing public. This is how a Beijing landlord in Zhejiangcun sees the issue of crime: "The situation is never as bad as what rumors paint. We have no reason to be afraid of them [migrants]. As long as you do not bother them, they usually will not bother you either. They are interested in their business, not fighting."

COUNTERDISCOURSE: CORRUPTION AS THE ORIGIN OF CRIME

There are a number of discrepancies between migrants' self-representation of their places and the dominant representation. For example, while migrant communities are portrayed as dirty and chaotic places that need to be eliminated or tightly controlled, these are precisely the places where migrants find shelter and a sense of order and security. Wenzhou migrants' big yards are represented as a source of disorder, but migrants see them as relatively safe places to live. A critical counterdiscourse has developed among Wenzhou migrants. It says that rather than focusing on the symptoms of crime, one needs to look at the structural conditions that help produce crime. In other words, the problem of crime should be sought in the existing social system, which perpetuates a particular form of crime culture, rather than in migrant dispositions or spatial mobility. Listen to how Chen, a Wenzhou migrant businessman, articulated this point:

> Beijing people only know that Zhejiangcun is disorderly, but they do not ask why. And they do not know what the real origin of such disorder is. . . . I can assure you that the majority of us are good, law-abiding people. The emergence of crime is closely related to recent societal changes. The problem is more serious here because no one can do anything to stop it. With *guanxi* and bribery money, criminals can easily get out of the police station. This way, lawbreakers are not afraid of anyone and can assault people again and again. In my view, the real origin of crime is rooted in the corruption of the police, as well as the entire legal system.

This account represents a widely shared view among Wenzhou migrants, who insist on differentiating criminals from victims. They believe that only by asking who commits crime against whom can one begin to move away from the tendency to criminalize the migrant group. In Zhejiangcun, most robberies are committed by a very small group of people. Criminals have learned that as long as they raid migrants only, they are less likely to be arrested by the police, who are primarily interested in protecting the locals. As a result, the majority of Wenzhou migrants like Chen have no legal protection and become victims of crime, rather than criminals themselves.

Wenzhou migrants subvert the dominant discourse by relocating the origin of crime in the disorder of the state bureaucracy. For them, the party-state, operating on the basis of the idiosyncratic power of officials (*quan*) rather than the rule of law (*fa*), is deeply corrupt. In the new era of marketization, local officials' incomes declined and they thus became more vulnerable to bribes and payoffs from gangsters and criminals. This rampant corruption in the local government allows crime and disorder to proliferate. Criminal groups that have formed direct or indirect associations with local authorities can bail their members out through large cash payments (as much as ten thousand yuan for each case). In some cases, disorder is even desired by some local police. A migrant explained: "If two parties get in a fight and are taken into custody, both parties have to send money to local authorities. The more you send, the lighter your punishment. Whoever sends more money will come out first. If there is no fight and everything is orderly and peaceful, how can those officials make money?" Corruption sends out signals to criminals that their activities are permissible. In many migrants' eyes, a police station is not the place to get justice done, but is where criminals are recycled and money is extracted. Migrants view the state as a regime of disorder and thus delegitimize it.

Although the origin of migrant crime is contested, migrant voices remain marginal and unheard in the city because they do not control the media. The remainder of this chapter provides a detailed ethnographic account of how drugs and robbery appeared in Zhejiangcun and how the majority of Wenzhou migrants grapple with this problem.

An Ethnography of Crime and Its Origins

In my interviews and daily conversations with Wenzhou migrants, I frequently asked them: What aspects of your life in Beijing concern or worry you most? Some said that it was "not being able to make enough money." But most replied, almost without hesitation, that it was personal safety and public security (*zhian*). In particular, those who lived outside the big yards received less local protection and thus felt more vulnerable than those within the housing compounds under the patronage of housing bosses. The following three excerpts from my interviews illustrate Wenzhou migrants' anxieties toward their families' safety:

> Public security is what worries me most. Sojourning at a place so far away from home and with my personal safety in danger, this is the biggest problem. This feeling is like a hidden disease in one's vital organ [*xinfu zhi huan*]. When we first came to Beijing, we were afraid of Beijing hooligans [*liumang*], who were ferocious to us. When they bullied us, we did not dare to say a word. Later, there were more and more of our Zhejiang people in this area, and we began to overpower Beijing hooligans. Now we are no longer afraid of Beijing *liumang*, but we are afraid of Zhejiang *liumang*. (A female migrant, owner and teacher in a family-run preschool)

> The thing that disturbs me most is the issue of personal safety and public security. Even if I am all right today, who knows what will happen tomorrow. Every minute, we live in constant fear of being robbed or even killed. If we

cannot feel safe and settled, how can we focus on our production and business? (A male migrant stall keeper)

Did you see that metal door? We installed it recently because we are afraid of being robbed and hurt. Public security here is very poor. There have been so many robberies in recent years. [LZ: Who are the robbers?] They are mostly drug addicts who come out at night with masks and knives. They break people's doors and force them to take out all the money. (A migrant who ran a small day-care center)

At the time of my interviews, these informants lived in local Beijing farmers' houses. They pointed out that because the local Beijing government was only interested in collecting fees, it provided them no protection against crime. People living in the housing compounds received some protection from their patrons, but those outside the compounds had none.

To understand how robbery and extortion became prevalent problems in Zhejiangcun, one must realize that the newly emerged drug culture is at least indirectly related to the majority of robbery cases. For this reason, Wenzhou migrants refer to robbers and other criminals by two specific terms: *chi dayan de* (those who eat opium) and *chou baifen de* (those who smoke white powder—heroin).

DRUGS AND SELF-DESTRUCTION

Drugs did not become a salient problem in Zhejiangcun until the 1990s. Because of the high concentration of private wealth and lack of government control, drugs are smuggled into the community daily. Beginning in the early 1990s, narcotics, mostly heroin and opium, began to spread among young Wenzhou migrants, those age sixteen to twenty-five. According to Xiang (1994–95), there were four to six underground drug trafficking spots and about two thousand drug addicts in this settlement by 1995. During my fieldwork (1995–96), the number of drug users increased steadily, and so did drug prices. One gram of heroin cost over a thousand yuan, more than one gram of gold. Since drugs are so expensive, it is not long before those who become addicted can no longer afford them.

The effects of drugs on the social fabric of the community are profound. Drug consumption creates tensions and conflicts between young drug users and their parents. When parents discover that their children are addicted, some deny them financial support or cut off their access to the family business. Some parents manage to place their addicted children in rehabilitation centers in their hometowns. But many parents are simply too busy to pay attention to their children's problems. Unable to bear the criticism and humiliation imposed by family members, some youngsters simply run away from their families and live with peers in similar situations. Struggling with destitution, some must turn to robbery to meet their increasing craving for drugs. Others find secret places to continue smoking heroin behind their parents' backs.

Parents of drug addicts feel ashamed, desperate, and helpless. They attribute the problem to the domination of commodities and money. In today's society, traditional parental authority has largely lost power over the younger generation who only respect the power of money. But when their children are arrested, many parents try to bribe officials to release them before they are convicted. Torn between her parental love and resentment toward her son, one mother said, "No matter how terrible his behavior is, after all he is my own child, my flesh and blood. How can I see him being locked in jail without giving him help?!" Given such mixed feelings, parents sometimes end up helping perpetuate the problem itself.

Drugs can also lead to the loss of the family business and to the disintegration of marriage and family ties. Some people begin with occasional use of a small amount of drugs and think that they can control their use and when to stop. But as their addiction increases, they begin to lose interest in their businesses and squander their savings on drugs. An addicted heroin user can spend up to four hundred yuan a day, over 100,000 yuan a year!

In most instances that I know of, young wives of addicted husbands demanded divorces and assumed responsibility for raising the children alone. In one instance, it was the wife who became a drug addict and lost custody of her two young children. When both members of a young couple became addicted to drugs and left their children unattended, their parents or relatives had to take the children in. These children were often subject to violence by their parents and suffered from depression.

Although I heard much about drug use and drug trafficking in Zhejiangcun in the first several months of my fieldwork, I did not speak directly to any drug users because their activities tended to take place covertly. Many questions puzzled me: Why did these people begin using drugs? Where did they get the drugs? How did they interact with their families and friends? The opportunity to gain some firsthand answers to these questions finally came unexpectedly.

It was a freezing winter day in Beijing. I went to visit my friend Lan, who had just moved into a small apartment. Lan was a young woman from a village in Hongqiao township, Wenzhou, and was one of my key informants.

That afternoon, we bought some vegetables and seafood in a local market-place to cook lunch together. When we returned to her room, there was a young man reclining on the sofa. He was short and skinny, and his face looked yellow and tired. Before I could even say hello, Lan winked at me and whispered into my ear: "Did you see what he is doing? But please don't say anything about it." I then realized that he was smoking heroin, "white powder" as it was called locally. Lan introduced me simply as a good friend of hers and did not mention anything about my research. I smiled at him and sat on the edge of the bed opposite him. He introduced himself as Zhou. Once he knew I was Lan's friend, not a reporter or stranger, he did not seem to mind my presence and continued to enjoy his magic powder. I did not say anything for a while and just watched him quietly.

Zhou was fully concentrated on what he was doing. He had a small piece of tinfoil in his hand. After carefully spreading the white powder evenly down the center of the tinfoil, he bent it into an arc shape with the powder in the middle. Then, with one hand he put a small tin straw in his mouth and lit a cigarette lighter with the other. As he moved the lighter beneath the tinfoil and the hot flame heated the heroin from below, he greedily sucked the powder into his body through the little tin straw. Finally, he ate a piece of apple to help him swallow the powder, which otherwise might be stuck in his throat. "That would be a waste if you do not get everything into your stomach, it is so expensive." That was the first thing he said to me. Now he looked more relaxed. Then he repeated the process several times. After a while he became quite relaxed and talkative. He began to ask me what I did for a living and why I was there. I said that I was a student studying Zhe-jiangcun. But he was primarily interested in talking and did not seem to pay attention to my answers. I asked him how he was feeling. With his eyes almost closed, he said in a state of hallucination: "It is the best feeling in the world. Now, whatever I think is real, and whatever I want is mine. Money and beautiful women are all within my reach."

Zhou was in his early twenties and unmarried, and came from the same village as Lan. His family had a profitable shoe store on the main street of Zhejiangcun. He had managed the store successfully and made a lot of money. But since becoming addicted to drugs, he could no longer concentrate on the business, and his sister had had to take over.

While he was taking a break from inhaling the drug, I was surprised to hear him say: "Actually this stuff is not good for the body; it is also too expensive, costing me a lot of money; but I cannot quit it." I asked him why, if he knew all these facts, he had started in the first place. He laughed:

Do you think that we paid money for this stuff at first and then became addicted? No, it is always the other way: some friends give you a little bit to smoke first without asking for any money. They let you taste it for a while, but once you become addicted, they will not give you any more for free. They even tell you that this stuff is not good for your health and you should not do it anymore. But if you are hooked on it, you cannot resist the craving, and you beg them to sell you some.

Not knowing where to get supplies, new addicts often turn to those who have led them into drugs in the first place. But this time they have to pay for it. The payment helps the older addicts support their own drug consumption. Thus a strange circle of drug consumption is formed. While we were talking, Zhou offered me a taste of his white powder. I tried to decline it in a polite way, but he sensed what I was thinking. "Elder sister, you are afraid of getting addicted to it, right? I tell you that it is not a problem just once or twice."[5] I thanked him but insisted on not taking it.

Given Zhou's apparently mixed feelings about drugs, I was curious whether he had ever tried to quit. His answer revealed a picture of how helpless youngsters like him struggled with the irresistible narcotic power:

Yes, I tried, but it did not work. The withdrawal period for somebody like me takes at least seven or eight days. This period is like an endless dark night in hell. At night when the craving comes, you do not want or care about anything else but smoking it. If you cannot get it, you cannot fall asleep for even a minute. I remember that my entire body ached unbearably and felt itchy. I was in agony.

The experience he described had taken place about half a year earlier, when his parents and siblings found out about his drug addiction and forced him to go through withdrawal. But not long after that, he could not resist the returning cravings and started up again. Feeling powerless to resist the drugs and ashamed in front of his kin, he became careful to smoke only in secret. He told me that some of his friends who tried to quit went to a drug rehabilitation center in his hometown.[6] "It costs about ten thousand yuan a shot to put somebody to sleep for several days. When they wake up, they seem to feel fine for a while. But after a few days, the addiction comes back again," Zhou continued. Thus, many people have lost faith in this sort of treatment, viewing it as a money-making machine rather than a solution to the problem.

When I met Zhou, he still had some money and was receiving an allowance from his parents and elder siblings. But that income was already not enough to meet his growing need for drugs. He admitted that some of his friends robbed and used extortion to get drug money, but he said that he had never done it. According to Zhou, when youth are caught by the police, their friends and families raise bribe money in order to set them free. That leads to more frantic robbery and extortion in order to compensate for the bribe. For this reason, they are not really afraid of the police despite increasingly stringent state drug laws. For them, being caught by the police was more of a financial loss than anything else. That was why, when I asked Zhou whether he was worried about being captured by the police, he replied: "No, as long as you have money to bribe them, you can be set free very quickly. A friend of mine is a local small drug dealer. He was caught recently for trading sixty grams of heroin. After being detained in the district police bureau for just one night, he was released with no criminal charges. These days, money makes it easier to negotiate with the police." In this context, what is legal or illegal as defined by law is not as important as how the law is enforced locally. Only those who cannot come up with bribery money or do not have the right kinds of *guanxi* are doomed to receive heavy punishment.

In Zhejiangcun, migrants' attitudes toward drug use are divided and ambivalent. While most of them see drugs as a waste of money and drain on business, some regard drug consumption as a status symbol and a measure of financial success. Although the migrants themselves say that typical drug addicts are youngsters like Zhou, some wealthy, middle-aged businessmen also smoke opium and heroin. Being able to afford drugs while not ruining the business is seen as a sign of affluence. One young Wenzhou migrant said: "If you really have plenty of money, smoking the white powder is not a problem. Say if you make five thousand yuan a day, smoking away a thousand or two thousand yuan is not a big deal. You can still use drugs without going bankrupt or turning to robbery."

Half an hour later Zhou became sleepy, not so talkative anymore. Eventually, he collapsed onto the bed and fell into a sound sleep. That was how our conversation ended. About four months later I ran into five or six youngsters again at Lan's apartment. They were smoking heroin in the same way that Zhou had. They told me similar stories about how they began to use drugs and how they tried to quit unsuccessfully. When they found out that my hometown is in Yunnan, a southern border province in China, they became extremely interested and asked me whether there was indeed a lot of white powder available there at a lower price.[7] They told me that they usually bought drugs from small local dealers in the community, but occasionally they bought outside because it was cheaper. Sometimes such excursions turned out to be a bad experience, as one of them recalled:

> I went to Xinjiangcun once. When I asked the restaurant boss whether he had any white powder, he said no and wanted to see my identification card. After making sure that I was not an undercover policeman, he sold me one small package of heroin for a thousand yuan. But only after I came back did I find out that I had been cheated. What I had in hand was white wheat flour.

Older Wenzhou migrants are deeply worried that Zhejiangcun is on its way to self-destruction if drugs continue to permeate the community. They draw an analogy between the current situation and the nation's tragic and humiliating historical experience during the Opium War, in which drugs became the most powerful destructive force in the Chinese nation. To change this situation, they suggest that at least three things need to be done: tougher control of drug trafficking in the border regions, reform of the corrupt bureaucratic system, and better education of the younger generation. The cycle of occasional police raid, arrest, and subsequent release of drug dealers and users can only encourage the drug culture to persist.

The drug problem among Wenzhou migrants is partly a consequence of the emergence of the transnational flows of commodities. It is no longer a secret that narcotics have reappeared in post-Mao China on a vast scale despite the state's effort to curb and eliminate them.[8] As China opens its doors to global capital and transnational commodity flows, it also creates new spaces for drug trade and consumption. Drugs are smuggled into China today primarily by two routes: through the famous Golden Triangle (*jinsanjiao*), an area where Burma, Laos, and Thailand intersect, via China's border province, Yunnan, then inland; and through what has been called "the golden new moon" (*jinxinyue*), a large area that covers Pakistan, Afghanistan, and Iran and is linked to China's Xinjiang Uygur Autonomous Region (*Beijing Evening Daily*, June 27, 1996).

In Beijing, even though Xinjiang migrants are stereotyped as ignorant, greedy drug dealers who are willing to risk their lives to make a quick fortune, the evidence from newspaper reports is that drug trafficking is an extremely complicated process often involving people of different backgrounds. While some Xinjiang migrants indeed engage in drug trafficking, many large drug deals are in fact handled by local Beijing residents who are better protected and subject to less surveillance than migrants.

ROBBERY, EXTORTION, AND THE MORAL DISTRIBUTION OF WEALTH

The companions of drugs are robbery and extortion, often combined with physical violence. Even though only a small fraction of the migrant population in Zhejiangcun is involved in such activities, the affliction they have created is pervasive.

Predators and Victims

Zhejiangcun is the target of drugs and crime for two main reasons: a high concentration of cash among migrant entrepreneurs, and corruption of local bureaucrats and their ineffective policing of order. Insofar as local Beijing residents are not harmed, the local police are very unlikely to undertake further serious investigation. There is another important consideration for not robbing local Beijing residents: their relatively lower incomes compared with those of migrant entrepreneurs. Most local farmers' income comes from rent, which usually does not exceed two thousand yuan monthly. Keeping on hand only enough for daily expenses, they put the remainder in the bank. By contrast, Wenzhou migrants are in general much wealthier than locals, and they often keep large amounts of cash on hand for business transactions. The presence of cash at homes makes in-door robbery easier.

A commonly held view among Wenzhou migrants is that the predators responsible for most robberies and extortion are young drug addicts, those who have lost their fortunes, and convicted criminals who have escaped from jail. These hedonists who "love leisure and despise work" (*haoyi wulao*) are a new by-product of a consumption-oriented society. Unlike the migrant patron-client networks I described earlier, the primary goal of such small criminal gangs is not self-protection but obtaining other people's wealth through violent acts. In most robbery cases, victims were middle-income migrant families living outside the housing compounds because they had the money to pay what was demanded by the predators, but they had little protection from patrons. The very wealthy households usually had more clout and their own followers for protection; those living in the housing compounds were under the patronage of powerful housing bosses.

Extortion and Indoor Robbery

Robbery takes place in both private and public spaces. But most of the serious crime is planned in advance. The time and the victims are carefully chosen. The robbers are usually familiar with the victim's finances and business. Some robberies involve face-to-face extortion combined with physical threat; others are done by masked robbers who may well be acquainted with their victims. "You know they are out there. They even say hello to you every day. But you never know when you will become their next target," a migrant explained.

The following is a typical extortion scenario.[9] Boss Huang was a wholesale dealer. He made a great deal of money in several major garment transactions in 1993. Somehow this information was passed to some local youngsters. One November evening, three young men came to his door. Huang recalled, "They said that there was someone named Chen from Furong township who owed them 100,000 yuan and that I had three days to turn the person over to them. I remembered that there was someone named Chen who did business with me once but then fled without paying me ten thousand yuan from that transaction. I had no idea where he went. So I dismissed those youngsters and did not pay much attention to it. Three days later, the three people came back and demanded Chen again! This time they did not waste time and immediately initiated a fight with me. I was lucky to have six or seven helpers in the store at the time. They helped fight back and drove them away. But ever since then I was cautious and closed down my shop for a week." Soon after he had reopened his store, a crowd of people showed up with knives. They dashed into his store, trashed everything, broke his cousin's legs, and left a mess behind. Huang was frightened. Instead of reporting to the police, he decided to settle the matter through a well-known local migrant patron. He ended up paying a large sum of cash and offering several banquets to treat those people involved. His total loss was nearly 100,000 yuan. Part of the cash payment went to the youngsters and part went to the local patron. Many migrants choose to settle extortion in this way because they do not have confidence in the police and they are afraid of further revenge.

What frightens Wenzhou migrants even more is indoor robbery (*rushi qiangjie*). Indoor robbery is frightening not only because it is violent but also because it intrudes on the private domestic realm, a space that in socialist China has always been relatively safe. "Indoor robbery" as a major crime category did not appear until the reform period, especially in the 1990s. The "March 20th case" reflects the experiences of many migrant families (see *Beijing Evening Daily*, June 9, 1996).

Wenzhou migrant Kong lived in Zhejiangcun, and his home was raided on the night of March 20. The day before the incident, Kong withdrew forty thousand yuan from the bank in order to buy some leather for his family business. Kong was a quiet person who never showed off his wealth. It turned out that the robber, Song, was his neighbor, a fellow Wenzhounese who had become addicted to heroin. Song had run out of money and had to rely on robbery to keep satisfying his craving for drugs. One day he happened to hear from his two neighbors that Kong's leather garment production was very profitable and that he had just taken a large amount of cash out of the bank to buy more leather the next day. Song was secretly delighted and thought that the chance of getting rich was finally coming. He went to talk to his uncle, who was also desperately in need of cash. A robbery plan took shape. Song first appeared at Kong's residence at about seven in the evening for a casual chat and visit. He tried to memorize how things were arranged in the house and then left. At about 3 A.M., when Kong's household members and workers were still working in front of the sewing machines, several masked robbers suddenly broke into the house. They ordered everyone to keep silent and demanded Kong's money. When Kong refused to give it to them, the robbers hit him on the head and knocked him to the ground. Then they searched the house until they found the 40,000 yuan and an additional 48,900 yuan that Kong's brother-in-law had left with him temporarily for their planned trip.

While indoor robberies are carefully planned and organized, street robberies are mostly random, involving not only cash but also more visible items such as expensive leather jackets, furs, and other clothing products. Wenzhou migrants usually transport raw materials and finished clothing products by pedicab from production sites (their residences) to the marketplace. The winding and narrow village alleyways are prime sites for crime. Robbers often stay in small motels adjacent to Zhejiangcun and go out in a group of three or four. When a good opportunity presents itself, they jump out of dark corners, seize the goods from the target, and flee quickly. Public spaces such as bathrooms are also a potential site for robbery, especially at night.[10] I have heard of many migrant women being assaulted in the bathrooms for their jewelry. Young female workers are particularly vulnerable because they tend to work late and use the bathrooms at night.

REACTION FROM THE POLICE

The following account by a Wenzhou migrant reflects a common problem with the police. As I have noted, the initial reaction of the police to crime and violence within the migrant population was to ignore it.

> They [police] are never there for you. If you are still alive and can manage to report to the police, the criminals have usually escaped. The last time my

family was robbed, I filed a report at the local police station. Instead of coming to the site immediately, they asked me who the criminals were and where they were. If I knew all that, why did I need their help? So I said I did not know. They accused me of lying about the case because I did not have enough evidence.

Since their duties are normally determined by the size of an area's permanent population, no extra government funding is available for police officers' salaries or to expand the police force for regulating migrants. When migrants poured into the area, their numbers were two to three times that of the local population, and the police were not equipped to regulate them. I once asked a local policeman why the regulation of the floating population is a chronic problem and whether he had any good ideas about how to improve it. He replied:

> No, I do not have any good ideas. No one does. This is a problem embedded in the current social-political system. To tell you the truth, we have never had any good methods of dealing with this new phenomenon [migration]. When so many people suddenly pour into the cities, our old social regulatory system cannot absorb these mobile people. Thus, we [the police] have always been in a position of passively coping with it, never actively tackling the problem because it requires some fundamental reforms in the existing system.

There are also cultural barriers in regulating the migrants. For example, the language difference can seriously impede the police's work during investigations. Lack of familiarity with Wenzhou migrants' social and economic practices also prevents the local police from picking up important signs and traces of criminal acts. Given this situation, the government of Yueqing, a subregion of Wenzhou, had voluntarily sent a small team of policemen to assist in the policing of social order in Zhejiangcun. But regional rivalries made this idea of cooperation between the sending and receiving areas unworkable. Soon after the arrival of the six Yueqing policemen, the two police corps (Beijing and Yueqing) entered into an ugly power struggle. Each side charged the other with covering up the evil deeds of its own people. Several confrontations occurred when the Yueqing police accused a local Beijing policeman of brutally beating a migrant suspect. Instead of collaboration, the result was conflict, misunderstanding, and hostility between the two sides. After two months, the Yueqing police were ordered by the Beijing government to leave. The Beijing officials claimed that Zhejiangcun was the duty zone of the Beijing police, not the Yueqing police. They feared that the emergent migrant leadership could be further empowered by the support of the Yueqing police.

In recent years, the local police have become more interested in handling criminal cases related to Wenzhou migrants because those relatively wealthy migrants provide a great opportunity for generating extra income. Corrupt policemen and local thugs have formed clientelist ties, which allow the latter to buy their freedom and bypass the law. For many migrants, the new local police "regulations" are more of an unofficial way of creating side-incomes for underpaid policemen than an effort to keep good public order and restore justice for migrants.[11]

Conclusion

"Migrant crime" and "disorder" are highly contentious issues in contemporary urban China. The dominant perception is that crime in the city is the fault of the migrant other, thus obscuring the larger picture of increasing crime facing the entire urban society. This view does not merely reflect or distort the reality, but is itself a form of social ordering, with real political consequences. Because the migrant population is constructed as a high crime group and to a certain degree a social anomaly (being out of place), it has been subject to arbitrary official campaigns of "cleaning and reordering." In Zhejiangcun, the cultural politics of representation resulted in a government campaign that nearly destroyed this migrant community.

While critiquing the majority's representation of the floating population, I do not mean to suggest that their views and perceptions were unfounded fantasies. My point is that "migrant crime" must not be viewed in isolation or simply be attributed to the cultural traits of rural migrants. Crime in migrant communities is an integral part of the structural problems in local governance in an era of commodified social relations. By essentializing criminality and attributing it to migrant *suzhi*, such discourse simply designates a scapegoat and thus fails to locate the structural origin of urban crime. In Zhejiangcun the majority of Wenzhou migrants are the victims of crime because, on the one hand, local state agents are bought off by criminals and thus unable to provide effective protection for the majority of law-abiding migrants; on the other hand, upper-level governments fear the migrant leadership and thus suppress its growth and role in local ordering. Better-organized, self-regulated migrant housing compounds could have provided a safer and more orderly environment for Wenzhou migrants. Yet the informal privatization of space and power was perceived by the central and city governments as even more threatening than crime. The next two chapters examine how these concerns about migrant crime and the growth of nonstate power led to a political campaign that shattered tens of thousands of Wenzhou migrants' lives.

7.   The Demolition of Zhejiangcun

In late 1995 the official campaign to "clean up and reorder" (*qingli zhengdun*) Zhejiangcun led to the expulsion of some forty thousand migrants from Beijing. Before they left, many watched as their newly built homes were bulldozed into piles of rubble. The scene was reminiscent of that described by Steinbeck as the homes of impoverished farmers in Oklahoma were destroyed by landowners in order to drive the farmers out:

> And the driver thundered his engine and started off. . . . Across the dooryard the tractor cut, and the hard, footbeaten ground was seeded field, and the tractor cut through again; the uncut space was ten feet wide. And back he came. The iron guard bit into the house corner, crumbled the wall, and wrenched the little house from its foundation so that it fell sideways, crushed like a bug. (John Steinbeck, *The Grapes of Wrath*)

After their homes were demolished, most of the Wenzhou migrants fled to nearby towns and the surrounding countryside; a small group temporarily returned to their home villages in Wenzhou.

The municipal government hastily announced its victory over migrant disorder and crime in Zhejiangcun and claimed full credit for protecting the interests and safety of Beijing residents by cleaning out socially "rotten" or "polluted" areas from the pure social body of Beijing. Though this event was officially represented as a triumph of good over evil, national and local media reports on the campaign were curiously restricted. Only a few short reports prepared by the party's propaganda agencies were released.[1] What actually happened behind the seemingly smooth and innocent picture painted by the official reports? What kinds of social conflicts emerged in this event and what did they tell us about the shifting relationship between the state and local society?

This chapter documents the political campaign to dismantle Wenzhou migrants' housing compounds. I pay special attention to the social and political conflicts that occurred on several levels. In analyzing the underlying political motivations of this campaign, I contrast the concerns of upper-level governments with the quite different rationale that motivated lower-level government officials. As I will demonstrate, their different emphases on economic gain and political stability were at the root of rising conflicts within the bureaucracy.

The demolition campaign provoked vocal expressions of emotion by the migrants, as well as reflections on urban citizenship, state power, and social belonging. Although widespread popular resistance to the government campaign was not formally organized, it was oriented toward the collective fate of Wenzhou migrants rather than individual losses. Meanwhile, the culturally specific notion of loyalty to native place was frequently appropriated by migrants to solicit political protection from their regional governments in negotiation with the Beijing government. The formation of informal political-economic coalitions between the migrants and their regional governments also indicated the growing disparity and instability within the "state" itself. Although popular resistance by migrants and local residents did not halt the campaign, its significance should not be discounted because it left a powerful influence on the city government's future strategy for dealing with this settlement.

In their study of compliance strategies in Communist China, Skinner and Winckler (1961) illustrated that the socialist state often shifted its strategy of control from exhortation to coercion in a cyclical manner. This cycle was reflected during the campaign to destroy Zhejiangcun. The government workteam first relied on normative power in an effort to persuade migrants to leave Beijing. When this failed, the workteam turned to coercion, physically removing migrants' houses to force them out of the community. A few months later when displaced migrants returned to the settlement, the government adopted a different regulation strategy based on the exchange of migrant compliance for material rewards via the mediation of local bosses.

Panic and Social Conflict on the Eve of the Demolition

No signs predicted the political storm in Zhejiangcun until late October 1995. Indeed, the migrants' garment businesses and community life were going very well. Thousands of migrant households had just moved into their large housing compounds and begun to enjoy a relatively stable, secure, and organized life. These entrepreneurial families were busy preparing for the annual "golden season" in the garment trade. Sales in the three months before the Chinese New Year (the Spring Festival, which fell around mid-February in 1996) usually generate the largest portion of annual profits. The hum of sewing machines around Zhejiangcun reminded one that a prosperous business season was coming. For the first time in their sojourning years, many Wenzhou migrants began to feel settled; they finally had their own marketplaces and residential space. A stall owner expressed his feelings with the traditional Chinese phrase, *anju leye*. It means that only when one has a permanent place to live can one begin to enjoy one's work or business. Yet just as this better life began, it was falling under a dark political shadow.

In late October, rumors spread among the migrants that the municipal government was determined to demolish all illegal structures (mainly migrant housing compounds) in Zhejiangcun and disperse the highly concentrated Wenzhou migrant group. This informal "alleyway news" (*xiaodao xiaoxi*) was leaked by local policemen (*pianjing*) via housing bosses. Although no official posters or announcements had been made public yet, this information immediately caused anxiety and panic among the migrants and local farmers. Soon migrants learned that the Beijing city government planned to demolish their housing compounds and that the decision had been personally endorsed by Premier Li Peng. Wenzhou migrants understood clearly that the state or government was composed of diversely situated agents whose interests might conflict. Therefore, there was always room for negotiation and maneuvering. If the campaign were to be carried out by the lower-level government, migrants would have more bargaining power because local officials shared many economic interests with them. When the migrants learned that this time the central and municipal governments were directly responsible for the campaign, they realized how serious the situation was.

As a prelude to the imminent large-scale demolition, district and city governments ordered some one hundred small clothing stalls on the main street of Zhejiangcun to be torn down. These makeshift stalls were mostly constructed by the local subdistrict government to generate extra income (*chuangshou*).[2] The official reason given was that these stalls were illegal structures and encroached on the street, which needed to be broadened to permit normal traffic flow. But many speculated that the demolition of the stalls was a test of how much popular resistance the campaign would encounter.

On the morning of November 1, as soon as I stepped out of the minibus at the entrance of Zhejiangcun, I sensed that something was wrong. There was a sense of tension floating in the atmosphere. The area where the makeshift stalls were concentrated was unusually crowded and noisy. There were many large cardboard signs in front of the stalls, and some read "Big

Moving Sale," "Discounts with Tears," or "Heart-Broken Sale." Stall keepers were shouting loudly in order to attract customers. They shouted until
their voices were hoarse. Thousands of buyers were pushing and shoving,
trying to get the best bargain. The prices were very low, about half of normal. As I joined the crowd buying flannel shirts and silk blouses, I asked one
of the stall keepers: "Why do you want to move? This is a great place for
business." He looked desperate and sighed: "We do not want to leave! But
the government suddenly ordered the removal of all the stalls. They said that
these are illegal structures that cause traffic jams. But these stalls have been
here for almost two years, and no one said anything before. It is crazy." I
asked him who had actually given the order. He said "some officials," but he
was not sure exactly which ones. Stall keepers were told to evacuate by
November 3, before the full-fledged demolition began the following day. He
went on, "They [officials] also said that all of Zhejiangcun will soon be
flattened and that migrants will not be allowed to do business in this area
anymore." I asked another stall keeper whether they had tried to appeal to
the local government collectively. She laughed and said: "No. Who will listen to us? We are outsiders who have no rights in the city. If this decision had
been made by the local district government, we might be able to negotiate
with it. But as far as we know, this order comes from the central and city
governments. So it will be extremely hard to disobey it."

While talking to the stall keepers, I learned that the majority of them were
actually from Anhui, not Wenzhou. Their stalls (about five square meters each)
were originally rented to Wenzhou migrants by the local Dahongmen subdistrict government (*jiedao banshichu*) at an annual rate of ten thousand yuan.
Later, many Wenzhou traders had rented their stalls to Anhui migrants who
wanted to do business there. But they raised the rent to thirty thousand yuan.

The dismantling of these clothing stalls instigated widespread conflict
involving the interests of three social groups: Anhui migrant stall keepers,
Wenzhou middlemen, and subdistrict officials. Local officials declared that
since the demolition was an unpredictable incident initiated by the higher-
level government and they themselves also suffered financial losses, they
could not reimburse the Wenzhou renters for the prepaid rent, except for a
small symbolic compensation fee (less than two thousand yuan for each stall).
To minimize their own losses, Wenzhou middlemen refused to reimburse
Anhui migrants for any prepaid rent. One day I saw two Anhui men arguing with a Wenzhou woman about the rent. They claimed that they had paid
a large lump sum of money for a twelve-month lease just three months earlier. Since the stall would be demolished and they could not continue their

business, they wanted part of the rental fee back. One of the men threatened to detain the woman until the money was paid. He cursed her for being heartless and greedy. The other man was too angry to say anything, but stood smoking silently. Like many other Anhui migrants, these two men had borrowed large sums of money from friends and relatives back home that now they were unable to pay back. The Wenzhou woman insisted that her family did not have the money because they had invested it in their family clothing business. But then she said that her husband had gone back to their hometown to borrow money. If they wanted the money back, they would have to let her go and wait for it. The two men did not trust her. Frustrated, she became hysterical and shouted at them:

> Boss so-and-so charged other people thirty thousand yuan for half a year's rent; other bosses also charged thirty thousand yuan for just seven or eight months' rent. I charged you much less for the entire year. How can you push me like this?! It is the state that wants to tear down the stalls. What can I do about it? I have nothing but my life. If you want take my life away, go ahead. I am right here!

Similar disputes were widespread in Zhejiangcun during that period. A few days later, when I was visiting a wealthy Wenzhou migrant, Yan, at his house, four Anhui migrants showed up at his door to demand the return of the money they had paid for a stall rental. A couple of years earlier Yan had rented a stall from the subdistrict officials for nine thousand yuan a year, which he in turn had rented to two Anhui migrant families. But not long after these Anhui migrants started their business, the stall was torn down.

Perhaps because of my presence, Yan tried to appear polite; he let the Anhui migrants into his living room. But they were obviously intimidated by Yan and did not even sit down. Yan asked the Anhui migrants what they wanted, even though he knew exactly why they were there. One of them answered carefully:

> Well, we know that you also suffered financial loss in this campaign. But you are a big boss and have a very strong financial capability. So such a loss cannot possibly weaken you. But for us, it is a matter of life and death. Now since we have nothing left, we would rather die than go back home because all the money we paid you was borrowed from other people. If you can just give us part of it back, it will mean a lot to us.

Boss Yan looked indifferent. He put his cigarette aside, slowly raised his eyes, and said:

You guys only lost twenty to thirty thousand yuan; but I will soon lose 200,000 to 300,000 yuan when they [state officials] come to destroy my big yard [He was a shareholder in the largest Jinou yard.] Where should I go to get my money back? I do not have any cash now. But if you want my house, go ahead and tear it apart, because sooner or later the government will order us to destroy it anyway! Yes, you can even sell the bricks. They are worth something.

The Anhui migrants were scared because Yan's words implied violence—tearing down his house. They tried a different strategy, threatening Yan with a lawsuit. But Yan knew that they could not afford a lawyer and had no *guanxi* with Beijing officials. He laughed hard and said: "Go ahead. This is just what I am waiting for. In fact, I will pay you to sue. But there is no legal contract between you and me. If you dare to sue me, I will sue you back for a false charge." At this moment, half a dozen youngsters living in the housing compound showed up. They shouted at the Anhui migrants: "What do you come here for? He [Yan] has nothing to do with you. If you do not get out of our place quickly, we will beat you up and throw you out." Given this bellicose atmosphere, the four Anhui migrants unwillingly left Yan's house.

While this dispute took place, I watched in silence, unsure what else to do. I felt uncomfortable and sad when the Anhui migrants left in despair. I kept wondering where they went and what they would do to pay their debts. In the overall scheme of migrant social and economic hierarchy in Beijing, Anhui migrants were lower on the scale than Wenzhou migrants. Thus, the conflict here articulated an asymmetric relationship between the two groups of migrants, both regionally and by class. This example was just one of hundreds of disputes in the local society before the full-fledged campaign began. As the demolition campaign deepened and more local people's interests were involved, social conflicts became even more pervasive and intense. Let us look at the political and social factors that contributed to this event.

The Motivations

One reason upper-level officials decided to "clean up" Zhejiangcun had to do with political power. The migrant community represented a new kind of spatialized power outside the official command. This migrant power was crystallized in an emerging group of local bosses who consolidated their power using traditional social networks, private wealth, and clientelist connections with officialdom. Therefore, this community appeared to the state to be threatening and out of control. As an official once observed to me, "A community with its own territorial ground [*dipan*] has the potential to become a separate regime of power." Because of its nature as a social and political anomaly, the Wenzhou migrant community could hardly be tolerated by upper-level officials who were deeply concerned with control and stability, and benefited little from the migrants directly.

Another motivation for the cleanup was the uneasy relationship between migrant enclaves and Beijing, the national capital. As elsewhere, there has always been a love-hate relationship between the migrant population and the receiving community in China.[3] Although urban residents and officials enjoy and even become dependent on the services and labor provided by migrants, they feel frustrated about the competition for limited urban resources. They tend to attribute all emerging urban problems such as over-crowding, pollution, and rising crime rates to the presence of migrants in the city. Further, Beijing is the emblematic heart of Chinese political power, modernity, and a popular national and international tourist destination. The crowded living conditions and poor hygiene in migrant enclaves damage the idealized modern image of Beijing and may eventually drain tourism and foreign investment.

A third motivation was closely related to the shift of power in the Beijing municipal government, which explained why the campaign occurred at that moment. Many migrants and local residents believed that the demolition campaign was used by the city government to regain its waning legitimacy in a period when popular distrust was at its height. In 1994, Mayor Chen Xitong and the vice mayor (who later committed suicide) had been forced to step down after a serious scandal was made public. The suicide of the vice mayor brought to light 2.2 billion yuan in missing city funds. After this incident, the Beijing municipal government underwent a radical power transition. The new leadership, appointed by the central state, attempted to recon-struct the administrative image by differentiating itself as sharply as possible from the shadow of the former regime. The attack on Zhejiangcun was one of the few promises that the new municipal government made to the Beijing public to improve public security and social order. Rumors circulated widely that Wenzhou migrants' construction of big yards had been tacitly approved by the former mayor, Chen, who had received under-the-table payments for this deal. Cleaning out Zhejiangcun had the symbolic significance of destroying the influence of the old regime. The claimed victory of eliminating a "high-crime" group and restoring social order helped the city government gain credibility.

The campaign directed by city officials could also please those top leaders who took a conservative stand. According to alleyway news, Premier Li Peng had seen several internal reports on the growth of private power in migrant enclaves, particularly in Zhejiangcun. In the summer of 1995, two migrants had been gunned down in the area. Many believed that this incident reinforced the negative attitude of some higher-level leaders toward the migrant community. Li Peng was said to have made pointed remarks on how to deal with migrant enclaves in the city and to have put pressure on the municipal government to curb the expansion of informal power in migrant enclaves. On July 8, 1995, a national conference on how to regulate the floating population was held in Fujian province. Officials at the meeting urged local governments to put combating migrant-related crime and disorder at the top of their agenda for safeguarding the socialist order and for political stability. The Beijing government was under strong pressure to take a leading role. By "cleaning up" Zhejiangcun, the new municipal administration could demonstrate its ability to get things done and its loyalty to higher authorities.

The Campaign Mobilization

On November 7, I had planned to interview Nanyuan township officials about the upcoming campaign, which had not yet been formally announced. On arriving at the township administrative building, I found that it was nearly empty. I was lucky to run into the last person there, a secretary who was leaving the office in a hurry. She said that everyone else had gone to a large mobilization meeting in a nearby military compound. I rushed to the meeting site but was blocked at the door by a middle-aged cadre with a yellow tag on his jacket. I explained to him that I was doing research on this migrant community and hoped to attend the meeting or talk to someone about the upcoming event. He pointed his finger to the yellow tag and said to me: "If you do not have this, you are not allowed to enter this hall. I work at the campaign headquarters. That is why I am here."

It was the first day of the Fengtai district campaign, which was formally announced as the "Cleaning Up and Reordering of the Dahongmen Area." The conference hall I went to was just one of the five mobilization sites. Several thousand local officials, village cadres, neighborhood committee members, and workers in state-owned sectors had been called to attend the mobilization meetings. I asked the official whether he could tell me more about the meeting. He said: "No. This is a 'closed' [*fengbishi*] event. . . . No news agencies or reporters are allowed to interview anyone or take any pictures. Only those approved by the central party's propaganda ministry can report this event." Although he kept me from entering the meeting, he wanted to show off his knowledge about what was going on, so after a pause, he continued: "The campaign will start tomorrow and last until the end of December. All Zhejiang people's big yards will be demolished. This is a fixed task [*sirenwu*] issued by the central party-state and must be accomplished. Premier Li Peng signed the order. A thousand armed policemen have arrived in this area waiting to be called in case a protest or uprising occurs."

This campaign was to be carried out in a "closed" manner because upper-level officials feared that if popular resistance arose during the housing demolition and violent suppression had to be used, media exposure would worsen the image of the party-state that claimed to be the protector of its people. It would also invite criticism from the international human rights community. Based on their experience with the 1989 student movement, the state authority was well aware of the power of the national and international media and press (Calhoun 1994). If this field of discourse was appropriated by migrants, they could gain wider social support to halt the campaign. By keeping the demolition hidden from the public gaze, the state would be able to reduce the visibility of any violence and cut off migrants' connections to the outside world.

By November 10, 1995, a formal government announcement was released to migrants and local residents in Zhejiangcun. It was called the "Public Announcement Regarding the Clean-Up and Reordering of the Dahongmen Area in Fengtai District" and outlined the urgency of the campaign and its rationale. Accompanying this was a propaganda flyer with similar but simplified contents. Numerous copies of the announcement and the flyer were posted on buildings in local streets and alleyways. Out of twelve rulings in the announcement, two are particularly worth noting. First, it pronounced that all the land-lease contracts between migrants and local villages or factories were considered invalid. Therefore, any housing constructed on these lands was illegal and would have to be demolished by the owners by November 30. Second, while claiming to protect the majority of law-abiding migrants with valid identification cards and temporary resident cards, it urged those who did not have proper documents to leave Beijing within fifteen days of the announcement. But in practice, the local police station was closed for unspecified reasons during this time, just as thousands of Wenzhou migrants needed to renew their temporary resident cards. Further, all neighborhoods in Beijing were informed by the public security offices not to accept any migrants coming out of Zhejiangcun so that those migrants would have no foothold in the city after losing their homes.

To create a strong campaign climate, trucks carrying loudspeakers moved through the community broadcasting information about the campaign. The propaganda represented the Dahongmen area as a dirty, crowded, and crime-ridden place, a spot that needed to be erased to ensure the purity and security of the city. The following is a typical description of this kind:

> The influx of outside workers and business people into Beijing has created the problem of overpopulation, which seriously hampers government regulation of social order in the Dahongmen area. There are traffic jams and poor hygiene. Villages are now being covered by trash piles and dirty water. The increase of unplanned population also put a heavy burden on the city's water and electricity supply. Migrants and local landlords make illegal profits by building massive illegal structures, which interfere with the implementation of Beijing's general city planning. In particular, there have emerged criminal cases involving the use of guns and other assault weapons. Drug use, drug trafficking, and other ugly social practices are becoming rampant. Criminal gangs with a strong flavor of the underworld have emerged. . . . Such an out-of-control situation will no doubt have a serious impact on the security and social stability of our national capital.

As I have argued earlier, such representations and truth-claiming are not simply a reflection of reality or of complaints by officials. Rather, they constitute part of the production of power. The discourse about disorder is a form of social regulation insofar as it creates the need for state intervention. Tens of thousands of pamphlets containing the twelve newly enacted stipulations were also distributed. The official rhetoric this time was to justify the demolition campaign by invoking the rule of law.

The official apparatus of the campaign was called the workteam (*gongzuodui*), composed of two thousand diversely positioned lower-, middle-, and upper-level government officials. The workteam was led by top Fengtai district officials under the supervision of the city government. Campaign activities were reported to the mayor and other central-party leaders via daily campaign newsletters.[4] The majority of the team members who did the day-to-day campaign work were lower-level district, township, and subdistrict officials, policemen, and village cadres. The major goal of this campaign was to destroy all the Wenzhou migrants' housing compounds as well as some other illegal buildings constructed by local farmers to accommodate migrants. The campaign was divided into three phases: (1) "educating" the masses through propaganda; (2) urging migrants and locals to tear down unauthorized housing by themselves; (3) forced demolition.

Unpacking the State

Throughout the campaign, upper- and lower-level officials had very different views about how to handle the relationship between political control and economic gain. For the former group, which received no direct economic benefits from Wenzhou migrants, maintaining political stability and state control was more important than anything else. They preferred to sacrifice local-level economic interest to ensure stability. In one official's words: "Economic loss cannot be compared with political loss in the larger scheme of things." By contrast, local officials regarded economic growth and prosperity as a true source of stability.

From the beginning, there were disagreements among lower-, middle-, and upper-level officials drawn into the campaign. Well aware of migrants' significant contribution to the district's revenue, many local officials did not want to drive them out and were thus personally opposed to the campaign. The police station, tax bureau, and the bureau of industry and commerce all benefited from the taxes, regulation fees, and bribes paid by migrants. But under the direct scrutiny of the city government, these officials had much to lose if they did not obey the order. Therefore, even if they opposed the campaign personally, district officials had to carry out the demolition campaign.

District officials were also disgruntled by the high cost of the campaign itself. The Fengtai district government was responsible for providing three million yuan for campaign-related administrative expenses, such as renting machinery and paying the workers who would move the thousands of tons of debris away. State-owned work units in this area were also responsible for all the meals and daily compensation (twenty yuan per day per person) for their workteam members.

The resistance and discontent of grassroots state agents was even stronger. Local township and village cadres and neighborhood committee members were unwillingly drawn into the campaign. Their economic interests, deeply entangled with those of migrants in the area, were now at risk, particularly since some of their own housing additions were targeted for demolition. During the economic reform period, with the rapid expansion of urban industry and commerce, agricultural production had drastically decreased as more and more farm lands in Beijing's suburbs were appropriated by the state for nonagricultural purposes. Yet many farmers in the area, especially the older generation, continued to be rural *hukou* holders and did not have the skills to take nonagricultural jobs. Their livelihoods thus depended on two sources of income: being able to rent housing to migrants, and their village pension. The pension was provided primarily by land-leasing fees charged to Wenzhou migrants. Thus, the proposed demolition of migrant housing compounds would eliminate this crucial source of income.

To express their discontent, local farmers demanded that the city and central governments cancel the demolition campaign. Some village heads and party secretaries took the lead and signed their names to these appeals. But there was no official response. These letters disappeared without a trace, like stones falling into the ocean (*shichen dahai*). I later interviewed two cadres of a local village where most migrant housing compounds were demolished. They described their loss as follows: "We are the most severely afflicted area [*zhong zaiqu*]. If this were a natural disaster, we could receive donations and help from the government. But this disaster is created by the government. Therefore, we have no place to turn for help and justice. Now we have nothing left to give to the farmers." In this village, more than 50 percent of the farmers lived partly on their private rental businesses and partly on the pension (seven to eight thousand yuan per person annually). After all the "illegal" housing was destroyed, the annual income per person was reduced to three thousand yuan, an amount too small to subsist on. The village used to be able to pay part of farmers' medical bills, but after the demolition it could hardly provide the basic money for food, let alone cover the medical bills. One cadre put it this way: "Driving Zhejiang people away and demolishing their big yards is no different from cutting off our sole means of survival. It is like killing us. Such a practice is contradictory to the reform policy and cannot gain any popular support in the local community."

Meanwhile, the campaign headquarters constantly called for unity, solidarity, and determination, demanding that local agents sacrifice their own economic interests for the higher goal of political stability. The possibility of punishment for those who would not comply was also announced. Upper-level officials repeatedly stressed the importance of "thought work" (*sixiang gongzuo*) in order to eliminate internal differences among lower-level cadres. The following two excerpts from upper-level officials' speeches to lower-level cadres articulated their eagerness to seek unity and suppress discord within the workteam:

We must mobilize local cadres and people to reach a common understanding [of the importance of this event]: that is a unified way of thinking and unified actions. All levels of leaders and cadres should work hard with conscience and enhance their own understanding of the event. They should start with their own villages. . . . Never sacrifice the overall interest of the capital city because of one's short-term local interests. (The general director of the campaign passing on the order by the central party-state to local party leaders)

Local party members and cadres should set good examples for ordinary people. Party members and cadres must be clear about our goal. . . . All the local units in this area must obey the larger political demand. Anyone who refuses to carry out his duty should be immediately reported to the city government. (The vice general director of the campaign)

During the early phases of the campaign, the workteam focused on two major tasks: entering individual households of migrants and local farmers to explain why the campaign was necessary, and identifying all the migrant housing compounds and other illegal construction by local farmers.[5] A giant white character, *chai* (to tear down, demolish, or remove), surrounded by a circle, was painted on the wall of the structures to be demolished. During that period, *chai* became the catchword haunting everyone's mind in Zhejiangcun.

Caught between the demands of migrants and local farmers and political pressure from higher up, many workteam members adopted elusive forms of resistance while performing their official tasks. For example, some expressed sympathy to migrants and local farmers privately: "The idea of tearing down your house comes from the government above us and has nothing to do with us. We are not willing to come to do this. It is a waste of our time." In so doing, they implicitly encouraged the migrants and locals to hold on to their housing. Some purposely neglected to mark their friends' houses to reduce the scale of destruction. But some of these practices were detected and severely criticized by the campaign headquarters.

The dilemma facing grassroots state agents is closely related to their dual role of mediating the relationship between the political center and the local community. This kind of tension has long existed in Chinese political history (see Chan et al. 1984; Friedman, Pickowicz, and Selden 1991; Li and O'Brien 1996; Mann 1987; Oi 1989; Shue 1988). With the advent of marketization, deeper and more varied economic alliances across the bureaucratic and nonbureaucratic spheres have been created. Socioeconomic alliances among local government, migrants, and locals as articulated in

Zhejiangcun complicate the neatly divided conceptual model of state versus society. The growing economic power of Wenzhou migrants and the shifting positions of diverse state agents require a more sophisticated way of understanding the changing nature of the Chinese state and the complexity of local politics in migrant communities. What was displayed during this campaign was not a simple conflict between migrants and monolithic state power, but multiple repositionings of diversely located state agencies and social elements.

Popular Resistance

As James Scott (1985) has pointed out, in order to gain a deeper understanding of local politics and power dynamics, it is important to examine not only large-scale, visible, organized protests, uprisings, and other political activities, but also everyday forms of resistance in less visible social domains. Particularly in a politically sensitive place like Zhejiangcun, where open, organized political actions by migrants were dangerous, informal resistance played a vital role in deflecting and dodging the efforts of the campaign. In the early stages of the campaign, unorganized popular resistance had already begun. Although these individual actions did not make national or local news, they were important parts of the micropolitics. While emphasizing popular resistance to the campaign, I am aware of the danger of romanticizing everyday resistance (see Abu-Lughod 1990; Ortner 1995). Hence, to give a more balanced picture and avoid oversimplifying local politics as state domination versus migrant resistance, I attempt to present an account of the multiple layers of conflict within the "state" and the community.

OUTSIDE THE HOUSING COMPOUNDS

When the workteam began to enter individual households in the villages, they encountered several types of resistance. Some farmers stared at the workteam officials with anger or simply refused to talk to them. Some locked their doors and went out for a stroll before the workteam came so that no one could enter their private courtyards. There were also landlords who purposely left their houses for days with only migrant renters working there. The absence of landlords made the workteam's task more difficult because officials were required to persuade landlords to tear down their own housing additions in order to reduce the possibility of violence caused by forced demolition. Some Wenzhou migrants pretended that they could not understand Mandarin and thus could not communicate with the officials. Migrants also closed down their private clinics and convenience stores temporarily to avoid inspection. These negative responses were recorded in an official report as follows:

> First, there was a general negative attitude toward demolishing private housing.[6] Some local landlords claimed: "The government can spread its propaganda any way it wants. But there is no way we will demolish our own housing because we depend on it to support our families." Second, some local cadres secretly sabotaged the campaign. Villagers in Shicun reported: "During a village meeting, some cadres told us not to say anything when the workteam came and see what they can do about it." Third, some local residents had doubts about the motivation of the demolition and believed that it would damage local farmers' interests. (Newsletter #22)

Although the hostility expressed by local farmers was not surprising to lower-level officials, it was disturbing to upper-level party leaders. Frustrated, the campaign leaders compelled all absent landlords to report to headquarters in person to explain their absence. If they failed to do so, they would be held responsible for all political consequences.[7] It was also announced that if no owners showed up to identify shacks that were unattached to houses in the village, those who lived there were responsible for tearing them down. After this official notice was sent out, however, few landlords obeyed the order to show up at the headquarters.

Resistance also came from some local factory workers who depended on rental housing. The newsletters recorded the following telling cases. A city worker and his wife rented ten private rooms to migrants. The rental income was the main income source for the family. On the first day the government campaign notice was issued, this couple explained desperately to workteam members: "We rely on these rooms to earn money for a living. If you tear down my rental rooms, we will go for a sit-down protest in front of the city government." A retired worker in his seventies who had lost his only son a few years earlier had just started a small convenience store to support himself and his young grandson. Now his store was also targeted for demolition. In desperation, he threatened to take his own life if his store were flattened. He protested: "Theoretically I support the cleaning up of migrant outsiders. But my pension from the village was only forty yuan a month and has just increased to a hundred yuan this November. Now if you drive all of them [migrants] away, nobody will rent my house. My basic livelihood cannot be guaranteed!" The situation was even more complicated when it involved the relationship between military units and civilians. For example, an air force branch leased thirty *mu* (two hectares) of land to Wenzhou migrants for their housing projects. This military unit sent a representative to the campaign headquarters, asking that the 140 migrant houses on their land not be torn down because doing so might sour the military–civilian relationship (*junmin guanxi*) that the party attempted to maintain.

The very act of marking "illegal houses" with the word *chai* (demolish) also invoked strong social friction. It was relatively easy to spot and mark migrant big yards because of migrants' non–Beijing resident status, but it was more difficult to decide the status of private housing additions built by the locals. The standards for deciding the illegality of these structures were not clearly specified, much depending on the location and date of construction and whether the owners had obtained proper papers from the village head and the district planning office. Some village cadres were able to create the necessary documents through their personal networks and power and thus could exempt their own housing additions from demolition. But this special treatment caused resentment among villagers whose housing additions were subject to demolition. Some people painted countermarks such as "*bu chai*" (refuse to demolish) on their houses and neighbors' houses to express their resistance. Others repeatedly erased the *chai* sign. The local police detained some resisters, charging them with hampering the state's effort to keep social order.

In addition to these everyday forms of resistance, people expressed their rage by burning and destroying the government notices about the demolition campaign. As I walked in streets and alleyways in Zhejiangcun a week after the campaign began, I noticed that almost none of the official announcements were intact. They had been removed from the walls, torn apart, or defaced by words such as "nonsense" or "disobey." According to the government workteam's report, by November 16 approximately a thousand public announcements had been either torn down or burned by migrants and locals.

In response, the upper-level government decided to take harsh measures to move the campaign beyond this impasse. Pressure was put on local officials and cadres to show some concrete signs of progress; they were warned that they could face serious political charges for not fulfilling their duties. Migrants and local farmers were notified that if they refused to flatten their own illegal housing, forced demolition would begin in December and they would be heavily fined and punished. Local cadres and party members were urged by higher authorities to set a good example to the community by demolishing their own illegal housing. Constantly pressed and even threatened by workteam members, some local residents did begin to tear down their housing additions. Once the destruction began in some areas, others thought that no one could stop the campaign and thus also began to dismantle their housing to avoid government persecution. By early December 1995, the majority of "illegal" housing additions by the locals had been demolished. Migrants who had lived in those additions were forced out, and many moved in temporarily with relatives whose housing had not yet been destroyed.

INSIDE THE HOUSING COMPOUNDS

Migrants in the housing compounds suffered most from the demolition campaign, but they also put up the strongest resistance. When the campaign first began, they were optimistic, believing that, given housing bosses' tight connections with various levels of officials, most compounds might eventually be allowed to remain. Also, since Wenzhou migrants were the majority population in this area and could be mobilized for collective action, they were not afraid of challenging the workteam. For example, two Wenzhou migrants confronted workteam members sent to do their thought-work like this: "The campaign you are carrying out is useless because we have a lot of money, and the central government consists of southerners such as Jiang Zemin, Qiao Shi, and Zhu Rongji who will support us. Some leaders in the Beijing government are also from the south. Just wait and see! Sooner or later we will get even with you guys." At that time, many of them thought that their economic power would help them bypass government rules and erode the campaign through *guanxi* and bribery. They overestimated the power of native-place identity in upper-level politics. Just because a few top party leaders originally came from China's southeastern coastal regions where Wenzhou is situated, these migrants assumed that those officials would provide them with the political backing to halt the campaign.[8]

The workteam members often felt uneasy and embarrassed, trying to dissociate themselves from the order they were unwilling to enforce. As one of them explained to migrants, "I told you that this is not my idea. I am just conveying the order from above and fulfilling my duty. Otherwise, I will lose my 'rice bowl' [*fanwan*, the means to survive] too." At the same time, the workteam was worried about being attacked by migrants in the compounds. Thus when a workteam branch entered a housing compound, it was accompanied by several policemen.

Migrant resistance was also expressed in verbal threats. For example, a housing boss made it clear in front of the workteam: "We built the houses piece by piece with our own hands. Now we are ordered to tear them down by our own hands. Our hearts hurt too much to do that. We will not move until forced demolition happens. If our houses are to be destroyed, we will commit suicide." Some claimed that they would organize a sit-down protest in front of the city hall and ask the administration to explain why it was flattening their homes.

As the campaign went on, semiorganized resistance grew. On November 18, migrants within one housing compound drafted an urgent appeal in the name of all migrants in the Dahongmen area and submitted it to the All-China Federation of Industry and Commerce (*quanguo gongshang lianhehui*) and the National Association for Independent Workers (*quanguo geti laodongzhe xiehui*). In the letter, migrants argued that migrant workers and entrepreneurs should also be protected by law because their work benefited the city's economy. The letter urged these organizations to help stop the campaign. The appeal predicted five possible tragic outcomes of the campaign: the loss of large amounts of capital; migrants unable to pay back their debts; migrant families unable to survive; increased crime; suicide due to great financial loss. Their choice to send the appeal to these organizations signified Wenzhou migrants' perceptions of potential political alliances. Since they identified themselves as part of newly emerged *getihu* or private manufacturers and merchants, they sought support from the organizations that were supposed to protect their interests. But as I discussed in an earlier chapter, almost all formal organizations and associations are controlled and led by the party-state in China. Thus the associations from which they sought support were not willing to risk their own political interests and chose to remain silent.

A few days later, migrants in the largest housing compound, Jinou, drafted another appeal and forwarded it to some top party officials and the State Council. The letter argued that the city government's decision to clean up Zhejiangcun would destroy ordinary migrants' normal economic activities and community life. Debunking the official representation of big yards as hotbeds for crime and disorder, the appeal stressed that migrant housing compounds actually had a better living and work environment and social order than the outside. By subverting the official image of big yards and the vision of order, migrants implicitly critiqued the city government as irrational and responsible for destroying rather than creating order. In an appeal to officials' conscience, the letter also underlined the possible tragic consequences of the demolition, including economic loss, the disruption of children's education, and large-scale social disorder.

But the top leaders insisted that migrant housing compounds were illegal and bred crime. They made it clear that political stability outweighed local economic loss. Other officials at the political center were unwilling to risk their own positions to speak out for Wenzhou migrants.

Native-Place Alliances

As Wenzhou migrants appealed to government organizations in Beijing unsuccessfully, they also actively sought political backing from their regional governments. The cultural notion of native place became a mechanism for the creation of political alliances between local government and migrants from the same place of origin.

Balancing power relations between central and provincial governments has long been a delicate issue in China. The central state needs to allow some autonomy and latitude to local government, but it also fears that too much local autonomy jeopardizes central state power. During the prereform socialist period, political power was highly centralized, leaving little autonomy for provincial and city governments. Since the post-Mao economic reforms, however, the political center (*zhongyang*) has begun to delegate more authority to local governments, particularly regarding economic development. The remarkable economic growth in the coastal regions such as Guangdong and Zhejiang provinces greatly empowered the provincial governments and also reinforced a resurgent regionalism. Wenzhou migrants took the opportunity to ask for their regional governments' support in negotiations with the central and Beijing governments.

The initial alliance between migrants and their regional governments was formed through informal personal connections with the liaison officers of the provincial and city governments posted in Beijing.[9] Officials in the liaison offices (particularly those from Wenzhou and Yueqing) became business partners of wealthy Wenzhou migrants and thus were highly motivated to hamper the campaign by using their political positions to negotiate with Beijing officials. The director of the Yueqing liaison office, for example, was one of the shareholders of Jinou. Two officials from the Wenzhou liaison office had invested a lot of money with a prominent local boss in a wholesale garment market. Their common financial interests were further strengthened by their shared native-place ties.

In addition to immediate personal interests, provincial and city officials had another stake in keeping Wenzhou migrants in Beijing. Every year migrant traders and workers sent large amounts of money to their families back home, where it was reinvested in private family businesses or spent on consumer goods, which helped stimulate the local economy. This financial source became so important that the Wenzhou and Yueqing city governments established special offices to facilitate out-migration and monitor the well-being of Wenzhou migrant diasporas in the country. To foster stronger connections between Wenzhou sojourners and their hometowns, the two city governments cosponsored a 1996 New Year's tea party with the theme "Maintaining Emotional Ties with Wenzhou, Creating Grand Achievements Together" (*Qingxi Wenzhou, Gongchuang Daye*). The goal was to interest Wenzhou migrants in reinvesting in their hometowns. Using the notion of native place, the regional officials pledged loyalty to the migrants to ensure a constant flow of remittances.

It was in this context that Wenzhou migrants in Beijing requested official support from their regional governments. Housing bosses played a critical role by representing Wenzhou migrants in the negotiation with officials from their native places. As the conflicts between the migrant community and the campaign workteam grew, the migrant leadership, previously centered on several big yard bosses, began to focus on Zhen. His home became the site of important meetings and negotiations that affected the fate of Zhejiangcun.[10]

In the early stages, contacts between Zhejiang and Wenzhou officials and migrant bosses remained at a personal level. They mobilized *guanxi* networks to influence township and district officials in the workteam. For example, the former head of a local police station was Zhen's good friend. He had been promoted to the district public security bureau but remained on good terms with Zhen. During the campaign, Zhen kept in close contact with this official, who regularly sent important campaign information to Zhen through a third person because their telephones were tapped. With inside information about the campaign schedule, official strategies, and leaders' attitudes, the migrant leaders determined what tactics to use in order to delay the demolition.

Half a month into the campaign, pressure from the upper-level government increased. Ordinary migrant families in the compounds still refused to abandon their homes, anxiously awaiting further instructions from their housing bosses. Everyone kept an eye on Zhen's compound. If it fell, people knew there was no hope for the smaller ones. Therefore, his compound,

Jinou, became a symbol for life and death to many Wenzhou migrants. At this time, migrants' call for protection from their regional government escalated. The Zhejiang provincial government began to take more serious measures to defend the interests of Wenzhou migrants. On November 20, the Zhejiang provincial liaison office delivered an appeal, titled "Special Urgent Suggestions Regarding the Demolition of Illegal Constructions in Zhejiangcun," to the Beijing city government. Zhou, the director of the liaison office and deputy secretary general of the Zhejiang provincial government, met with two vice directors of the campaign. In a tension-charged meeting, the two campaign directors refused to stop the campaign. Instead they demanded unconditional support from the Zhejiang provincial government to ensure its successful on-time completion. They stressed that this task had been assigned by the central and Beijing government and that any refusal to comply with the order would be tantamount to an antiparty/ state act. Intimidated, Zhou backed down and said that the provincial government would obey orders by the State Council but strongly recommended that the workteam allow the Wenzhou migrants more time to relocate. He emphasized that forced demolition in such a short period of time would inevitably cause a number of social and economic problems. This negotiation may not seem striking to people in the United States, where dissension between state and federal governments is common. But in socialist China an open confrontation between a provincial government and the central state is startling. The meeting ended with no agreement.

Two days later, the Zhejiang government sent a formal delegation of eight officials to Beijing for further negotiations. This time the chief director and other important officials of the campaign headquarters met with the delegation. The delegation suggested allowing some major housing compounds to stand, instead of wiping all of them out at once. The Beijing side quickly rejected this idea, reiterating that all local governments should obey the orders of the higher authority to ensure the political stability of the capital. Realizing that the demolition was inevitable, the Zhejiang delegation changed its focus and asked for more time for migrants to prepare for relocation. The vice mayor of Wenzhou pointed out:

> Premier Li Peng did not specify the deadline for demolition in his order. Is it possible to be more lenient regarding the deadline? We hope that the cleaning and reordering work can adopt practical methods to face the reality. Impatience and excessive pressure can only cause undesirable incidents to happen. Tearing down law-abiding production households' housing and

making them unable to produce and survive will not only cause huge economic loss but also disobey the ultimate goal of maintaining the capital's stability. (Newsletter #67)

Again, this second proposal was turned down. Most members of the Zhejiang delegation left Beijing in anger and disappointment. A few demanded to see the central party leaders directly, but this request was ignored. Zhejiang and Wenzhou governments' support for their migrants and their failure to obey higher political orders further reinforced upper-level officials' determination to wipe out migrants' housing compounds quickly, before the conflict intensified.

The Demolition

In late November, having learned that the official negotiations had failed and that most housing bosses had given up their resistance, migrants in some twenty smaller housing compounds began to leave in large numbers after doing their own "self-demolition" (*zichai*). Some families were able to obtain rental trucks to carry their household items, sewing machines, and unfinished products away from Zhejiangcun, but they did not know exactly where they should go. Some headed for remote suburbs or adjacent provinces to hide from further persecution; other poorer families who could not immediately find new shelter became homeless for several days. They slept on street corners in the community while the temperature dropped to below zero centigrade. Several days later, many housing compounds were demolished and Zhejiangcun was covered by massive ruins (see Figure 15). As I walked over broken bricks and wooden boards, I could hardly recognize the place. It looked like a war zone. Housing compounds, food stands, corner stores, and busy marketplaces had suddenly vanished, as had the familiar sound of thousands of sewing machines. There were few people on the street, and most local households kept their doors shut tightly. A once vibrant community had lost its vitality.

One morning I entered a torn-down big yard and heard someone calling my name. It was Boss Wu, whom I knew very well. He looked tired and desperate. The workteam had ordered him to destroy all the roofs within his compound to show that nobody was living there any more. But even after the migrant families had gone, he stayed on secretly, unable to leave his compound behind just yet. "I lost several big yards at once. How can my heart not hurt so much?! I want to stay here to see what they will do next to my

15.   Ruins of a migrant compound after demolition

big yards. I will not leave until they flatten them." As we walked through the torn-apart compound, he asked me to take photographs and to at least write something to show the outside world what the government had done to them: "Xiao Zhang, I tell you that the media people are all cowards and controlled by government. And officials are corrupt. So no one has the guts to speak for us. Perhaps you can do something about it someday because this part of history should not be erased."

Torn golden-colored strips of wallpaper were blowing in the wind. As they hit the collapsed walls and beams, they made a strange sound. It was a sound of sorrow. I felt as if I were at a Chinese funeral. The drifting paper in the air was lamenting the destruction of a once vibrant migrant community. Like many other housing compound bosses, Wu was now saddled with huge debts. He might never be able to return to his hometown. His future looked gloomy.

While the majority of housing compounds had been emptied and demolished, a few large ones at the southern frontier of Nanyuan township were still intact at this point. Boss Zhen and several other influential housing bosses still hoped that the workteam would feel satisfied with the fact that most of the compounds had been destroyed and thus would spare theirs. Their covert political patrons in the local government also encouraged them to hold on as long as possible. But after the negotiations between the Zhejiang and Beijing officials broke down, the workteam was pressed by the city government to complete the campaign by the Chinese Spring Festival. They feared that further delay could invite unexpected nightmares (*yechang mengduo*). Thus, leading officials of the workteam took turns pressing and threatening Zhen at his home every day because they knew that migrant renters would listen to him. But they did not want to press him too much; they were afraid that desperate migrants might revolt.

When Zhen refused to cooperate after many days of exhortation, the officials detained him once as a warning and then released him. Zhen was seriously concerned about his own safety and decided to hide away from home. His wife, Lin, stayed at home to meet with the officials. Lin was a brave and wise woman. She talked to visiting officials about how hard it was for migrants to make a living in Beijing and how much damage the campaign had caused. When the officials asked her where Zhen went, she said that she did not know. They asked her to page him. She did, but there was never any response. She told me later that she and her husband had agreed that he would not return her page; instead he would call her when necessary. While in hiding, Zhen searched with his friends for a potential relocation site, since the final demolition appeared inevitable.

The forced demolition took place suddenly on the afternoon of Saturday, December 2. Migrants in Jinou compound did not expect the government workteam to come that day because it was a weekend. So they were actually relaxing a little bit after days of officials' pushing and thought-work. Toward noon, the workteam suddenly appeared with about two dozen armed policemen and a large yellow bulldozer. They were going to remove the office of the Jinou regulation committee at the center of the compound. Several hundred migrants came out and surrounded the office. A leader of the workteam shouted at the migrants, warning them to retreat and not to obstruct their work. The policemen formed a circle to push people away so that the bulldozer could move forward.

A few migrants were talking to the policemen, trying to persuade them to leave. Most of them did not respond. One official said to the migrants: "What we are doing is good for you. After reordering and cleansing, you will feel safer." His words caused a strong reaction. Someone in the crowd yelled: "How can you say this is good for us?! You tear down our houses, leaving us homeless, and kick us out of Beijing. What is good about it?!" A

16.　Panicked Wenzhou migrants tearing down their own roofs and leaving Zhejiangcun on the eve of the demolition

few regulation committee members asked the workteam to give them some time to move the furniture, TV, and house plants out. Four people were allowed to enter the circle formed by the police to remove things from the office. I remembered how happy these migrants had been so recently, just after moving into Jinou. Now it seemed that everything—their houses, plants, and hopes—was about to vanish.

As soon as the last piece of furniture was taken out, the yellow bulldozer moved forward. Its giant iron blade ruthlessly hit, grasped, and shook the little house, and a big chunk of the building crumbled to the ground (see Figures 16 and 17). Amidst the flying dust from breaking glass and bricks, the fear, despair, and wrath in the eyes of the Wenzhou migrants was evident. The bulldozer backed up a few yards and then moved forward again several times until the house was completely shattered. Then it moved toward another house across the street, where youth played pool and arcade games. In less than a minute, this building too was turned into rubble. While all this was happening, the entire place was strangely quiet. Most migrants stood there speechless; a few women were sobbing. One middle-aged woman, a mother of two and a good friend of mine, broke down and began to cry

17.   The Jinou compound after demolition

aloud. She was desperate because her family had a share (about 200,000 yuan) of this compound. Since her family was not wealthy, they had borrowed all the money. But now everything she had was gone. As the workteam and bulldozer went away, she crawled on the ground crying as if she were trying to follow something that had vanished.

In this context, the yellow bulldozer was more than a machine; it was the embodiment of state power. The destruction of the Jinou housing office also had deeper symbolic meanings: it was not simply the demolition of a house; rather it was the destruction of an emerging popular regime of power. The officials knew very well that Jinou was the emblematic heart of Zhejiang migrant leadership; thus destroying it in front of the migrant public was a manifesto of state power against any perceived potential oppositional social forces. Further, by demolishing this center, officials predicted that migrants in other compounds would finally give up and leave the area. In this they were correct. By December 12, half of Jinou's residents had moved out and were dispersed among suburban communities in Beijing's remote peripheral areas and other surrounding towns. On a snowy day the rest followed Boss Zhen to their new relocation site in Hebei province.

The workteam sent in half a dozen bulldozers to finish the demolition.

By late December, Jinou and several other large migrant housing compounds were completely flattened. As I walked through the ruins by myself, I felt extremely sad. A once-wonderful, dynamic migrant community was gone. The only thing left was the main gate, standing by itself. I could still recognize a few broken words painted on its upper part: "Welcome to the Jinou Big Yard of Leather Products." The wind swirled the dust on the ground. For some reason, I did not want to leave the ruins just yet. Perhaps it was because I knew that after a few days even the rubble would disappear. This was my last trip to Jinou, and I was saying farewell to it.

8.   Displacement and Revitalization

On the eve of the massive housing destruction, Zhejiangcun became chaotic. Panicky migrant families hastily packed their essential household belongings and garment production equipment as they made ready to flee. Tens of thousands of migrants who had lost their homes shivered in the chilly wind on their way out of the city.

In this chapter I document their mass exodus and coping strategies at the relocation sites. I also examine the continuing salient role of the migrant leadership in selecting the major relocation sites and reorganizing migrant social and economic life. My analysis focuses on the negotiation and temporary alignments established between migrant leaders and local government officials in the relocation areas. In contrast with the political concerns of the central and Beijing governments, lower-level government officials in Hebei province (where many migrants fled) were very interested in the economic gains migrant entrepreneurs might bring. They embraced displaced Wenzhou migrants in hopes of getting them to stay. Yet despite the willingness of local Hebei officials to cooperate with Wenzhou migrants on new commercial developments, their ambitious attempts to create a large garment production and trade center in Hebei failed. I will offer some speculations on the logic of the market that led to the failure of this project.

The second part of the chapter turns to the social and economic alliances recreated between returning migrants and local government agencies or state enterprises in Beijing during the period of radical urban economic restructuring. In particular, the acceleration of state enterprise reform created new opportunities for Wenzhou migrants to use closed-down state factories and other resources to rebuild their community. With the growth of marketization and commodification, more state agencies and state-owned enterprises were turning into profit-seeking, businesslike units willing to engage in unconventional alliances with migrant entrepreneurs. More important, the Beijing government began to modify its strategies for controlling the

Wenzhou migrant community, gradually incorporating migrant leaders as mediators in local affairs. These changes made it possible for returning migrants to regain a foothold in the city and rebuild their community on a larger and more permanent scale.

Coping with Relocation

During and after the campaign, the Beijing government ordered all the urban and suburban neighborhoods and police stations not to host any migrants from Zhejiangcun. Thus, the Wenzhou migrants had to rely largely on kin and friendship networks for housing and financial assistance. Some former housing bosses continued to act as business brokers by negotiating with Beijing work units and villages for temporary rentals for migrant families. Only a small portion of them managed to stay in run-down suburban factories, out-of-business motels, and remote villages. The majority of migrants were dispersed in rural counties outside the city proper, and some went to Tianjin as well as cities and towns in Hebei province (such as Baoding, Langfang, and Sanhe). Daxing County, for example, a major relocation site adjacent to the southern frontier of Zhejiangcun, was largely a rural area covered by extended farmlands and villages. Therefore, housing space was available in local farmers' houses there, and government control was relatively weak.

To learn how the migrant families coped in relocation, I followed two groups of them: one that fled to a suburb of Beijing, the other to Hebei province. The first group consisted of several hundred Wenzhou migrants and their workers who went to Datun, a transitional suburban community in the Chaoyang district of Beijing. Datun was primarily a farming area, but an up-scale private housing development had recently been built there. The relocation was secretly arranged by two Wenzhou migrant bosses who had personal connections with local officials. The migrant families were settled at two different places: a closed-down motel owned by a local village, and a housing compound that had once been used by a state work unit to accommodate families waiting to move into new apartment buildings.

Why were these migrants allowed to stay in this community given the official order not to accept any Wenzhou migrants? Two Beijing residents working in the regulation office of the housing compound explained to me:

> These Zhejiang people came to look for empty rooms and asked us to let them stay. They also brought their relatives and friends—it was like snow-

balling. We felt sorry that they had lost their homes and thought that we could also make some money by renting out these empty rooms. So we talked to the local police and promised them that we would keep good order and not let any trouble occur.

Here "talking" to the police was just an indirect way of saying that they had bought off the police through bribery and *guanxi*.

Actually many grassroots community leaders in Beijing wanted to attract Wenzhou migrants because they anticipated that their entrepreneurial activities would stimulate the local economy and generate sizable revenues. Contrary to official and media portrayals, which equated migrants with crime and disorder, the locals saw migrants as a source of prosperity. Residents in Datun were impressed by the Wenzhou migrants' hard-working spirit; one of them said: "Almost as soon as these Wenzhounese arrived, they began to set up production in the households. For a while, there was no electricity available in their rooms. But that did not stop them from working; they did their sewing in the dim candlelight." How can we reconcile the sharply different views held by these local residents and the urban public? I suggest that the differences derived mainly from the fact that the locals based their opinions on direct, personal contact, while the city residents based theirs on media representations.

The distance between Datun and the clothing markets in Zhejiangcun created problems. Although the migrants' housing compounds had been destroyed, their major marketplaces were intact and remained the center of private garment trading in Beijing. Since clothing produced at the relocation sites had to be delivered to the markets in Zhejiangcun (usually by taxi), transportation added significantly to the general production costs. Time was another major concern. Clothing products could not always reach the markets on time and thus became less competitive. For these reasons, prospects for migrant businesses at the several relocation sites were dismal. Some households eventually had to stop production and return to Wenzhou, waiting for the chance to return to Beijing. Unable to predict whether they would be discovered and ejected by the government again, displaced migrants lived in constant fear. They tried to reduce their visibility by limiting their activities outside the shelters.

The other group of migrants I followed went to Sanhe, a small city in Hebei province. Although Sanhe had recently been designated a city, it had a large farming area. The specific site of the resettlement was Yanjiao, a newly designated economic and technological development zone, about six hours by bus from Zhejiangcun. Approximately three thousand migrants followed their patron, Zhen, to this place, creating the largest relocation site for Wenzhou migrants. Among them, some one hundred households were arranged in an old state-run liquor factory that was soon to be shut down. The factory agreed to accept these migrants because it could collect fifty thousand yuan in monthly rent for its three abandoned buildings. I visited the families there and found the living conditions miserable: overcrowded, dark, and cold. Since the buildings were designed as a production shop, not as residences, several families had to share a large open room without heat, water, or bathrooms. The air was filled with a strong brewery smell.

The other three hundred migrant households were placed in a nearby "commodity housing" building (*shangping fang*, commercial apartments) that had been recently completed but not yet put on the market. Boss Zhen rented five of these apartment buildings from the developer and then sublet them to ordinary migrant families, presumably for a profit. The rent for each apartment was high, between eighteen hundred and two thousand yuan a month, depending on the floor location and size. To reduce costs, two families might share a three-bedroom apartment.

Migrant daily life at the Yanjiao relocation site was filled with hardship. Since the buildings had just been constructed, water and electricity had not yet been fully connected. Without power, semiautomatic sewing machines could not operate and thus no work could be done. If the migrants could not meet the terms of their contracts with buyers, their credibility would suffer and eventually lead to the loss of future business deals. The lack of heat was another serious problem. The temperature was often below minus ten centigrade at that time of a year. Some workers' hands became cracked and swollen from the long-term exposure to cold. Water pipes frequently froze or broke, causing flooding and water shortages.

To resolve the transportation problem, the migrants themselves established a new bus route between Zhejiangcun and Yanjiao. A couple of Wenzhou businessmen contracted with two Beijing minibus drivers to run the route. Each van held about twenty passengers and ran two round trips a day. The two drivers were paid eight hundred yuan daily regardless of how many people actually took the vans. A round-trip ticket was thirty yuan. On a normal day, the migrant bosses could make a net profit of seven to eight hundred yuan after paying for the driver and gasoline. These transportation arrangements helped migrant families keep their businesses going; but in the long run, the commute was too expensive and time-consuming.

Finally, the difficulties of relocation life affected migrants' emotional state.

Their financial losses and gloomy economic future led to severe depression among some migrants. The woman whose family had lost nearly 200,000 yuan in Jinou became hysterical and then fell into a long-term depression. She wept every day without speaking a word. Her family was unable to pay back the large amount of money borrowed from relatives and fellow villagers and thus could not return to their home village for fear of being harassed by those who had lent them money.

Migrant Leadership at Work

When news of the demolition campaign spread, many local governments and business enterprises outside Beijing actually encouraged Wenzhou migrants to bring their families and businesses to their areas. Some even sent representatives to Zhejiangcun to advertise the potential for private business development in their regions. Two women from a large real estate corporation came to distribute advertisement flyers with colorful pictures of a giant commercial center.[1] This center, covering 425 acres of land in the city of Yuci in Shanxi province, was nearly completed. It consisted of several interconnected commercial buildings, commodity trading markets, residential buildings, and supplementary public facilities. Its developers saw the official campaign to displace Wenzhou migrant entrepreneurs as a great opportunity to lure these shrewd business people to their commercial center. Meanwhile, other local government enterprises in Hebei also advertised among the Wenzhou migrants, claiming that their places were ideal for private economic development. Many promised to provide housing and favorable policies to incoming migrants. But most Wenzhou migrants remained skeptical about these warm invitations. While talking to the two women from Shanxi, several migrants said to them: "Show us some red government seals on your documents. If you do not have them, how do we know that we will not be kicked out again someday?! You had better go back to get the red seal first before asking us to go to your place."

Among the many potential places for relocation, Zhen and his followers chose the Yanjiao district because of its relatively convenient location, its special status as an economic and technological development zone, and the local government's support. Before the demolition, Zhen and his men made several trips to Yanjiao, investigating its potential as a new garment production and trade center. Two important elite-level meetings regarding the relocation took place on November 29 and 30.[2] The first meeting was at Zhen's home in the Jinou compound. Ten people were present, including the mayor of Sanhe city (in which Yanjiao was located), his secretary, the director of the Wenzhou government liaison office, Zhen, and a few of Jinou's shareholders. The atmosphere was friendly and cooperative, in contrast to the meetings with the campaign workteam. There was a certain tension during the meeting, but it was more economically oriented than political. The Sanhe officials focused on possible economic alliances with Wenzhou migrants and did not mention anything even remotely related to political stability. The liaison officer played a mediating role between Sanhe and migrant leaders because of his position as a government official and his native-place tie with Wenzhou migrants.

Both sides agreed on a two-stage blueprint for relocation. During the first phase, Zhen would mobilize a large group of migrants to go to Sanhe with him, while the Sanhe government would guarantee the migrants' safety and help arrange their resettlement. During the second phase, both sides would cooperate to establish a new garment trade center in Sanhe. The focus of the meeting then shifted to the question of short-term housing space for incoming migrants. Sanhe officials proposed to utilize an abandoned factory and at the same time assemble temporary shelters. Migrant leaders accepted the proposal but insisted that the Sanhe side be responsible for all construction-related matters. They would only rent because they did not want to risk investing in another real estate project just yet.

The next day (three days before the demolition of Jinou), a second meeting between migrant leaders and Hebei officials took place. Six of us—Zhen, his wife, one of Zhen's business partners, two Jinou shareholders, and myself—drove to Sanhe. Later, three more Wenzhou bosses joined us. The negotiation was held at the best hotel in the area. When we arrived, I noticed a big sign reading "Reception Station to Welcome Zhejiang Industrialists and Merchants" at the front gate of the hotel. The choice of such terms as "industrialists and merchants" was important because it showed respect for the Zhejiang migrants. This welcoming gesture contrasted sharply with the rejection in Beijing.

The negotiation lasted about three hours and focused on the proposed temporary shelters. The Sanhe side included the director of the Yanjiao development zone, who had control over the right to land allocation and price, two managers of a housing construction company, and four managers of local electricity and water supply companies. Although the pursuit of profits was what brought these officials, managers, and migrant bosses together, they all had their own agendas. Sanhe officials and managers wanted Zhen to ensure that he would bring a large number of migrants so that they could build more temporary shelters for greater profits. They also wanted to raise prices for land use and housing rentals. The head of the housing construction company began by pressing Zhen: "After all, how many households can you bring here? How many square meters of temporary housing do you want?" Zhen replied: "About a thousand households. Let us say forty square meters of shelter for each household. That is a lot already." The two managers were not quite satisfied but decided to settle for the moment. Then they discussed what kind of materials should be used for the construction. They first agreed to use concrete, but then the managers changed their minds and suggested bricks instead (bricks are cheaper and easily obtained in China). Migrant bosses knew that although bricks cost less and crumble more quickly than concrete, the rental price would remain the same, so they insisted on concrete. After bargaining back and forth, they finally agreed on concrete. Then it came to the focal point of setting rental fees. The construction company proposed fifteen yuan per square meter. This would amount to six million yuan for the entire proposed construction space, not including other fees such as land use and the installation of water and electricity. The migrant bosses talked to each other in their own Wenzhou dialect and decided to reject this offer.[3] They pointed out that what would be built were simple makeshift dwellings, not permanent apartment buildings, while the proposed rental price was as high as that for permanent apartments. They further argued, "If Sanhe really welcomes us, you should offer a better price to show your sincerity."

The construction managers eventually agreed to lower the price, but they were worried that there would not be as many migrants coming as Zhen predicted. If the new housing were not fully occupied and Zhen could not collect enough rent, the company would lose money. They thus suggested signing a contract with Zhen specifying that they would finish the project on time and that Zhen was solely responsible for renting all the rooms. Zhen agreed, but he also made it clear that his men would be in charge of making rules and collecting fees and that the local government would not interfere. The leading official of the Yanjiao district completely agreed with this proposal: "All I am concerned with is profit. As long as you can bring enough people here, maintain order, and make our local economy prosperous, our government will not interfere with anything in your place. We trust you." The agreement to let migrant bosses regulate their own socioeconomic space nourished a sense of trust between the local government and incoming migrants.

At this point, both sides decided it was time to go to look at the land for the temporary housing. The site suggested by Sanhe officials was a large piece of farm land of three hundred *mu* (twenty hectares) recently designated for nonagricultural development. Everyone seemed satisfied with its location and size, which was only five kilometers from the center of town and adjacent to a major interprovince highway. A newly built modern water park and golf course were nearby, which could attract more people to the area.

At dusk, the negotiation finally ended and we headed back to Beijing. I was excited about the possibility that a large new migrant community would appear in Hebei. While I asked Zhen when they would sign the actual contract, surprisingly, he said, "I am not sure, at least not just yet." It turned out that this entire afternoon's negotiation was simply a business strategy to test what kind of deal they could get. Once the other side made the offer, migrant bosses would do more investigation and think it over. Further, they revealed to me that temporary housing was only a short-term plan; what they really wanted was more ambitious—to develop a multifunctional commercial center in Yanjiao.

I later found out that on November 24, 1995, a document titled "The Report on the Feasibility of Building the Zhejiang North Commercial City in Hebei" was drafted by a special committee. The report proposed to build a giant multifunctional commercial center in the Yanjiao district, which would contain five wings for production, market, storage, residence and service, and education. The entire project would cost about one billion yuan and would absorb the businesses of at least ten thousand families. The goal was to create a safe, stable, and permanent socioeconomic space for displaced Wenzhou migrants and to "facilitate the spread of the Zhejiang commercial spirit nationwide so as to help push China's market economy forward," the report claimed. The planning of this project involved a wide range of agencies and people: the Zhejiang provincial government's liaison office, the Wenzhou municipal government's liaison office, local Hebei government agencies, two private Wenzhou corporations, and Wenzhou migrant representatives. An independent corporation was formed to raise funds and take charge of the operation. Although there were government agencies involved, they only acted as subeconomic units, but their participation gave the project a certain legitimacy and thus political protection.

This attempt to reproduce a larger version of Zhejiangcun in a relatively peripheral area did not go very far. To begin with, the plan was initially promoted by a few migrant bosses and Zhejiang and Wenzhou government officials who wished to gain from it financially. Although some migrants were also interested in the project, they had serious doubts about its feasibility. Yanjiao, a small, underdeveloped district outside Beijing's consumer market, was not an ideal site for developing private businesses. The disadvantages of the location became obvious during the migrants' three-month stay in Yanjiao. Initially, a few garment wholesale dealers and buyers traveled to the relocation sites because the prices offered by migrants were lower than those in Beijing. But because of the cost and inconvenience of long-distance transportation, fewer and fewer buyers came later. Their declining sales reinforced many migrants' lack of enthusiasm about a large-scale commercial center in Hebei. Therefore, most families were not willing to invest in the project for fear it would turn out to be an empty city (*kongcheng*). Instead, they prepared to return to Beijing. Indeed, like most other political campaigns in China, the cleansing of the Wenzhou migrant community was like a tornado. It came quickly, did a lot of damage, and disappeared just as fast as it had come. Three months after the campaign, most of the migrant households had gradually trickled back to Zhejiangcun.

Without strong grassroots support, the plan for building a large commercial center in Hebei failed. The failure suggested that market development had its own inner logic. The formation of Zhejiangcun had taken more than ten years and had been based on expanding social networks among ordinary migrants. Further, Zhejiangcun enjoyed a great location—close to downtown Beijing, with a vast consumer market and an existing transportation system that linked it to hundreds of cities by train and bus. By contrast, Yanjiao had none of those features and no existing large consumer market. The planners of the Hebei project failed to realize that private market developments were not just about the physical construction of the buildings, but also about the nurturing of business seeds and networks.

"New Bottle, Old Wine"

By April 1996, most migrants had returned to Zhejiangcun. What puzzled me most was how they managed to find new residential and production space given that their previous housing compounds no longer existed. I eventually identified three sources of migrant housing. One was space in local private homes, but since most of the available space in local villages was already rented to other migrants, returning migrants turned to neighborhoods adjacent to Zhejiangcun. In desperation, some even sought housing in nearby high-rise apartment buildings with higher rents.[4] But living in urban apartment buildings could be a problem for the production households. These families needed space to set up their sewing machines, store materials, and accommodate workers, but it was hard to find large rooms in the high-rise buildings; even if rooms were available, the cost was prohibitive. Further, urban residents in the buildings constantly complained about the migrants' noisy sewing machines. When conflicts with neighbors intensified, migrants could be forced to leave.

Others, using the name of a local government agency, started seemingly legitimate businesses and then built apartments on the acquired space. These new covert big yards were no longer called *dayuan*, but were given a new name—*gongsi* (company).[5] I discovered one covert migrant housing compound self-marked as a clinic. The owner, Boss Chai, told me that this was a joint business project funded by his family but sponsored by a state-run company under a central government ministry. Because the building was registered under the name of a state enterprise, official approval for leasing the land for three years was granted by the district's city planning bureau. Chai continued, "We use its [the company's] title to register and have all the necessary legal documents. With such support and the economic interest of the ministry involved, I do not think the Beijing government will touch this place."

Ownership of this compound was divided into ten large shares. Chai's family and another family owned eight shares; the other two shares were held by the sponsoring state enterprise. Because the enterprise secured a construction permit by using its title, it did need to provide initial capital but was entitled to 20 percent of the profit. In other words, Wenzhou migrants purchased legitimacy and protection from a state enterprise that in effect leased its official title. As I walked around in the compound, I noticed that in addition to the clinic there were about fifty apartments inhabited by Wenzhou migrants. Just before I left, Chai reminded me not to tell any Beijing people that there were residential units in this compound: "Make sure you say that it is just a hospital."

The third and most important way of creating housing was to use space in local state-owned enterprises. The appropriation of this urban space was made possible by the recent acceleration of state enterprise reform. In the mid-1990s, many inefficient and unprofitable medium-sized and large state enterprises were forced to close down or cut back their workforces (Zhong 1998; Research Team of the CCP School 1998). In 1996, 8.14 million urban state enterprise workers were laid off, and in 1997 the number rose to 13.7 million (20–30 percent of the total urban work force) (*China News Digest*, November 3, 1997).[6] Many urban workers suddenly found themselves unemployed and without meaningful support from the state. Rumors flew that some unemployed workers were planning protests. A group of laid-off workers in Beijing demanded that the central and city governments put their livelihoods at the top of the political agenda. They articulated their concerns through this down-to-earth slogan: "We need to eat, to live, and to support our parents!"

In Zhejiangcun, several state-run factories faced shutdown. This situation presented an unusual opportunity for migrants to form new economic alliances with the factories struggling on the edge of a late-socialist society. As a result, three or four factories in the area were turned into covert migrant housing compounds (see Figure 18). One of them, Dongfeng Factory (a pseudonym), was a subunit of a Beijing government bureau with approximately sixteen hundred workers. During the years of the centrally planned socialist economy, this factory, like many others, received raw materials from designated state suppliers and provided finished products to designated state buyers. Profit-making was not the chief concern as long as the factory fulfilled the quota set by the higher authority. But as market reforms deepened in the 1990s, the state decided to gradually reduce its role in state enterprises and asked some of them to operate on their own financially. In the face of intense market competition, this factory had lost money for several consecutive years. The situation worsened in late 1995. The factory manager told me that they had tried to keep production going for a few months because "we worried that if so many workers suddenly lost their jobs and became floaters, it would cause instability in society; we also hoped that the state would eventually do something to help us out." But no support came through. Higher-level bureaucrats decided that this factory was not worth saving, and therefore it was ordered to halt production. In our conversation, the word *shiye* (unemployment) was never mentioned. Instead, echoing the standard official rhetoric, unemployment was referred to as *xiagang*, which literally means "stepping down from one's post."

Though the state did not take much responsibility for its former employees' welfare, heads of individual factories felt a moral responsibility to continue supporting their own laid-off workers for about two years.[7] It was during this time that new commercial alignments appeared. As this factory manager put it: "All human beings need to eat and drink, thus they will find ways to fulfill such basic needs. When some Zhejiang migrants took the initiative and asked to rent our factory, we naturally agreed because this deal can benefit both sides." The factory leaders did not actually deal with individual migrant households; migrant bosses negotiated the contract and then rented

18.   A closed-down state factory rented as a covert migrant housing compound

the space to other migrants for a profit. I asked the factory manager what would happen if the local or city government found out about such arrangements. He replied: "I do not know, but I do know that our workers have to live. Also, this is only a short-term contract, and we got the approval from officials above. If the future looks good, we will extend the contract."

The factory was divided into two separate parts by a street. The south part was used mainly for production workshops with heavy machines, while the north part was designed for administration and storage. When I visited the factory in June 1996, the north part, which contained six rows of one-story office structures and a two-story administrative building, was already fully occupied by fifty or sixty Wenzhou migrant households. Each room had been turned into a residence. On the wall near the front gate, several large painted characters read: "Leather Jackets for Sale Inside." I spoke to several families living there and found out that most of them had moved in the previous week. But I noticed that most of them had already renovated the rooms by adding a wood platform in part of the room to maximize the use of space. Although migrant bosses rented the rooms from the factory for two to three hundred yuan, the monthly rent per room for these families was seven to eight hundred yuan. Assuming these figures were accurate, the secondary housing bosses could make at least four hundred yuan profit per room in a month.

In spatial and social organization, this factory-turned-housing-compound was not much different from previous big yards. The main difference was that this compound was not built by the migrants themselves. An old Chinese saying describes the situation: *xinpingzi zhuang jiujiu* ("new bottle, old wine"), meaning that the superficial appearance has changed but the essence remains the same. Another difference was how this housing compound was regulated. As the factory manager explained, the factory wanted to partially oversee what was going on there: "We have provided security guards to help them regulate this place because after all this is our factory site. We cannot let them [the migrants] turn it into a little independent kingdom for themselves."

In sum, there was an intensification of "the commodification of urban space": state work units turned their space into a commodity. Through new alliances with state units, some Wenzhou migrants were able to find relatively stable and safe places to live and work. At the same time, the unemployed workers received rent money from migrants, which could help ease workers' soaring discontent with the state. For this reason, such collaborations were tacitly approved by local and even city-level authorities concerned about potential social unrest.

Closer Collaboration or Deeper Control?

In the postdemolition recovery of Zhejiangcun, a variety of commercial collaborations between Wenzhou migrants and government agencies flourished. These new collaborations were concentrated on the development of garment marketplaces. This trend of seeking alliances with local agencies was closely related to migrants' acute awareness of their unstable and inferior position in the city. And local officials participated in or even initiated collaborations with them for financial returns. Three kinds of commercial alliances were most important.

First, there appeared several large-scale "early-morning markets" (*zaoshi*) set up by the township, streetship, and village cadres as low-cost trading spaces for migrants (see Figure 19). These marketplaces usually ran from 5 A.M. to 8 A.M. in parking lots, closed factories, or other temporarily free space. Each one could accommodate several hundred retailers. It cost practically nothing for local government agencies and villages to set up these

19.   An open-field marketplace for garment sales

markets, but the returns were good. Since the sellers paid only a small fee for
a slot (three to five hundred yuan a month), they could afford to charge relatively low prices for their products and thus attracted tens of thousands of
customers daily.

   The second kind of collaboration was through the construction of a new
garment center initiated by the Beijing city government. On December 21,
1995 (at the peak of the demolition event), Vice Mayor Zhang Baifa held a
meeting to discuss the blueprints for reconstructing a large central garment
trade center in Dahongmen. Later, in early May of 1996, a ceremony to lay
the foundation stone for this future garment center was held in an open field
in Zhejiangcun. The ceremony was carefully orchestrated as one of the
biggest local events. This field had once been used to store the debris of
houses from the demolition and thus had a particular symbolic significance:
It symbolized the death of a migrant space and the birth of another kind of
officially sanctioned socioeconomic space. This government act indicated
that the ultimate intention of the campaign to clean up Zhejiangcun was not
to erase the community altogether, but to weaken its formation of nonstate
power and turn it into a regulated regime of private capital. When I

20.   A new garment trade plaza constructed in the postdemolition period

returned to the United States in September, construction had not yet begun. I later learned that the garment center was being built.

Sixteen months later, in January 1998, I revisited Zhejiangcun. I was amazed by the number of new market developments in the area. Rather than declining or disappearing, the community had expanded rapidly. An enormous modern plaza called Dahongmen Garment City was housed in a newly completed six-story building; this garment manufacturing and trade center was the realization of the city and district governments' plan (see Figure 20). It contained several thousand trading stalls and several hundred apartments to be rented to migrants. Hotels, restaurants, entertainment facilities, and other services were also included in the plaza. It was predicted that there would be tens of thousands of customers coming to this garment center daily. The building of this garment city had been initiated by the Beijing municipal government, but the actual work was carried out by the Fengtai district government. And the investment and business participation of Wenzhou migrants was crucial. In the beginning, the Fengtai government agencies were unable to persuade individual migrant families to invest in the project and sign up for a stall because most Wenzhou migrants no longer trusted the government that had demolished their housing compounds. The district officials therefore had to seek help from migrant leaders like Zhen. In the beginning, migrant leaders were not willing to offer help or partici- pate either, but soon they realized how much they had to gain. Thus they again acted as brokers to coordinate the investment process. In return for his mediating role, Zhen, for example, was able to obtain several stalls in the new market building at a discount and acquired special government approval to reconstruct two private housing compounds. In this way, the role of de facto local migrant leaders was partially restored.

Two additional large garment trade buildings were also nearly completed. One was a modern ten-story building designed to replace the old Longqiu market, which was soon to be torn down to make way for the construction of the fourth ring road around the city. This market was privately owned by Wenzhou bosses. The other one was also permanent and even larger, funded by both Wenzhou migrants and their regional government. In front of this construction site, a large eye-catching banner read "the Wangfujing in the Southern Part of the City." Traditionally, Wangfujing, located in downtown Beijing, has been the best known and most prosperous commercial center in the city. This banner thus demonstrated the ambition of Wenzhou migrant entrepreneurs to expand their businesses on an unprecedented scale and remain in Beijing.

In sum, the emerging economic collaborations between government agencies and migrants indicated a different kind of governmentality at work, one not characterized by antagonistic exclusion of migrant leaders but by cooperation. The construction of the garment city in the name of the gov- ernment provided a legitimate space for migrant trade, but at the same time, by bringing migrants into this state-organized space, the state was also able to exercise closer surveillance and political domination over them. The new rule of the game was this: as long as the migrant community could be brought under the government gaze and its commercial activities formalized, the "golden goose" that was Zhejiangcun could be allowed to exist and even grow.

To what extent would the government assume the role of policing order in these new market spaces? Which level and division of the bureaucracy would be responsible for the regulation? Would the migrant leadership con- tinue to grow, change shape, or eventually dissolve given further state pene- tration of the community? These important questions about the changing power dynamics in postdemolition Zhejiangcun will be explored in my future research.

Conclusion

The story of Zhejiangcun continues to unfold in surprising ways, which makes the task of bringing this ethnography to a conclusion particularly challenging. Zhejiangcun and other unofficial migrant communities have become more deeply entangled with China's larger economic transformation and changing political culture. Although the fates of these communities are unpredictable, I will attempt to highlight the important issues and discuss their relevance for rethinking socialist transformations.

Space-Making as Higher-Level Social Change

Social space exists at several levels: the micro level, which includes architecture, neighborhood, housing, and street; the middle level, which involves town, city, and rural-urban asymmetry; and the macro level, which encompasses national and global organizations and strategies. This book has primarily examined the micro-level spaces in a migrant community as manifested in the politics of migrant housing and marketplace developments. But it is also concerned with the mid-level spatial relationship between the city and the countryside caused by migration. The migrants' emerging power is both conditioned by and derived from the migrants' spatial mobility and the production of their own social space. What we have seen is a highly contested process in which existing socialist spaces (villages, factories, and other state-dominated sites) were transformed into different kinds of spaces more suitable for private economic practices and capital accumulation by migrant entrepreneurs. Because rural migrants in China are defined as outsiders and strangers in the cities and denied formal urban membership and substantive rights, their creation of a new social space outside the regime of official planning has profound social and political implications.[1] Such spatial transformations are not just about physical space, but are integral, dynamic aspects of the late-socialist transformations that will reshape the economic and social trajectory of

Chinese society (see Zhang 2001). Lefebvre has pointed out that all political, economic, and social formations are underpinned by configurations of social space, and that the rise of both capitalism and socialism was inseparable from the production of new social spaces (1990: 401–3). By differentiating two levels of social change—the production of things in space and the production of space itself—he suggests that altering things in space is social change on a lower level and that only the production of new spaces and spatial relations brings about a higher-level social transformation. From this perspective, all fundamental societal transitions are closely linked to the reorganization of social spaces through which new kinds of social relations are made possible.

In China, dramatic spatial reconfigurations have resulted from the shift from a centrally planned socialist economy to its current hybrid form. The existing spatial structures could no longer meet the needs of the new economy and social life. The same is true for migrant communities such as Zhejiangcun. The informal migrant economy and an alternative way of life without urban citizenship have demanded a different kind of social space, one that can nurture innovative commercial activities and private communal life. Chinese migrants' production of residential, manufacturing, and trading space has thus been an essential basis of emerging migrant entrepreneurial power. But this level of change (that is, a fundamental reordering of the existing social space) is precisely what the party-state fears because it further challenges the established order. Spatial reconfigurations in societies in transition have historical precedents in China. When the socialist regime came to power, its planners, too, profoundly reconfigured both urban and rural space. The *danwei* system transformed urban space into self-sufficient, spatially demarcated work units. Rural collectivization and antisuperstition campaigns destroyed or transformed temples, lineage halls, and other sites into collective dining halls, commune offices, nurseries, and so forth (see Jing 1996; A. Chan, Madsen, and Unger 1984; Friedman, Pickowicz, and Selden 1991).[2]

Two larger processes in late-socialist China made migrants' spatial reproduction possible: the commodification of space and the commodification of bureaucratic power. First, even though land and property cannot be freely sold or purchased under most circumstances, the ability to rent space (*dipan*) over the short term and lease it over the long term are among the most prominent changes in China since the late 1980s. From the business world to officialdom, for enterprises run by the state and collective and those run by private individuals, urban space has become a special type of commodity that can be rented or leased to generate profits. Never before in socialist

China has the commercialization of space been as pervasive and frantic as it is today. Despite the government's attempt to limit what kinds of space can be used for income-generating purposes, individuals and state-owned units have developed tactics to bend or evade the rules. It was in this context of pervasive commodification of space that numerous migrant communities thrived in urban China.

Second, the commodification of space is also linked with the changing nature of the Chinese bureaucracy. Since the early 1980s, many government agencies have begun to engage in commercial activities that will increase informal revenue.[3] As local governments turn into profit-seeking agents, their primary activity has shifted from administrative regulation to commercial facilitation. In Zhejiangcun the local state agencies turned to entrepreneurship in their pursuit of commercial alignments between local officials and successful Wenzhou migrants via migrant bosses.

Some people might argue that the partial destruction of Zhejiangcun by the government campaign indicates the utter powerlessness of these migrant traders in the face of coercive state power. This observation was true for migrant spatial politics at that moment. But in looking at migrant community-making over time, we are more likely to arrive at a different conclusion. Within a few months of the demolition campaign, thousands of displaced migrants managed to return to the settlement; they quickly found new ways to rebuild their community on an even larger scale. Without their previously established economic power, enduring social solidarity, and sustained connections with the residents and state agents in the receiving community, such a quick return and revitalization would not have been possible.

In my analysis of the reconfigurations of power relations in this migrant community, I have sought to integrate insights from two classical theorists: Marx and Weber. According to Marx, the key to gaining power is to seize control over the means of material production, which constitutes the core of class struggles in capitalist society (Marx and Engels 1988; O'Laughlin 1975). This framework is useful for understanding the social and political struggles of China's rural migrants, but it is important to expand the meaning of "means of production" to include not only material production but also the production of social space and the discursive production of categories and knowledge. I am by no means the first one to call for such an attempt. Many theorists and anthropologists have demonstrated the importance of analyzing spatial production and the production of meaning as forms of the means of production.[4] Moreover, while a political-economic account of power dynamics tends to emphasize the importance of impersonal bureaucracy and social institutions, it often ignores or downplays the role of "informal" social networks and personal traits in the production of political and social power. Power thus becomes disembodied. This study demonstrates that migrant leaders built up their influence by simultaneously drawing on three types of power as defined by Weber: traditional, charismatic, and bureaucratic power (see Weber 1981). Thus I have highlighted the social connections of migrant leaders, including kinship ties, native-place networks, and patron-client relationships, while taking into account masculinity-based charisma through the concept "prowess" (*benshi*).

Clientelism as a Mode of Governmentality?

Despite the deepening of a market-based economy and the emergence of regimes of private capital and migrant power, the Chinese party-state remains highly visible and central in regulating newly formed migrant communities under late socialism. It would be misleading to conclude that state power has diminished in the face of market forces, or that it has retreated from migrant social and economic life simply because migrants have succeeded in creating alternative communities without direct state intervention. Their struggle to develop Zhejiangcun is a testament to the fact that state power still figures centrally in the migrants' social and economic worlds and that clientelist politics in the local power dynamics is not a thing of the past.[5]

It was not my original intention to study clientelism in the Wenzhou migrant settlement. But as the lives of Chinese migrant entrepreneurs and traders unfolded before me, I realized that the dynamic, vertically integrated clientelist networks among local officials, migrant leaders, and ordinary migrants were central to an understanding of state-society relations. Clientelist politics was the primary vehicle by which migrants struggled to create and reorganize a social space of their own in the city. While drawing on kinship, native-place, and other social networks, this emerging migrant clientelism was highly commercialized, often measured by market exchange value, and was closely tied to the increased commodification of state power.[6] These seemingly traditional yet highly commercialized clientelist networks enabled new modalities of governance. Since rural migrants were not counted as true constituencies of the urban government, informal patron-client relationships became the primary conduit for regulating and sustaining public order, market relations, and social relations in the floating population. In Zhejiangcun, housing bosses and market bosses, backed up by their personal connections with officialdom, were the de facto regulators and facilitators of local affairs.[7]

In comparison with other forms of clientelist politics in socialist China, three distinct features of migrant clientelism are worth elaborating. First, the migrant clientelist networks I have described in this book were usually triadic and relatively unstable. By contrast, patron-client relationships formed in the prereform socialist context were relatively structured and stable. For example, in the socialist urban work units, party-clientelist networks were created by the party-state and were highly institutionalized (see Walder 1986). In villages, peasants were also heavily dependent on their team leaders and had little choice of patrons (see Oi 1989). Members of the mediating social stratum that linked individuals with the state were formally appointed or backed up by higher-level political authorities, even though the mediators shared many common socioeconomic traits with their clients.

The clientelist networks in Zhejiangcun were created by migrant entrepreneurs out of their sense of insecurity and inferior social position in the city. Migrant bosses recruited local officials to act as their patrons in gaining access to spatial and other resources (albeit at high market prices). At the same time, ordinary migrant families considered these bosses their patrons for local protection and access to housing and market spaces. Migrant patrons were not officially appointed but had close informal connections with officialdom. Therefore, the mediating stratum between migrant communities and the state was no longer a single group but two structurally different yet informally connected groups—de facto migrant leaders and grassroots cadres and officials. In other words, it was not a dyadic but a triadic relationship—among officials, local bosses, and migrants—that constituted migrant clientelist networks. Further, these triadic clientelist networks were unstable and fluid. Ordinary migrants could choose their preferred patrons, even though in practice their choices were largely shaped by existing kin and geographic ties. Here there is a great deal of similarity between today's unofficial mediating status of migrant bosses and the role of local patrons in both rural and city politics during the republican era (see Duara 1988; Helen Siu 1989; Strand 1989).

Second, migrant clientelism was clearly marked by the politics of place. Clientelist networks were largely built on migrants' shared native-place ties. The relationship between migrant patrons and their clients was mediated primarily through their common geographic origin, which served as an enduring social bond between these two vertically positioned groups. But just as native-place identity played an important role in the development of a collective identity and group solidarity among Wenzhou migrants, the same notion divided them into different subgroups, also according to geographic origin. Their competing interests thereby set limits on the development of a more centralized migrant leadership and collective action.[8]

The politics of place was also reflected in the dual mediation by urban officials and migrant bosses, because the former shared few common social and economic traits with migrants. The most important factors dividing them were their *hukou* classification (rural or urban) and place of origin. These differences made it difficult for Beijing officials to penetrate the migrants' provincial enclaves and compelled them to seek migrant leaders as brokers to regulate migrant communities. While lower-level officials were fully aware of the need to incorporate the power of migrant leaders, upper-level officials were worried that the de facto recognition of migrant leadership would encourage uncontrolled growth of migrant power that would ultimately displace local government rule. This was the main reason for "cleaning up" Zhejiangcun. Yet despite the direct intervention of upper-level officials to remove the spatial underpinning of growing migrant power, clientelist networks continued to flourish in the postdemolition years. It was actually through the mediating role of migrant bosses that the Fengtai district government was able to mobilize migrants to participate in new, officially organized commercial projects. In this manner, local government authorities also restored some of the power and authority of migrant leaders.

Third, the mode of dependency and the needs of patrons and clients in migrant communities differed from that of prereform socialist clientelism. On the one hand, official patrons no longer demanded political support from migrant entrepreneurs; instead they wanted commercial goods, money, and other tangible economic benefits. On the other hand, migrants wanted not specific goods but access to space—namely local cadres' tacit permission to create their own housing and market spaces.

Ironically, the flourishing of clientelist politics today is often accompanied by a new kind of official rhetoric that emphasizes the rule of law. The ten official regulations enacted by the Beijing city government in 1995 were supposed to be the guiding legal principles for governing migrants. Yet this new vision of governmentality, based on "impartial" law (*fazhi*) rather than arbitrary governance, exists only on paper, given the pervasiveness of asymmetric clientelist networks. Instead, another kind of impersonal force—money—combined with patronage networks recasts everyday power relations and social domination in late-socialist China.

Rethinking Socialist Transformation

The spatial and social reconfigurations within China's floating population provide a good empirical basis for pondering the nature and trajectory of future late- and postsocialist transformations. Two questions are of particular concern here: Is the current periodization of socialist transformation a useful tool in thinking about social changes in countries like China? What is the meaning of the "transition to a market economy" in the Chinese social context, and how should we conceptualize the relationship between market, capitalism, and democratic development?

Let me begin with the first question. In this book I have referred to the current condition of Chinese society as "late socialism" rather than "postsocialism." I do so not because I believe that one can actually pinpoint these stages or epochs in time. By using the term "late socialism" I simply want to resist the assumption that current societal transformations in China will necessarily lead to the demise of the socialist regime. "Late" conveys less a sense of breakdown, rupture, and death of the existing system than a condition characterized by some fundamentally new developments mixed with the legacies of the old system. Hence, late socialism is similar to Jameson's conception of late capitalism in that "what 'late' generally conveys is . . . the sense that something has changed, that things are different, that we have gone through a transformation of the life world which is somehow decisive but incomparable with the older" (Jameson 1997: xxi). It is under such a condition, I suggest, that alternative societal forms (outside the strictly socialist or capitalist) are likely to emerge.

With regard to the second question, this study questions the scenario of "triumphant markets and capitalism," in which the free market is constantly represented as a foreign force transplanted from the outside into socialist countries. There is an implicit assumption that market forces will eventually erase traditional forms of social relationships and practices. Yet as this ethnographic account of the formation of migrant enclaves in China indicates, "the market" is not necessarily an alien economic form imported from the West. The kind of petty capitalism engaged in by Wenzhou migrants grew out of indigenous practices and was built on traditional social networks and clientelist connections with the socialist bureaucracy. Such indigenous petty capitalism coexists with state-owned enterprises and managed foreign capital, which together reshape the contours of Chinese society, one that is based on the interplay of market forces, traditional social relations, and state regulatory power.

Further, in this book I have argued against the notion that economic privatization and the growth of free-market forces will lead inevitably to the decline of state power and an increase in horizontal social ties and trust. Stark and Bruszt (1998) have shown that in Hungary, while old socialist state power may be eroding, the state has been able to reconstitute itself through new governing strategies.[9] In this process of "restatization," the reconstituted state becomes the *manager* of planned social change. Thus, as Verdery puts it, "socialism's centralized political economy could be dismantled only by further strengthening the state so it could manage the process of its own dissolution" (1996: 213). This form of planned and managed socioeconomic change is best exemplified in China as the state takes up the role of the ultimate supervisor and designer of the "socialist market economy." Within migrant communities the reinvented and recrafted regulatory and managerial role of the state was played out mainly through clientelist politics. In the remaining pages I turn to a brief examination of current developments in Zhejiangcun and the fate of migrant enclaves in Beijing in a time of changing urban economic structure and political climate.

Repositioning the Floating Population in Recent Urban Restructuring

Since the completion of my primary fieldwork in 1996, many important social changes have taken place in urban China that have affected the fate of rural migrants. In Chapter 8, I only briefly pointed to some of the new trends. Now I would like to discuss in greater detail how recent urban economic restructuring and political events in Beijing are reshaping the future of Chinese rural migrants and their enclaves in the city, and to explore the implications for rethinking the relationships among space, power, private capital, and governmentality.

In the early 1980s and the mid-1990s, creating effective strategies for managing the floating population was high on the agenda of the Chinese government. Although regulating rural migrants remains important, another set of problems facing the reform state has become even more pressing. The privatization of state enterprises has generated tens of millions of unemployed workers who now constitute a massive urban underclass and a source of instability. How to absorb this extraordinarily large group of laid-off workers and maintain social stability has become a central concern of the Chinese party-state. The effects of this radical restructuring of the urban economic system are far-reaching. My discussion here is primarily concerned with how urban unemployment and potential social unrest affect government policies toward migrants and their community development.

The first thing that must be noted is that the effects of urban restructuring on the migrant population are paradoxical and uneven. On the one hand, in 1998 the state urged unemployed urban workers to "learn from rural migrants" to be "on their own": that is, to take up temporary hard work such as construction and services that are traditionally rejected by most urbanites, or to create their own jobs by starting small businesses. In this official rhetoric, rural migrants, who were once represented as a social problem, are used by the state to denounce and silence the discontent of the unemployed urban population. On the other hand, many city governments have begun to limit the kinds of jobs migrants are allowed to take because migrant workers are believed to compete for jobs with laid-off workers. For example, in Beijing since 1998, migrant workers have been banned from entering twenty specific work sectors as a way of easing job competition for unemployed urban workers (Eckholm 1998; O'Neil 1998). Similarly, the Guangdong government has established strict regulations on the number of rural migrants allowed to settle there in order to make it easier for the hundred thousand local laid-off workers (presumably permanent urban residents) to find business opportunities and employment (*China News Digest*, January 6, 1999).

These stringent rules on employment in the cities have directly affected migrant laborers who depend on wage work, but migrant traders and entrepreneurs who have their own businesses and thus do not compete with laid-off workers are affected only indirectly. In some cases, they even provide jobs for urbanites. For example, in Zhejiangcun some local laid-off women make a living by taking care of Wenzhou migrants' children at home; some work in the large new trading centers. But migrant street vendors compete with urbanites who start small retail businesses. Therefore, local governments in some areas have made it more difficult for migrants to get business permits in order to reserve small business opportunities for the locals. To combat worsening unemployment, governments in several large cities have also begun to demolish migrant shelters and street markets in order to expel small rural traders. These new attacks on migrant space are "part of a master plan to cut the number of rural migrants living and working in the cities" (Eckholm 1999).

In addition, the shifting geopolitics of Beijing also affects the fate of migrant enclaves. On October 1, 1999, the People's Republic of China celebrated its fiftieth anniversary by holding a grand ceremony in the capital.

To prepare Beijing for the commemoration of this important event, the city government mobilized another great cleanup campaign. This "beautification" program aimed to tear down 2.6 million square meters of illegally built structures, most of which were temporary housing, stores, restaurants, and street markets established by migrants or shanties rented out to migrants. Beijing Mayor Liu claimed that because "the illegal structures are the major cause of the untidy appearance and visual pollution in certain parts of the city" they needed to be removed. He also urged district officials to carry out daily inspections to make sure that no such buildings would be rebuilt. Clearly, this official vision of a modern urban aesthetics for metropolitan Beijing—the emblem of a revitalized new China—clashed with the untidy petty migrant businesses, even though Vice Mayor Wang admitted that "Beijing depends on the help of workers from outside the city."

As a result, many migrant neighborhoods in Beijing once again became targets for demolition. From late January to early February 1999, one of the city's largest migrant communities, Xinjiang Village, located in Weigongcun and Ganjiakou, was bulldozed by the Haidian district government. This place had been home for more than a thousand Uygur migrants, a Muslim minority from the northwestern Xinjiang Autonomous Region. During the 1990s they had established about fifty family-run restaurants serving Xinjiang-style food. An eyewitness to the demolition of one migrant community described this campaign: "The disfigured specter of modernization has raised its ugly head and is once again preparing to strike down a beloved Beijing institution." Many other migrant congregating zones, such as the Sanlitun area, and hundreds of spontaneously formed small migrant marketplaces were also subject to the cleanup. The most frequently used pretext for such campaigns was the need to widen streets, reduce traffic pressure, and thus beautify the capital for the fiftieth anniversary. Migrants without urban resident status were most vulnerable to state-initiated expulsion at times like this because they had no rights and nowhere to appeal or complain. But even though this great cleanup erased numerous street markets and migrant communities, migrant entrepreneurs and traders returned to rebuild their markets and communities after the campaign died down.

The fate of Zhejiangcun in the midst of China's changing political economy is different from that of other migrant enclaves, however. Since the displaced Wenzhou migrants returned in 1996, they have gradually gained a more secure position in the city than before. By renting closed-down factory spaces and turning them into housing compounds, these migrants became the primary providers of income for several thousand unemployed urban workers in the area. Thus if the city government wants to expel Wenzhou migrants again, it would mean taking away the "rice bowl" of local unemployed urban workers. Further, the several newly completed large garment plazas in Zhejiangcun now provide both business opportunities for Wenzhou migrants and jobs for some suburban residents. Since the economic interests of urban unemployed workers are more deeply entangled with those of migrants than before, it becomes more and more difficult for the city government to displace Wenzhou migrant entrepreneurs.

While the mutual entanglement of the Wenzhou migrants and the local community deepens, the nature of the migrant social space is also changing. With the establishment of several large, modern market buildings sponsored and managed by local governments via migrant leaders, this place begins to have more and more of what the city government aims to promote in the capital: formalized, well-managed private businesses and modern commercial developments operating under the gaze of the state. But even though unofficial migrant communities may be partly under state scrutiny, migrant struggles for power and control will continue because no gaze is all-encompassing. In addition, the nature of the gazing agents itself may also be transformed by their subjects. At the beginning of the twenty-first century clientelist politics in late-socialist China has not disappeared. It is a mode of governmentality that is at once archaic and modern and that continues to obscure the boundaries between state and society.

Appendix: Notes on the Conditions and Politics of Fieldwork

In *Reflections on Fieldwork in Morocco* (1977), Paul Rabinow suggests that ethnographic knowledge is profoundly mediated by the complex relationship between the ethnographer and the cultural other and is conditioned by specific local and larger sociopolitical circumstances. In recent years, even though more and more "native" anthropologists like myself have returned to their countries of origin to conduct ethnographic fieldwork—a familiar yet also strange social context—problems inherent in the relationship between self and other have not simply disappeared. At the same time, political and social conditions in the destination countries continue to shape the possibility and contour of the fieldwork by "homecoming" anthropologists in different ways. Such was the case for my anthropological research among the floating population in China.

Because my fieldwork site was an unofficial migrant enclave, it was viewed by the Chinese authorities as a problematic product of recent market reform. As a result, research on this community by both domestic and foreign scholars was largely discouraged by city officials. Conducting long-term fieldwork in the area was complicated, especially for someone like me: at that time I was still a Chinese passport holder, yet I came from a foreign university. During the government campaign to demolish Wenzhou migrant housing compounds—a time charged with political tensions and conflicts—my ethnographic account of this community became further politicized.

Needless to say, having grown up in China, I had many advantages in conducting field research in my home country. Because I speak Mandarin and also understand several Chinese regional dialects, I could blend in easily with other Chinese people in the migrant community and elsewhere. Yet establishing a local institutional affiliation to support my research was not easy. Because of my status as a Chinese citizen holding a permanent U.S. residence card, I was considered neither a foreigner nor a true Chinese. At first, no institutions in Beijing were willing to officially host me as a visiting researcher because I could not be accepted as a *liuxuesheng* (a foreign student studying in China) through the *waiban* (the foreign affairs office) or as a native Chinese student. Without a proper place in the existing categorical order of people in China, I became, in effect, a floater without *danwei* (work unit) affiliation. Yet everyone who has lived in China knows that an institutional affiliation is essential for doing research there, especially for interviewing officials and gaining access to libraries and archive materials. Eventually I was able to work around the bureaucratic rules by using my own *guanxi* networks to arrange an informal affiliation with Peking University. The fact that I had graduated from Peking University made it justifiable for officials there to approve my informal affiliation should higher authorities have questioned it later.

Ideally, a researcher conducting ethnographic fieldwork lives temporarily among the informants so as to observe and participate in their daily activities and community events. But this living arrangement was not feasible in my case because of the politicized nature of the migrant community. As mentioned, research in Zhejiangcun was largely discouraged by government officials and the police. Living in the community would have entailed unnecessary direct encounters with the police and local officials who periodically carried out "night inspections." Second, housing was extremely scarce in the area. One often had to wait a long time and work through networks of kin and friends to find a place. Given this situation, I decided to commute to Zhejiangcun daily from my dormitory at Peking University. Later on, when I developed friendships with migrant families, I was able to stay with some of them from time to time.

As a researcher without a locally recognized productive role, I felt awkward in the beginning. Many migrants also were uncomfortable with formal interviews. I thus tried to establish some productive roles for myself within the community and interviewed a good portion of my informants in a casual way. For example, two months into the fieldwork I became a casual English language tutor for some migrant children of wealthy families. This role gave me ample opportunity to interact with their families and get to know them personally. Sometimes, I looked after their clothing shops while they ran errands, or helped restaurant owners prepare food (such as dumplings) during our conversations. In the end, interviews in those circumstances were much richer and more telling than the formal ones.

The majority of my interviews with migrants were semistructured with open-ended questions. I memorized most key questions so that I would not intimidate my informants with a printed questionnaire in hand. To protect the safety of my informants, tape-recording of interviews was not appropriate. But to preserve the substance of the interviews, I was usually able to write down key words and sentences and then, from memory, expand on them immediately afterward. Hence, most quotations from my interviews in the book are not verbatim, but they are very close to the actual conversations. To protect my informants' identities, all the names used in the book are pseudonyms.

Most anthropologists today would agree that no fieldwork site (either a relatively localized or a translocal space) is like a "natural laboratory," in which the researcher can collect "objective" data and leave without disturbing the setting. In reality, an ethnographer is highly visible in the place where he or she carries out long-term fieldwork. Therefore, an ethnographer is inevitably entangled with local culture and politics. I was no exception. From the first day of my fieldwork, and especially during the demolition campaign, I had to reposition myself constantly and be positioned by my informants. The notion that an ethnographer could remain neutral, unbiased, and distant from local politics was simply a myth. As I argue several places in the book, discursive production of knowledge and representation of migrant enclaves had real, concrete effects on migrants' lives. Because most Chinese rural migrants had little formal education, they had virtually no access to print or broadcast media, which played a powerful role in shaping the image of migrants and their communities. Many Wenzhou migrants expected me—a university student who could read and write well—to speak for them by writing articles about the positive aspects of the community. During the demolition campaign, such expectations became even higher. Several housing bosses urged me to publish articles in national and Beijing newspapers that would debunk the dominant representation of Zhejiangcun as a crime-ridden place. Their expectations put me in an extremely difficult situation. On the one hand, I felt strongly that the interests of Wenzhou migrants should be defended. On the other hand, I had to avoid direct confrontations with officialdom in order to continue my research. Yet my perceived reluctance to act as a spokesperson for Wenzhou migrants at a time when the fate of their community was at stake made some of them begin to have doubts about my position. Soon, however, the government announced that newspapers would not be allowed to publish articles or reports on Zhejiangcun that had not been officially sanctioned, and this decision helped alleviate the pressure on me. But the uneasy feeling stayed with me throughout my fieldwork.

Another legal and ethical dilemma presented itself when I had the opportunity to speak with young drug users at a migrant friend's home (see Chapter 6). The police randomly raided migrant houses for drug trafficking and consumption. According to the rules set by the Beijing authorities, anyone who knew about a drug-use site was required to report it to the police. And anyone caught at a drug-use site could be charged with the same crime facing a drug user. Luckily nothing of that kind happened, but the possibility was there like a shadow.

Finally, as a young Chinese woman working alone in a large community, I also experienced gender-specific problems. Zhejiangcun had about one hundred thousand residents, and naturally, not everyone knew me. Besides those migrant families I hung out with, I also frequently interacted with "strangers." Oftentimes, simply because I was alone and eager to talk to people, migrant businessmen mistook me as interested in sex trafficking because women were not supposed to interact with unfamiliar men alone in their local cultural milieu. Near the beginning of my fieldwork, I had a rather disturbing encounter with a male migrant entrepreneur at his clothing shop. Despite my repeated explanations that I was a student researcher interested in migrant lives for academic purposes, many thought that I was simply too embarrassed to tell the truth. Even as an ethnographer, I could not escape the local assumptions about gendered boundaries and moral codes.

In sum, while striving for "thick description" (Geertz 1973), an ethnographer's descriptions and interpretations are inevitably shaped by his or her subject position through direct or indirect moral, political, and emotional engagement. Ethnographic knowledge is necessarily a form of "local knowledge" mediated by the self/other relationship and the political and social context. Thus my account of Wenzhou migrants' lives and struggles was inevitably shaped by my own subject position and the surrounding social and political forces.

A final note: I took all of the photographs in this book during my research in China.

Notes

Introduction

1. This is only an estimate provided by official and unofficial reports. Because migrants tend to move frequently with the changing demand of markets, accurate large-scale survey data are extremely difficult to obtain. For a detailed discussion of the sources of the numbers and the difficulty of counting rural migrants in China, see Solinger 1999a and Ma and Xiang 1998.

2. Although it has become common for scholars to use the term "postsocialist" to describe reform-era China, I prefer to use "late socialist" to characterize this period of transformation because the one-party Communist political system continues to dominate. This is not to say that there have been no important changes within this political regime or in the way it operates. Indeed, this book explores these changes. Yet such changes have not amounted to a fundamental alteration of one-party rule, and the state apparatus continues to expand.

3. For more about how Wenzhou migrants raised their initial capital before migrating to Beijing, see Chapter 2, as well as Tsai's extensive study of capital-raising strategies and informal financial institutions created by China's rural private entrepreneurs (Tsai 1999).

4. For example, Fukuyama's notion of "the end of history" (1989) predicts the ultimate demise of socialism and triumph of market capitalism and liberal democracy as the final and universal form of political-economic structure for all human societies. Although this view has been criticized by many social scientists, it continues to influence popular political discourse in the West.

5. Some examples of this growing body of literature critiquing a monolithic and progressive treatment of postsocialism are Verdery 1996, Bridger and Pine 1998, Bunce and Csanadi 1993, R. Watson 1994, Winckler 1999, and Stark and Bruszt 1998. Some scholars even question whether a generalized model of socialism is possible at all, given that diverse forms of socialism existed in different countries (see Sampson 1991; Hann 1994).

6. Some recent studies of urban space in post-Mao China include Rofel 1999, Davis et al. 1995, and Hershkovitz 1993. Several excellent works by

China historians explore the role of urban space in shaping everyday social life and city politics in the early twentieth century, including Dong 1996, Esherick 2000, and Lu 1999.

7. In socialist China, land is either state owned or collectively owned. In the city, land-use rights are usually allocated by the state to collectives or state work units. In the reform era, however, land and space are increasingly commodified.

8. In analyzing Chinese politics, Dittmer (1978) also points out the difference between *quanli* and *shili* as two types of political power in the upper-level bureaucratic realm. He contrasts *quanli* as formalized power based on rank and posts in the party-state hierarchies, with *shili* as informal power based on prestige and qualification. I think that this distinction is largely sound, and even though *shili* is often translated as "influence," viewing it as a culturally specific form of power can highlight the centrality of informal social networks and cultural capital in the political sphere. This does not mean that *shili* should be equated with power; rather my point is that the Western concept of power needs to be disaggregated and made more specific in the Chinese cultural context.

9. On the changing state-society relations in China, see Perry 1989, 1994 and Shue 1988, which inspired my inquiry into this complex field.

10. Much excellent work has been done in this spirit. See, for example, Shue 1988, Walder 1986, Oi 1989, Solinger 1992, White 1993, Wank 1999, and A. Chan, Madsen, and Unger 1984.

11. See Anagnost 1997, Brownell 1995, Rofel 1999, Helen Siu 1989, and Mayfair Yang 1994 for examples of everyday and symbolic forms of state power in post-Mao China. These studies were influenced by and contribute to a growing body of anthropological literature that seeks to bring the "state" back into the analysis of culture and society (e.g., Borneman 1992; Gupta 1995; Herzfeld 1992; Mitchell 1991; Taussig 1992; and Verdery 1996).

12. I borrow the concept of political brokerage developed by scholars such as Barth (1959), Vincent (1971), Schneider and Schneider (1976), and Swartz (1969) in their discussions of leadership in local politics. In her study of rural revolution in China, Helen Siu (1989) applies this concept to the role of local party-state cadres in mediating the relationship between the state and the rural populace.

13. I define commodification as a process in which products, land, space, time, labor, social relations, and power become commodities whose exchange value encompasses use value (see Marx 1977).

14. The ability of Wenzhou migrants to create commercial alliances with bureaucrats is inseparable from their increased economic power as private entrepreneurs who have gained most in the post-Mao economic order. For accounts of the changing relationship between private entrepreneurs and the

state, see Wank 1999, Young 1995, Solinger 1984, Gold 1989, 1990, Bruun 1993, Pearson 1997, and Gates 1996.

15. Henan Village in the Chaoyang district and Anhui Village in the Haidian district are composed of migrants engaged in recycling, vegetable retailing, and other small-scale repair work. Xinjiang Village is in two different locations (Ganjiakou in the Xicheng district and Weigongcun in the Haidian district), where Uygur migrants from the Xinjiang Autonomous Region operate family restaurants (see Ma and Xiang 1998 for a fuller account of these enclaves).

16. I use present tense to describe this place because many of its social and economic aspects are the same today, after the rebuilding of this community, as they were before the government campaign.

17. The Wenzhou municipality is a prefecture-level city, which refers to a large administrative area. Yueqing is a county-level city that contains extensive rural areas and the city proper, which is about the size of a township.

18. This term was first used by economists analyzing the Eastern Bloc's economic changes (see Grossman 1977). Later China scholars borrowed the term to refer to "the entire range of economic activities outside the formal, centrally planned economy, including private construction, manufacturing, commerce, transport, handicrafts, repairs, services, and moonlighters whose off-hours work is for private gain." (Nee and Young 1990: 3).

Chapter 1

1. Rumors circulated widely in 1994 that the Chinese government would soon do away with the two-tier household registration system as a result of mass labor migration (see *Wall Street Journal*, April 26, 1994).

2. It is important to note that two seemingly analogous concepts, *renkou liudong* and *liudong renkou*, need to be differentiated. The former is an all-encompassing demographic term referring to various kinds of spatial and social mobility; the latter refers specifically to displaced people in the city who are unable to change their official residential status in the *hukou* system, in other words, the floating population. The meaning of "floating population" thus goes beyond spatial mobility and is associated with a sense of disorder and abnormality in the Chinese order of things (see Wang 1991).

3. For detailed discussion of migration and changing state policies during the 1950s, see Solinger 1999a, Cheng and Selden 1994, and Davin 1999.

4. There is a large body of literature examining the origins, functions, and socioeconomic consequences of *hukou* in China (see Cheng and Selden 1994; Dutton 1992; Kam Wing Chan 1994b; Christiansen 1990; Zhang Qingwu 1988; Selden 1993; Solinger 1999a; and Potter and Potter 1990).

5. It is not my intention here to delve into a detailed discussion of the causes for present-day migration. For those interested in a fuller explanation of

post-Mao Chinese internal migration, see, for example, the following studies: Banister 1986, Goldstein and Goldstein 1985, Liang and White 1996, Xiushi Yang 1993, Yan Yayu 1994, Yi and Shao 1995, Solinger 1999a, Mallee 1988, Davin 1999, Scharping 1997.

6. Surplus rural laborers existed in Maoist China, but they remained invisible because of the collective farming system and tight rural-to-urban migration control. Post-Mao agricultural reforms intensified the problem of surplus laborers and made them more visible (see Taylor 1988; Davin 1999).

7. A comprehensive list of major research, newspaper articles, and books on the floating population published between 1984 and 1995 is provided by Yi and Shao 1995.

8. Although technically the floating population refers both to short-term travelers and visitors who have left their homes temporarily and to long-term rural migrants working in the cities, it is the latter group that serves as the basis of the image of floaters.

9. I wish to thank one anonymous reviewer for bringing my full attention to the dehumanizing aspect of the discourse on the floating population. I also want to point out a striking similarity between the dehumanizing discourse on Chinese migrants and the discourse on refugees (see Malkki 1996) and world hunger (Escobar 1995: 103–4).

10. A similar argument regarding the making of the internal other has also been made by Gladney (1991) and Schein (1997) in their analyses of the positions and identity politics of ethnic minorities in contemporary China.

11. The shed people were migrants (mostly Hakka migrants) who lived in makeshift huts.

12. For example, Laozi, the Taoist master, described his vision of utopia as "enjoying his food and clothes, being able to enjoy his stable residence and local customs . . . but never going to visit or interact with adjacent countries." Mengzi, a Confucian master, also proposed that one should "never move out of the hometown" but should farm the land and help out friends in the same community until death. These images and notions have been selectively appropriated by the state to serve present needs.

13. *Waidiren* (outsiders) is another common term for the floating population. Floaters are rarely called migrants in China because they are not granted official permanent *hukou* in the receiving areas. Therefore they are products of the Chinese household registration system. For a discussion of the terminology associated with this social group, see Solinger 1999a.

14. Although the migrant population as a whole may have more children per couple than urbanites, migrants tend to have lower fertility rates than the rural population that does not migrate, because of postponed marriages, marital separations, long working hours, and the high cost of raising children in the city (see Davin 1999: 130–33).

15. For instance, the Fuzhou municipality imposes a fine of at least one thousand yuan for the first unauthorized child; three thousand yuan for the second; and ten thousand yuan for the third (Chen Shubi 1990: 24).

16. Direct intervention in residents' private residential space was also common during Mao's time. But in the reform period most urban residents are no longer subject to such intervention in their everyday lives.

17. What a floater looks like is often determined by the cultural stereotypes of migrants as poor and dirty; or they may be marked by their rural clothing style.

18. The Chinese phrase is: "*Wenzhouren xiang taiyang, zoudao nali nali liang.*" This is an intentional adaptation of a popular revolutionary saying about Chairman Mao: "*Maozhuxi xiang taiyang, zoudao nali nali liang*" (Chairman Mao is like the sun. Wherever he goes, he brings sunlight to brighten the place).

19. Similar phenomena whereby migrants simultaneously maintain important social and economic ties with their home communities while developing new involvements in other places are observed by Chavez (1992), Ferguson (1992), Rouse (1991, 1992), and James Watson (1975) in both international and internal migration contexts.

20. This is part of a general new trend in post-Mao China that material consumption has become an increasingly important domain for articulating and negotiating identity, status, and social belonging among Chinese people (Davis 2000; Jing 2000). This observation, however, can be easily extended beyond China. See, for example, Mills 1999 on gender and migration in Thailand, which demonstrates the centrality of commodity consumption in reshaping rural migrant women's senses of self and experiences of modernity.

21. The average household income of Wenzhou migrants is very high. About 80 percent of the seventy households that I interviewed claimed an annual income above 200,000 yuan, which is roughly twenty times the annual income of a middle-class Beijing household.

Chapter 2

1. The dialectical relationship between structure and agency is articulated not only within the Wenzhou migrant group but also within the entire migrant population in China (see Solinger 1999a). Kate Zhou (1996) makes a similar point regarding the agency of Chinese peasants in shaping social changes during the post-Mao reform period.

2. Wenzhou people speak the Wu dialect. Wu is different enough from Mandarin that most Mandarin speakers cannot understand it (see Norman 1988; DeFrancis 1984).

3. There are 6.6 *mu* to an acre and 15 *mu* to a hectare. The transportation

system in the region was particularly underdeveloped. There was no airport before July 1990 and no railway running through the region until the mid-1990s.

4. Helen Siu (1990) has pointed out that not all regions evenly experienced
an increase in spatial mobility during the reform period. Migration was determined by specific local and historical circumstances.

5. Such ideas were echoed in the official state ideology during Mao's years,
which valorized peasants as the essence of the Chinese nation and criticized
petty trade as "profiteering."

6. In the mid-1950s and early 1960s, there appeared a few state policies that
supported the role of small tradesmen (*xiaoshang xiaofan*) in the socialist economy (see Chinese State Administration and Regulation Bureau of Independent
Economy 1987). During this period small business and trade recovered briefly
but were soon crushed by ultra-leftist political forces (see Solinger 1984 and
Young 1995).

7. In 1987 there were sixty thousand Wenzhou natives living abroad (Parris
1993: 243).

8. On August 16, 1992, *Economic Daily* published an important article
titled, "It Is Time to Conclude That Wenzhou Is Socialist, Not Capitalist,"
which concluded the long debate over the Wenzhou model.

9. This idea echoes Furnivall's (1956) conception of a market relationship
as allowing individuals to act as strangers and temporarily separate their social,
economic, cultural, and political backgrounds from their business transactions.
The only thing that matters in market exchange is the principle of
equivalence.

10. In her critique of the literature on Chinese "entrepreneurial familism,"
Greenhalgh (1994) has pointed out the danger of neglecting the micropolitics
of gender, ethnicity, and other inequalities in the Chinese family firm.

11. Charles Tilly defines "chain migration" as involving "sets of related individuals or households who move from one place to another through a set of
social arrangements in which people at the destination provide aid, information, and encouragement to the newcomers" (1990: 88).

12. Before the mid-1980s, it was considered capitalist exploitation, and was
deemed illegal, for private entrepreneurs to hire workers. In 1982, Premier
Zhao Ziyang first confirmed that taking on a few helpers (if no more than
five) and apprentices was acceptable. Then in 1984 a series of rules regarding
rural individual entrepreneurs passed by the State Council formally approved
Zhao's proposal (see Chinese State Administration and Regulation Bureau of
Independent Economy 1987). But in practice, it took some time to change
people's skepticism about hiring wage workers. See also Young 1995.

13. For a detailed study of the effect of state policies on migration, see Wan
1995, Chaoze Cheng 1991, and Kam Wing Chan 1994b.

14. In China the service sector is called *disan chanye*, the third-tier econ-

omy; the first tier is agriculture, and the second tier is industry and construction. Services have often been provided through what has been called the "informal sector" (Portes 1983).

15. Commercial reform in Beijing was an extremely complicated process. This account simply outlines a few critical moments that made it possible for Wenzhou migrants to live and work in the city. For more on Beijing's commercial reform and the development of the service sector, see Duan et al. 1989. For more on changes in state policy toward the private economy on a national scale, see Sabin 1994, Solinger 1984, and Young 1995.

16. Some local farmers and officials said that the area was ignored by the state because the communities there were not only poor but also densely populated by farming households. It would have been too expensive for the state to relocate the large number of farming households into state-subsidized housing if their land had been used for urban development.

17. See more accounts provided in Xiang 1994 and Wang Chunguang 1995, and a newspaper report in the *Qianjiang Evening Daily* (May 6, 1993) for this near-mythical story about the origin of Zhejiangcun.

18. "Making three calls at a cottage." This phrase comes from a well-known classical novel, *The Three Kingdoms* (*Sanguo Yanyi*), in which a famous military leader, Liubei, went repeatedly to the hut of a legendary sage and mastermind, Zhuge Liang, to invite him to be his chief military adviser. The story implies the power of persistence and sincerity.

Chapter 3

1. Chinese migrants in other enclaves normally rent rooms from the locals, rather than constructing their own housing. And the situation in Zhejiangcun is very different from that of the spatially demarcated shantytowns or squatter settlements commonly found among migrants in other countries. For comparison, see Perlman's (1976) account of squatter settlements in Rio de Janeiro, and Chavez's (1992) description of the "Green Valley" shantytown of Mexican immigrants in the United States.

2. Gradually during the urban housing reforms of the 1990s, many urban residents were asked to buy back state-allocated apartments in which they lived at a discounted rate significantly lower than the market value. Although some newly constructed commercial housing is available on the market, to purchase a commercial apartment one must have a local urban *hukou*, and the price is far beyond most ordinary people's means.

3. According to a survey of 4,714 migrants in Shanghai, in 1995 nearly half of them rented temporary housing (see Wang and Zuo 1996). This is a general pattern of lodging within the migrant population in urban China today (except among migrant factory workers).

4. *Dadui* was the term used before the decollectivization. Now it is called *xingzhengcun* (an administratively defined village), and it is overseen by the *cunweihui* (village committee). But people today continue to use the old term.

5. For details about regulations, see the collection of official documents on Beijing city planning and construction (Beijing City Planning and Regulation Bureau 1993). Even though the reform of real estate property in Beijing had already begun in the early 1990s, it did not have much effect on rural migrants' access to land for housing construction. As *waidiren*, they were still excluded from the formal regime of urban real estate.

Chapter 4

1. For a systematic study of the history and political-social functions of the *danwei*, see Lu and Perry 1977. See also Walder 1986, Whyte and Parish 1984, and Dutton 1992. These scholars show that the Chinese work unit is a powerful institution through which the state organizes and controls urban society while seeking political loyalty from citizens.

2. For accounts of close connections between secret societies and other popular associations, and between peasant rebellion and revolutions, see Chesneaux 1972; Perry 1980, 1993; Hershatter 1986; Zhou and Shao 1993; and Honig 1986.

3. During my fieldwork I became an English tutor for Zhen's two children and thus a close friend to his family. I spent a lot of time with them and had numerous opportunities to observe their everyday activities and social interactions.

4. This enterprise is called the Nanyuan-Dahongmen Union Company of Agriculture, Industry, and Commerce (*nanyuanxiang dahongmen nong gong shang lianhe zonggongsi*). It is a special entrepreneurial entity used to generate financial resources for the township government.

5. I use the term "marketplace" (*shichang*) in a narrow sense to refer to the actual markets where trade is conducted, rather than to the "market system" as defined in regional analysis (see Smith 1976; Skinner 1964–65).

6. None of the people I interviewed was married to a Beijing resident. Almost all told me that their spouses came from the same village, township, county, or Wenzhou region as their own. Only one of my informants—a merchant from Yueqing—was married to a woman from Hubei; she had once work for him in his retail store.

7. In his study of lineage and secret societies in southeastern China, Freedman points out that secret societies tended to cut across lineage organizations and displayed a sense of class solidarity against the solidarity of lineages (1958: 121–24). In the case of Wenzhou migrant *bang* today, such informal groupings also cut across lineage, but they do not mark the line between the rich and the

poor. Rather, the relatively poor and weak are drawn into the *bang* structure under the power umbrella of the rich and strong.

8. The migrant *bang* I am discussing here shares some common features with the *hui* in the Qing period described by Ownby (1993), but the *bang* is a more casual and loosely defined social organization than the *hui*. In a *bang* rituals of fictive kinship and blood oath may be practiced by some migrants, but they are not a key component in the *bang* formation today.

9. For comparison with the personification of power among "big men" in the context of Melanesia, see Godelier and Strathern 1991.

10. Most provincial and city governments establish a liaison office (*lian-luochu*) in Beijing to represent their own interests and mediate affairs involving both Beijing and local governments.

11. The majority of Wenzhou migrants practice popular Buddhism, but a small number are Christians.

12. Such dual roles are also an important feature of overseas Chinese leadership, as Skinner's study of the Chinese communities in Southeast Asia has convincingly shown (1968). But key community leaders such as the Kapitan among overseas Chinese were given certain authority by the state and were thus agents of the state. Such was not the case for Wenzhou migrant leaders in Beijing; they are not recognized by the state despite their de facto mediating role. To further compare the role of Wenzhou migrant leaders with the role of "power brokers" played out by leaders in other alternative social structures in a larger scope, see studies by Blok (1974), Hess (1973), and Schneider and Schneider (1976) on mafiosi in western Sicily.

Chapter 5

1. I define "patriarchy" as a changing social and ideological institution in which senior male figures exercise domination over women and other junior members (see also Stacey 1983).

2. In demographic surveys by local governments in the countryside, household members who migrate to the city are also considered members of their rural households.

3. Whether private business owners (*getihu*) should be granted permission to hire helpers was a highly debated issue in the beginning of economic reform. It was over a long period of time that government policies shifted from defining the private employer-employee relationship as an exploitative, capitalist class relationship to allowing a limited number of helpers (see Chinese State Administration and Regulation Bureau of Independent Economy 1987; Young 1995).

4. Many multinational corporations similarly use female docility and man-

ual dexterity as part of their employment strategy (see Fernández-Kelly 1983; Lim 1983; Ong 1987).

5. The treatments and discipline of migrant workers in this enclave, however, is perhaps not as severe as that of other migrant workers hired by private and foreign-owned enterprises elsewhere in China (see, e.g., Anita Chan 1998; Lee 1998).

6. Pun (forthcoming) has provided an interesting analysis of how a new genre of resistance by young migrant factory workers in southern China can lead to an odyssey of human freedom.

7. On the relationship between mental health and recent social changes in China, see Lee, Kong, and Kleinman, n.d.

Chapter 6

1. This event, known as *yanda*, lasted for over a year, during which local public security bureaus were pressured to solve a specific number of criminal cases and to arrest a specific number of criminals. The first government crackdown on crime took place in 1983. Since then similar campaigns have been mobilized several times, but none was as far-reaching as the one in 1996.

2. A similar process of criminalizing marginal groups also takes place in the postsocialist states of Eastern Europe (see Borneman 1997).

3. In China, major newspapers and magazines are still controlled by the government and thus reflect official views. But media agencies also want to report things that attract readers, even if they must occasionally disobey official orders.

4. During my fieldwork, I collected hundreds of newspaper clippings on crime related to the floating population from the *Beijing Evening Daily*. Every day there were at least two short articles about crimes committed by floaters.

5. Elder sister (*dajie*) is a polite way of addressing a woman regardless of her age.

6. The problem of drug consumption is also reflected in the number of newly established drug rehabilitation centers (*qiangzhi jiedusuo*). According to the Central Chinese Television News, there were 695 such centers in China at the end of 1997.

7. Yunnan Province is a main entry point for drugs smuggled into China from the Golden Triangle.

8. A rule called "Decisions Regarding Drug Prohibition" was passed in December 1990. According to it, a person found carrying fifty grams of heroin or a thousand grams of opium is subject to a minimum of seven years in jail plus a heavy fine. The death penalty can be given to drug traffickers.

9. This account is taken from Xiang 1994–95.

10. Since most households do not have their own in-house bathrooms, people have to go to public bathrooms.

11. The base salary of a local police officer is usually less than eight hundred yuan a month, while a middle-income Zhejiang migrant businessman can make ten or twenty times that amount. The striking difference in their incomes compels local government agents to seek additional income by abusing their power.

Chapter 7

1. These brief reports, which appeared in the *Beijing Evening Daily*, *Beijing Youth Daily*, and *Beijing Daily*, had virtually identical content and used similar rhetoric because they were all sanctioned by the city government.

2. This is a typical example of how local state agencies enter the market sphere to make extra money and become profit-making entities. This phenomenon is widely found in reform-era China (see Solinger 1984 and Pieke 1995).

3. This ambiguous relationship is common among migrants and immigrants in other cultures. For example, see Chavez 1992 on undocumented Mexican immigrants in the United States, Ferguson 1992 on migrant workers in Africa, Oxfeld 1996 on Chinese immigrants in Calcutta, and Lowe 1996 on Asian immigrants in the United States.

4. These newsletters (about 170 issues) were not released to the general public at the time, but became accessible after the campaign. They provide a detailed account of how the campaign was carried out and what resistance the workteam encountered from the perspective of the local officials. In this chapter, I use information from these newsletters to help reconstruct this event.

5. Farmers had built many additional rooms for extra rental income. Almost every farmer's household had one or more additions.

6. "Private housing" (*sifang*) here specifically referred to the rooms added by the locals for rental, not their own preexisting houses.

7. Such standard official rhetoric did not specify what those consequences might be or any possible punishment. The vague wording was designed as a threat, and it also allowed the government to press whatever charges it wished later.

8. There is a broadly defined southern identity among people from the southeastern coastal region. People speculate that, in the power dynamics of the central government, tension and differences exist between leaders from the north and those from the south.

9. There were three liaison offices, one established by the Zhejiang provincial government, one by the Wenzhou city government, and one by the Yueqing city government.

10. To gain some insight into how migrants made informal alliances with their regional governments and negotiated with Beijing officials, I lived with

Zhen's family for about a week and spent most of that time in his big yard before the demolition. I was able to meet officials from their place of origin who were identified by migrants as "our own people."

Chapter 8

1. This center was a joint venture between an industrial corporation in Shanxi Province and a Hong Kong–based real estate development company.

2. Women were generally excluded from such important meetings and political negotiations. But Zhen's wife and I were allowed in the meetings because of her persistent requests and my research status.

3. This was an intentional business negotiation strategy. Because the Wenzhou dialect is fundamentally different from Mandarin and the Hebei dialect, Sanhe officials were unable to understand what the migrants were discussing among themselves.

4. Rent in these buildings tended to be close to double what farmers charged. But the living conditions were better, since each apartment was equipped with running water and toilets.

5. A more detailed account of this new type of big yard in Zhejiangcun can be found in Jeong 2000.

6. The large-scale reform of state enterprises was formally announced by the central party-state at its Fifteenth Party Congress of October 1997.

7. Since then, the Chinese government has realized the urgency of establishing a new social welfare system. Most cities and towns today have established some sort of pension system to help those whose incomes are below the poverty line, but the amount of money provided barely covers basic living costs and is often unreliable (see Solinger 1999b; Wang and Chen 1998).

Conclusion

1. See Holston and Appadurai 1999 for a thorough discussion of the relationship between formal membership and substantive rights regarding citizenship.

2. I wish to thank Sara Friedman for bringing my attention to these historical precedents of spatial transformation in the early socialist period.

3. This new phenomenon is discussed in great detail by Pieke (1995) as the meshing of bureaucratic, market, and personalized spheres. Most striking is the People's Liberation Army's creation of more than twenty thousand companies under its control dealing with transportation, real estate, entertainment, hospitality, and other types of business; these generate commercial revenue that exceeds the state's military budget (see *Chinese News Digest*, July 29, 1998). In

1998 the central state ordered the closing of these military-run enterprises to curtail the political corruption.

4. For spatial production as a means of production, see Lefebvre 1991. For the production of meaning as a means of production, see Comaroff 1985 and Turner 1980. Although Foucault does not speak of the means of production and class struggle, his insights regarding knowledge and power remain central to anthropologists who attempt to incorporate an analysis of discourse and power into an account of the political economy (see Ong 1987; Povinell 1993).

5. Some scholars have proposed using the model of state corporatism to conceptualize emerging state-society relations in certain segments of the whole system (see, e.g., Pearson 1997). Although this model is useful for understanding the role of the state and the dynamics of political power in joint ventures and urban private enterprises, I feel it is less helpful in explaining the relationship between small, family-based migrant businesses and the state pre-cisely because no state-licensed intermediary associations exist in the latter cases. Instead, the highly commercialized form of clientelism in the migrant community links officialdom with the migrants on a personal basis and thus can shed more light on the changing modes of governmentality in China today.

6. My findings are similar to those in Wank's (1999) study of commercial clientelism between state officials and urban private businesses in reform-era China.

7. Compare Strand's (1989) account of quasi-governmental functions per-formed by local elites and civic organizations in republican Beijing.

8. In her historical study of the politics of Chinese labor, Perry (1993) has pointed out a similar situation: though mobilization of native-place identity was what made the modern Chinese labor movement possible, the divisions and fragmentations created by such place-based identity also set boundaries to such movement. Strand's (1989) study of labor politics in republican Beijing also shows a simultaneous presence of factionalism and cohesion among guilds.

9. According to Putnam (1995), building community-based horizontal ties and social trust is crucial for the formation of civic power independent of the state.

Glossary

Anhuicun	安徽村	Anhui Village
anju leye	安居乐业	to have a secure place to live and to enjoy one's business
baifen	白粉	white powder; heroin
banguan banmin	半官半民	semiofficial; semipopular
bange laoxiang	半个老乡	one who is considered by others a partially native fellow
bang	帮	gang; coalition
banghui	帮会	ganglike association
baogao wenxue	报告文学	reportage literature
baojia	保甲	household registration system and mutual surveillance used in late-imperial and republican China
ben mo	本末	in Confucianism, the fundamental/essential and the incidental
benshi	本事	ability, prowess
bulao er huo	不劳而获	to reap without sowing; illegal ways of making money
cengci di	层次低	low class
chaye	查夜	night inspection
chai	拆	to tear down; to demolish
changzhu renkou	常住人口	permanent resident
chengbao	承包	to contract
chengxiang jiao-jiedai	城乡交结带	urban-rural transitional belt
chi dayan de	吃大烟的	those who smoke opium
chou baifen de	抽白粉的	those who smoke white powder, heroin

chumen	出门	to leave home
chuanmen	串门	to visit friends or relatives casually
chuangshou	创收	to create extra income
chunjie	春节	Spring Festival; Chinese New Year
cungongsuo	村公所	the office of an administratively defined village, which usually includes several smaller naturally formed villages
cunweihui	村委会	village committee
cunzhang	村长	the head of a village
dachuanlian	大串联	mass travel to establish ties among the Red Guards during the Chinese Cultural Revolution
dadui	大队	brigade; a production unit under the Maoist commune
dageda	大哥大	cellular phone
dagongde	打工的	migrant wage workers
dagongmei	打工妹	migrant working sisters
dajia	打架	to fight
dahu	大户	big household; wealthy household
dakuan	大款	very wealthy people
dashehui xiao-zhengfu	大社会, 小政府	a big/strong society with a small government
dayuan	大院	big yard; migrant housing compound
dai	带	to take along and look after junior relatives
dai hongmaozi	戴红帽子	to wear a red hat; to seek protection by affiliating with a collective or state unit
danwei	单位	work unit
daobi	倒闭	bankrupt
daoyi	道义	the Confucianist ideal and morality
daozuofang	倒坐房	the reversed room, located on the south side of a courtyard residence
difang zhuyi	地方主义	regionalism or localism
dipan	地盘	territory; a sphere of influence

disan chanye	第三产业	third-tier economy; the service sector
dixia gongchang	地下工厂	underground factory
diyuan	地缘	place bond
dongfang de jipusairen	东方的吉普赛人	the Oriental Gypsy
dongfang de youtairen	东方的犹太人	the Oriental Jew
dongluan	动乱	instability and disorder
du	堵	to block; a strategy used by the Chinese state to stop migration
erdeng gongmin	二等公民	secondary citizen
fanwan	饭碗	rice bowl; means of living
fanzui	犯罪	crime; to commit a crime
fengbishi	封闭式	closed; not open to the public
ganbu	干部	cadre
getihu	个体户	independent or individual entrepreneur
gong	公	public
gonganju	公安局	Public Security Bureau
gongshangju	工商局	Bureau of Industry and Commerce
gongshangyezhe	工商业者	industrial and commercial entrepreneur
gongshe	公社	commune, abolished in the early 1980s
gongzuodui	工作队	workteam
gudong	股东	shareholder
gufenzhi	股份制	shareholder system
guahu	挂户	hang-on household; independent family firm associated with public enterprises
guanli	管理	to regulate
guanshang heliu	官商合流	the merging of official and merchant power
guanxi	关系	personal connections
guanxihu	关系户	established partners for exchanging favors in personal networks

gui	鬼	ghost
guojia	国家	state
haoyi wulao	好逸恶劳	to love leisure and despise work
hefa	合法	legal
Henancun	河南村	Henan village
heishehui	黑社会	black society; the underworld
hongweibing	红卫兵	Red Guard
hu	户	household
huji	户籍	household registration status
hukou	户口	household registration system
huahua shijie	花花世界	flashy world
huantang buhuan-yao	换汤不换药	to change only the soup but not the medicine; no fundamental change
hunyuzheng	婚育证	marriage and fertility certificate
jiguan	籍贯	native place, usually determined by one's patriline
jihua shengyu	计划生育	family planning
jinu	妓女	prostitute
jia	家	family; home
jiating zerenzhi	家庭责任制	family responsibility system
jiawuhuo	家务活	domestic chores
jianshimian	见世面	to see the outside world
jianghu pianzi	江湖骗子	swindler
jiedao banshichu	街道办事处	streetship government office; the smallest official unit governing the urban population
jieshaoxin	介绍信	letter of introduction
jinhai	禁海	to close up the sea to foreigners
jinsanjiao	金三角	the Golden Triangle; a large opium-growing and -trading area where Burma, Laos, and Thailand intersect
jinxinyue	金新月	the golden new moon; an opium-growing and -trading area that extends to Pakistan, Afghanistan, Iran, and neighboring countries

jingshang	经商	doing or conducting business
jingshen wenming	精神文明	spiritual civilization
jingwen aixin she	京温爱心社	Beijing-Wenzhou Loving Heart Society
jirenlixia	寄人篱下	living under someone else's roof
jiufu	舅父	mother's brother
jujudian	聚居点	congregating zones
jumin	居民	residents
juweihui	居委会	neighborhood committee
junmin guanxi	军民关系	military-civilian relations
kaifang gaohuo	开放搞活	to open up and enliven the economy
kongcheng	空城	empty city
laoban	老板	boss
laobanniang	老板娘	wife of the boss; female boss
laogong	老公	husband
laojia	老家	native place; home origin
laoxiang	老乡	fellow natives
liqihuo	力气活	strenuous physical work
lianluochu	联络处	liaison office
lianse	脸色	facial expression, usually unhappy
liegenxing	劣根性	dark and poor dispositions
lingdao	领导	leader; boss
liucuan	流窜	to flee from place to place
liudong renkou	流动人口	floating population
liudong renkou fanzui	流动人口犯罪	crime by the floating population
liudong renkou jihua shengyu xunjiandui	流动人口计划生育巡检队	patrol teams that monitor the floating population's birth control practices and birth rate
liudong renkou jujudian	流动人口聚居点	congregating zones of the floating population
liudong renyuan	流动人员	floater; floating people
liudu	流毒	a pernicious influence
liufang	流放	to exile
liukou	流寇	roving bandits

liumang	流氓	hooligan; rogue
liumin	流民	wandering homeless people
liuwang	流亡	to exile
liuxuesheng	留学生	foreign students
loufang	楼房	buildings with more than one floor
luohou	落后	backward
majiang	麻将	mahjong, a Chinese gambling game
mangliu	盲流	blind flow; undirected or unregulated flow [of migrants]
mimi shehui	秘密社会	secret society
mianzi	面子	face; respect
mingong	民工	peasant worker
minjian	民间	among the people; popular or nongovernmental
minjian zuzhi	民间组织	popular or nongovernmental organization
mingqi	名气	prestige
mingsheng	名声	reputation
mu	亩	a unit of area that is equal to about 0.1647 acre
nongmao shichang	农贸市场	a marketplace that specializes in agricultural products
nongmin	农民	peasants
ouyue wenhua	瓯粤文化	the Ouyue culture in southern Zhejiang province
paichusuo	派出所	a branch office of the Public Security Bureau
pianjing	片警	a police officer in charge of a specific area
pingfang	平房	a one-floor home
Qianmen	前门	the most prosperous traditional commercial district in downtown Beijing
qiansong	遣送	to deport
qianxi	迁徙	to move or migrate; relocate
qiangzhi jiedusuo	强制戒毒所	drug rehabilitation center
qinqi	亲戚	relatives

qingli	清理	to clean up
qingxi Wenzhou, gongchuang daye	情系温州，共创业大	to maintain emotional connections with Wenzhou, and to create grand common achievements
quzhu	驱逐	to expel
quanguo geti lao-dongzhe xiehui	全国个体劳动者协会	National Association for Independent Workers
quanguo gong-shang lianhehui	全国工商联合会	All-China Federation of Industry and Commerce
quanli	权力	bureaucratic power
quanshi	权势	influence built on bureaucratic power
renkou liudong	人口流动	population mobility
renkou yidong	人口移动	population movement
renminbi	人民币	the Chinese unit of money, yuan
renqing	人情	human feelings; favors
renren guanwo, wo guan renren	人人管我，我管人人	everyone else polices me, while I police everyone else
ren yu fa	人与法	people and law
rushi qiangjie	入室抢劫	indoor robbery
sandeng gongmin	三等公民	a third-class citizen
san gu mao lu	三顾茅庐	making three calls at a cottage; showing sincerity
sanguo yanyi	三国演义	*The Three Kingdoms*, a classical Chinese novel
shamao	傻帽	a silly hat; a fool
shanqing shuixiu	山青水秀	green hills and clear waters; beautiful scenery
shangpinhua	商品化	commodification
shangshan xiaxiang	上山下乡	up to the mountains and down to the countryside; the movement in which urban youth were sent down to the countryside during the Cultural Revolution
shangyehua	商业化	commercialization
shehui jiandu	社会监督	societal surveillance
shehui zhi chuang	社会之窗	a window into society
shenshang	绅商	gentry-merchants

shenshi	绅士	gentry
shengchan jianshe bingtuan	生产建设兵团	production and construction corps
shibowu	市舶务	an official agency that regulated overseas trading during the Southern Song dynasty
shichang	市场	market; marketplace
shichang jingji	市场经济	market economy
shichen dahai	石沉大海	stones falling into the ocean without a trace; no response
shili	势力	influence
shimin shehui	市民社会	civil society
shi mong gong shang	士农工商	scholars, farmers, artisans, merchants; the four basic occupations in traditional China
shiwei	市委	the party committee of a municipal government
shiye	失业	unemployed
shouren	熟人	a familiar acquaintance
shuji	书记	party secretary
sifang	私房	private house
siheyuan	四合院	residential housing, consisting of a courtyard surrounded by rooms
sirenwu	死任务	fixed task that has to be finished
sishengzi	私生子	illegitimate child
sixiang gongzuo	思想工作	thought-work; persuasion
suzhi	素质	quality of a person
taitu	太土	too earthy
tanshengyi	谈生意	business negotiation
tanwei	摊位	stall; counter
tiao kuai	条块	the vertical system and the horizontal locality; the socialist gridlock of control
tiegemen	铁哥们	iron brothers
tinghua	听话	docile
tongxiang hui	同乡会	native-place association

toujidaoba	投机倒把	illegal profit-seeking
tuanhuo fanzui	团伙犯罪	organized crime
tuiqin	退亲	to cancel an engagement to be married
tuzi buchi wobiancao	兔子不吃窝边草	A rabbit never eats the grass around its own nest; one should not take advantage of one's own folks
waiban	外办	foreign affairs office
waidiren	外地人	non-natives; outsiders
wailai renkou	外来人口	population that arrives from outside; migrants
Wangfujing	王府井	a downtown commercial district of Beijing
weishengfei	卫生费	environmental cleanup fee
Wenzhou moshi	温州模式	the Wenzhou model
Wenzhouren xiang taiyang, zoudao nali nali liang	温州人象太阳，走到哪里哪里亮	Wenzhou people are like the sun; wherever they go, they bring sunlight to brighten the place
wu	巫	witch
wuzhi	无知	ignorant
ximin	徙民	migrating people
xiagang	下岗	to step down from one's post; to become unemployed
xian	县	county
xianhui	贤惠	virtuous
xiang	乡	township
xiangfang	厢房	side rooms in a square courtyard
xiangqingfu	享清福	to enjoy life without doing anything
xiang zhengfu	乡政府	township government
xiao Hangzhou	小杭州	little Hangzhou
xiaodao xiaoxi	小道消息	alleyway news; informal news
xiaodui	小队	small team; the smallest production unit in a commune
xiaoshang xiaofan	小商小贩	small tradesmen and peddlers
xinfu zhi huan	心腹之患	a hidden disease in one's vital organ; serious hidden trouble

Xinjiangcun	新疆村	Xinjiang village
xinpingzi zhuang jiujiu	新瓶子装旧酒	new bottle, old wine
xinshiji	新世纪	new century
xinxue	心血	heart and blood; complete efforts
xingxiang	形象	image
xingzhengcun	行政村	an administratively defined village
xuehanqian	血汗钱	money earned with blood and sweat
xueyuan	血缘	blood bond; consanguinity
xuzhi	须知	must-know rules; important points
yanda	严打	crackdown
yandangshan	雁荡山	a famous scenic area in Zhejiang province
yangqi	洋气	foreign flavor; Western style
yimin	移民	migrants; immigrants
yipan sansha	一盘散沙	a plate of loose sand; unorganized
yiqi	义气	personal loyalty
yingchou	应酬	activities of exchange for mutual benefit
Yongjia xuepai	永嘉学派	the Yongjia School of Thought
youqi	游乞	wandering beggars
youqian nengshi guituimo	有钱能使鬼推磨	If one has money, one can make the devil push the mill
yumei	愚昧	unenlightened
yuan	圆	the Chinese monetary unit; renminbi
Yueqing	乐清	a county-level city in Zhejiang province
zang luan cha	脏乱差	dirty; chaotic; miserable
zaoshi	早市	early-morning marketplace
zhadui	扎堆	people with similar backgrounds sticking together, as in a tight bundle
zhanzhu renkou	暂住人口	temporary resident population
zhanzhu zheng	暂住证	temporary resident card
Zhejiangcun	浙江村	Zhejiang Village
zhen	镇	town
zhengdun	整顿	to straighten; to reorder

zhengfang	正房	main or master rooms in a square courtyard
zhian	治安	public security
zhibian	支边	to support the border areas
zhifu guangrong	致富光荣	getting rich is glorious
zhong-xiao hu	中小户	lower- or middle-income household
zhongyang	中央	the central state
zhong zaiqu	重灾区	severely afflicted area
zhuazhu mingyun de yanhou	抓住命运的咽喉	to control the throat of fate
zhuanqian	赚钱	making money
zibenzhuyi de weiba	资本主义的尾巴	the capitalist tail; minor capitalist practices
zichai	自拆	self-demolition
zirancun	自然村	naturally formed village
ziwo fazhan, ziwo guanli, ziwo wanshan	自我发展, 自我管理, 自我完善	self-development, self-discipline, and self-perfection
zoutianxia	走天下	traveling all over the world
zulin	租赁	to rent or lease
zuzhi	组织	organization
zuoshengyi	做生意	doing business

References

Abu-Lughod, Lila. 1990. "The Romance of Resistance: Tracing Transformations of Power Through Bedouin Women." *American Ethnologist* 17(1): 41–55.

Anagnost, Ann. 1995. "A Surfeit of Bodies: Population and the Rationality of the State in Post-Mao China." In Faye D. Ginsburg and Rayna Rapp, eds., *Conceiving the New World Order*, 22–41. Berkeley: University of California Press.

———. 1997. *National Past-Times: Narrative, Representation, and Power in Modern China*. Durham, N.C.: Duke University Press.

Anderson, Benedict. 1991. *Imagined Communities: Reflections on the Origin and Spread of Nationalism*. London: Verso.

Averill, Stephen C. 1983. "The Shed People and the Opening of the Yangzi Highlands." *Modern China* 9(1): 84–126.

Ba Liang and Ma Lun. 1989. "Taojinzhe de Meng" (The Dream of Gold Searchers). *Tequ Wenxue* (Literature of Special Economic Zones), no. 4: 48–66.

Banister, Judith. 1986. *Urban-Rural Population Projections for China*. Washington, D.C.: Center for International Research, U.S. Bureau of the Census, No. 15, March.

Barth, Fredrik. 1959. *Political Leadership Among Swat Pathans*. London: Athlone Press.

Beijing City Planning and Regulation Bureau. 1993. *Chengshi Jianshe Guihua Guanli Fagui Wenjian Huibian* (Collection of Legal Codes and Government Documents Regarding the Regulation of the City's Construction and Planning).

Beijing Municipal Government. 1995a. *Beijingshi Waidi Laijing Wugong Jingshang Renyuan Guanli Wenjian Huibian* (Collection of Regulation Documents Regarding Migrant Workers and Merchants in Beijing).

———. 1995b. *Guanyu Qingli Zhengdun Fengtai Dahongmen Diqu de Tonggao* (Public Announcement Regarding the Cleaning Up and Reordering of the Dahongmen Area in Fengtai District).

Beijing Municipal Planning Committee Research Team. 1995. *Beijingshi Liu-dong Renkou Guanli Duice Yanjiu* (A Study of Regulation Strategies Regarding Beijing's Floating Population). *Shoudu Jingji* (The Capital's Economy) 5: 14–17.

Beijing West-District Government. 1996. *Waidi Jinjing Wugong Renyuan Peixun Jiaocai* (Training Materials for Migrant Workers in Beijing).

Bernstein, Thomas P. 1977. *Up to the Mountains and Down to the Villages.* New Haven, Conn.: Yale University Press.

Billingsley, Phil. 1981. "Bandits, Bosses, and Bare Sticks: Beneath the Surface of Local Control in Early Republican China." *Modern China* 7(3): 235–88.

Blok, Anton. 1974. *The Mafia of a Sicilian Village, 1860–1960: A Study of Violent Peasant Entrepreneurs.* Oxford: Blackwell.

Boretz, Avron. 1996. *Martial Gods and Magic Swords: The Ritual Production of Manhood in Taiwanese Popular Religion.* Ph.D. dissertation, Department of Anthropology, Cornell University.

Borneman, John. 1992. *Belonging in the Two Berlins: Kin, State, Nation.* Cambridge: Cambridge University Press.

———. 1997. *Settling Accounts: Violence, Justice, and Accountability in Postsocialist Europe.* Princeton, N.J.: Princeton University Press.

Boserup, Ester. 1970. *Woman's Role in Economic Development.* New York: St. Martin's Press.

Bourdieu, Pierre. 1977. *Outline of a Theory of Practice.* Cambridge: Cambridge University Press.

———. 1990. "The Kabyle House or the World Reversed." In *The Logic of Practice*, trans. Richard Nice, 271–83. Stanford, Calif.: Stanford University Press.

———. 1991. *Language and Symbolic Power.* Cambridge, Mass.: Harvard University Press.

Bridger, Sue, and Frances Pine, eds. 1998. *Surviving Post-Socialism: Local Strategies and Regional Responses in Eastern Europe and the Former Soviet Union.* London: Routledge.

Brook, Timothy, and B. Michael Frolic, eds. 1997. *Civil Society in China.* Armonk, N.Y.: M. E. Sharpe.

Brownell, Susan. 1995. *Training the Body for China: Sports in the Moral Order of the People's Republic.* Chicago: University of Chicago Press.

Bruun, Ole. 1993. *Business and Bureaucracy in a Chinese City: An Ethnography of Private Business Households in Contemporary China.* China Research Monograph 43. Berkeley: Institute of East Asian Studies, University of California.

Bunce, Valerie, and Maria Csanadi. 1993. "Uncertainty in the Transition:

Post-Communism in Hungary." *East European Politics and Societies* 7(2): 240–75.

Calhoun, Craig. 1994. *Neither Gods Nor Emperors: Students and the Struggle for Democracy in China*. Berkeley: University of California Press.

Castles, Stephen, and Godula Kosack. 1985. *Immigrant Workers and Class Structure in Western Europe*. New York: Oxford University Press.

Chan, Anita. 1998. "Labor Relations in Foreign-Funded Ventures, Chinese Trade Unions, and the Prospects for Collective Bargaining." In Greg O'Leary, ed., *Adjusting to Capitalism: Chinese Workers and the State*, 122–49. Armonk, N.Y.: M. E. Sharpe.

Chan, Anita, Richard Madsen, and Jonathan Unger. 1984. *Chen Village Under Mao and Deng*. Berkeley: University of California Press.

Chan, Kam Wing. 1994a. "Urbanization and Rural-Urban Migration in China Since 1982." *Modern China* 20(3): 243–81.

———. 1994b. *Cities with Invisible Walls: Reinterpreting Urbanization in post-1949 China*. Hong Kong: Oxford University Press.

Chang, Chung-li. 1955. *The Chinese Gentry: Studies on Their Role in Nineteenth-Century Chinese Society*. Seattle: University of Washington Press.

Chavez, Leo R. 1992. *Shadowed Lives: Undocumented Immigrants in American Society*. Fort Worth: Harcourt Brace Jovanovich College Publishers.

Chen Shubi. 1990. "Yi Liurudi Weizhu Zhuahao Liudong Renkou Shengyu Guanli" (To Better Manage Birth Control in the Floating Population in the Receiving Areas). *Renkou yu Jingji* (Population and Economics) 1: 23–24.

Chen Youquan. 1988. "Liudong Erbaiwan" (Two Million Floating People). *Shanghai Tan* (The Shanghai Beach), no. 8: 24.

Cheng, Chaoze. 1991. "Internal Migration in Mainland China—The Impact of Government Policies." *Issues and Studies* 27(8): 47–70.

Cheng, L. 1996. "Surplus Rural Laborers and Internal Migration in China—Current Status and Future Prospects." *Asian Survey* 36(11): 1122–45.

Cheng, Tiejun, and Mark Selden. 1994. "The Origins and Social Consequences of China's Hukou System." *China Quarterly* 139: 644–68.

Chesneaux, Jean, ed. 1972. *Popular Movements and Secret Societies in China, 1840–1950*. Stanford, Calif.: Stanford University Press.

Chi Zihua. 1996. *Zhongguo Jindai Liumin* (Floaters in Modern China). Hangzhou: Zhejiang Renmin Chubanshe (Zhejiang People's Publishing House).

Chinese State Administration and Regulation Bureau of Independent Economy. 1987. *Geti Gongshangye Zhengce Fagui Huibian, 1957–1986* (Collection of Policies and Legal Rules Regarding Independent

Industry and Commerce, 1957–1986). Beijing: Jingji Kexue Chuban-she (Economic Science Publisher).

Christiansen, Flemming. 1990. "Social Division and Peasant Mobility in Mainland China: The Implications of the Hu-k'ou System." *Issues and Studies* 26(4): 23–42.

Ch'u T'ung-tsu. 1962. *Local Government in China Under the Ch'ing*. Cambridge, Mass.: Harvard University Press.

Cohen, Myron L. 1970. "Developmental Process in the Chinese Domestic Group." In Maurice Freedman, ed., *Family and Kinship in Chinese Society*, 21–36. Stanford, Calif.: Stanford University Press.

———. 1976. *House United, House Divided: The Chinese Family in Taiwan*. New York: Columbia University Press.

———. 1993. "Cultural and Political Inventions in Modern China: The Case of the Chinese 'Peasant.'" *Daedalus* 122(2): 151–70.

Comaroff, Jean. 1985. *Body of Power, Spirit of Resistance: The Culture and History of a South African People*. Chicago: University of Chicago Press.

Comaroff, John, and Jean Comaroff. 1987. "The Madman and the Migrant: Work and Labor in the Historical Consciousness of a South African People." *American Ethnologist* 14(2): 191–209.

———. 1991. *Of Revelation and Revolution: Christianity, Colonialism, and Consciousness in South Africa*. Vol. 1. Chicago: University of Chicago Press.

Constable, Nicole. 1997. *Maid to Order in Hong Kong: Stories of Filipina Workers*. Ithaca, N.Y.: Cornell University Press.

Crissman, Lawrence W. 1967. "The Segmentary Structure of Urban Overseas Chinese Communities." *Man* 2(2): 185–204.

Davin, Delia. 1999. *Internal Migration in Contemporary China*. New York: St. Martin's Press.

Davis, Deborah, ed. 2000. *The Consumer Revolution in Urban China*. Berkeley: University of California Press.

Davis, Deborah, Richard Kraus, Barry Naughton, and Elizabeth Perry, eds. 1995. *Urban Spaces in Contemporary China*. Cambridge: Cambridge University Press.

Davis, Deborah S., and Julia Sensenbrenner. 1997. "Bourgeois Childhoods in Working Class Shanghai." Paper presented at the conference "Urban Consumers and Consumer Culture in Contemporary China," New Haven, Conn. January 9–12, 1997.

Davis, Mike. 1992. *City of Quartz: Excavating the Future in Los Angeles*. New York: Vintage Books.

De Certeau, Michel. 1984. *The Practice of Everyday Life*, trans. Steven Rendall. Berkeley: University of California Press.

DeFrancis, John. 1984. *The Chinese Language: Fact and Fantasy*. Honolulu: University of Hawaii Press.

di Leonardo, Micaela. 1991. "Introduction: Gender, Culture, and Political Economy: Feminist Anthropology in Historical Perspective." In Micaela di Leonardo, ed., *Gender at the Crossroads of Knowledge*, 1–48. Berkeley: University of California Press.

Dittmer, Lowell. 1978. "Bases of Power in Chinese Politics: A Theory and an Analysis of the Fall of the 'Gang of Four.'" *World Politics* 31(1): 26–60.

Dong, Yue. 1996. *Memories of the Present: The Vicissitudes of Transition in Republican Beijing, 1911–1937*. Ph.D. dissertation, Department of History, University of California, San Diego.

Douglas, Mary. 1966. *Purity and Danger: An Analysis of the Concepts of Pollution and Taboo*. London: Routledge.

Du Weidong. 1988. "Beijing Chengli de 'Jipusai' Ren" (The 'Gypsy' in Beijing). *Xin Guancha* (New Observations), nos. 7–11.

Du Wulu. 1986. "Beijing Shiqu Liudong Renkou Wenti Tantao" (An Exploration of the Problem Regarding Beijing's Floating Population). *Renkou yu Jingji* (Population and Economy), no. 1: 12–14.

Duan Binren et al., eds. 1989. *Beijing shi Gaige Shinian, 1979–1989*. (A Decade of Beijing's Reforms, 1979–1989). Beijing Chubanshe (Beijing Publishing House).

Duara, Prasenjit. 1988. *Culture, Power, and the State: Rural North China, 1900–1942*. Stanford, Calif.: Stanford University Press.

Dutton, Michael R. 1992. *Policing and Punishment in China*. Cambridge: Cambridge University Press.

Eckholm, Erik. 1998. "On the Road to Capitalism, China Hits a Nasty Curve: Joblessness." *New York Times*, January 9.

———. 1999. "As Beijing Pretties Up, Migrants Face Expulsion." *New York Times*, April 18.

Eisenstadt, S. N., and L. Roniger. 1984. *Patrons, Clients and Friends: Interpersonal Relations and the Structure of Trust in Society*. Cambridge: Cambridge University Press.

Engels, Frederick. [1891] 1972. *The Origin of the Family, Private Property, and the State*. New York: Pathfinder Press.

Escobar, Arturo. 1995. *Encountering Development: The Making and Unmaking of the Third World*. Princeton, N.J.: Princeton University Press.

Esherick, Joseph, ed. 2000. *Remaking the Chinese City: Modernity and National Identity, 1900–1950*. Honolulu: University of Hawaii Press.

Esherick, Joseph, and Mary Backus Rankin. 1990. "Introduction." In Joseph Esherick and Mary Backus Rankin, eds., *Chinese Local Elites and Patterns of Dominance*, 1–24. Berkeley: University of California Press.

Fan, Cindy, and Youqin Huang. 1998. "Waves of Rural Brides: Female Marriage Migration in China." *Annals of the Association of American Geographers* 88(2): 227–51.

Fei, Hsiao-Tung. 1953. *China's Gentry*. Chicago: University of Chicago Press.
———. 1974. *Peasant Life in China: A Field Study of Country Life in the Yangtze Valley*. London: Kegan Paul, Trench, Trubuer.
———. 1985. *Xiang Tu Zhong Guo* (Earthbound China). Beijing: San-Lian Publisher.
Fengtai Local History Office. 1994. *Beijingshi Fengtaiqu Jie Xiang GaiKuang* (Introduction to Streetships and Townships in the Fengtai District of Beijing). Beijing: Zhishi Chubanshe (The Knowledge Publishing House).
Ferguson, James. 1992. "The Country and the City on the Copperbelt." *Cultural Anthropology* 7(1): 80–92.
Fernández-Kelly, María Patricia. 1981. "Development and the Sexual Division of Labor: An Introduction." *Journal of Women in Culture and Society* 7(2):268–278.
———. 1983. *For We Are Sold, I and My People: Women and Industry in Mexico's Frontier*. Albany: State University of New York.
Flap, H. D. 1990. "Patronage: An Institution in Its Own Right." In Michael Hechter, et al., eds., *Social Institutions: Their Emergence, Maintenance, and Effects*, 225–43. New York: Aldine de Gruyter.
Fortes, Meyer, and E. E. Evans-Prichard. 1958. *African Political Systems*. London: Oxford University Press.
Foster, George M. 1963. "The Dyadic Contract in Tzintzuntzan, II: Patron-Client Relationships." *American Anthropologist* 65(6): 1280–94.
Foucault, Michel. 1972. *Power/Knowledge*. New York: Pantheon.
———. 1978. *The History of Sexuality: An Introduction*. Vol. 1. New York: Vintage.
———. 1979. *Discipline and Punish: The Birth of the Prison*. New York: Vintage.
———. 1984. "Space, Knowledge, and Power." In Paul Rabinow, ed., *The Foucault Reader*, 239–56. New York: Pantheon.
———. 1991. "Governmentality." In Graham Burchell, Colin Gordon, and Peter Miller, eds., *The Foucault Effect: Studies in Governmentality*, 87–104. London: Harvester/Wheatsheaf.
Freedman, Maurice. 1958. *Lineage Organization in Southeastern China*. New York: Humanities Press.
Fried, Morton. 1953. *The Fabric of Chinese Society*. New York: Praeger.
Friedman, Edward, Paul Pickowicz, and Mark Selden. 1991. *Chinese Village, Socialist State*. New Haven, Conn.: Yale University Press.
Fukuyama, Francis. 1989. "The End of History?" *The National Interest* 16: 3–18.
Furnivall, John S. 1956. *Colonial Policy and Practice: A Comparative Study of Burma and Netherlands India*. New York: New York University Press.

Gates, Hill. 1987. *Chinese Working-Class Lives: Getting By in Taiwan*. Ithaca, N.Y.: Cornell University Press.

———. 1996. *China's Motor: A Thousand Years of Petty Capitalism*. Ithaca, N.Y.: Cornell University Press.

Geertz, Clifford. 1973. *The Interpretation of Culture*. New York: Basic Books.

Giddens, Anthony. 1979. *Central Problems in Social Theory: Action, Structure, and Contradiction in Social Analysis*. Berkeley: University of California Press.

Gilroy, Paul. 1991. *There Ain't No Black in the Union Jack: The Cultural Politics of Race and Nation*. Chicago: University of Chicago Press.

Gladney, Dru. 1991. *Muslim Chinese: Ethnic Nationalism in the People's Republic*. Cambridge, Mass.: Council on East Asian Studies, Harvard University.

Godelier, Maurice, and Marilyn Strathern, eds. 1991. *Big Men and Great Men: Personification of Power in Melanesia*. Cambridge: Cambridge University Press.

Gold, Thomas B. 1989 "Guerrilla Interviewing Among the Getihu." In Perry Link, Richard Madsen, and Paul G. Pickowicz, eds., *Unofficial China: Popular Culture and Thought in the People's Republic*, 175–92. Boulder, Colo.: Westview.

———. 1990. "Urban Private Business and Social Change." In Deborah Davis and Ezra F. Vogel, eds., *Chinese Society on the Eve of Tiananmen: The Impact of Reform*, 157–78. Cambridge, Mass.: Council on East Asian Studies, Harvard University Press.

Goldstein, Sidney, and Alice Goldstein. 1985. *Population Mobility in the People's Republic of China*. Honolulu: East-West Population Institute.

Goodman, Bryna. 1995. *Native Place, City, and Nation: Regional Networks and Identities in Shanghai, 1853–1937*. Berkeley: University of California Press.

Gordon, Colin. 1991. "Governmental Rationality: An Introduction." In Graham Burchell, Colin Gordon, and Peter Miller, eds., *The Foucault Effect: Studies in Governmentality*, 1–51. London: Harvester/Wheatsheaf.

Gramsci, Antonio. 1971. *Selections from the Prison Notebooks*. New York: International Publishers.

Granet, Marcel. 1975. *The Religion of the Chinese People*. New York: Harper and Row.

Greenhalgh, Susan. 1988. "Families and Networks in Taiwan's Economic Development." In Edwin A. Winckler and Susan Greenhalgh, eds., *Contending Approaches to the Political Economy of Taiwan*, 224–45. Armonk, N.Y.: M. E. Sharpe.

———. 1994. "De-Orientalizing the Chinese Family Firm." *American Ethnologist* 21(4): 746–75.

Grossman, Gregory. 1977. "The Second Economy of the USSR." *Problems of Communism* 26(5): 25–40.

Gupta, Akhil. 1995. "Blurred Boundaries: The Discourse of Corruption, the Culture of Politics, and the Imagined State." *American Ethnologist* 22(2): 375–402.

Gupta, Akhil, and James Ferguson, eds. 1997. *Culture, Power, Place: Explorations in Critical Anthropology*. Durham, N.C.: Duke University Press.

Hall, Stuart. 1985. "Signification, Representation, Ideology: Althusser and the Post-Structuralist Debates." *Critical Studies in Mass Communication* 2(2): 91–114.

Handelman, Stephen. 1993. "Why Capitalism and the Mafia Mean Business— Inside Russia's Gangster Economy." *New York Times Magazine*, January 24: p. 12.

Hann, Chris. 1994. "After Communism: Reflections on East European Anthropology and the 'Transition.'" *Social Anthropology* 2(3): 229–49.

Hann, Chris, and Elizabeth Dunn, eds. 1996. *Civil Society: Challenging Western Models*. London: Routledge.

Hao Zaijin. 1992. "Zhongguo Liudong Renkou Baogao" (Reports on China's Floating Population). *Jiefang Ribao* (Liberation Daily).

Harrell, Stevan. 1985. "Why Do the Chinese Work So Hard? Reflections on an Entrepreneurial Ethic." *Modern China* 11: 203–26.

Harvey, David. 1989a. *The Urban Experience*. Baltimore: Johns Hopkins University Press.

———. 1989b. *The Condition of Postmodernity: An Enquiry into the Origins of Cultural Change*. Oxford: Blackwell.

Henderson, Gail, et al. 1996. "The Meaning of Work (Gongzuo): Interviews from Towns and Villages in Hubei Province, 1995." Paper presented at conference on Gender, Households, and the Boundaries of Work in China, University of North Carolina, Oct. 25–27, 1996.

Hershatter, Gail. 1986. *The Workers of Tianjin, 1900–1949*. Stanford, Calif.: Stanford University Press.

Hershkovitz, Linda. 1993. "Tiananmen Square and the Politics of Place." *Political Geography* 12(5): 395–420.

Herzfeld, Michael. 1992. *The Social Production of Indifference: Exploring the Symbolic Roots of Western Bureaucracy*. New York: Berg.

Hess, Henner. 1973. *Mafia and Mafiosi: The Structure of Power*. Farnborough, England: Saxon House.

Ho, Ping-ti. 1959. *Studies on the Population of China, 1368–1953*. Cambridge, Mass.: Harvard University Press.

———. 1962. *The Ladder of Success in Imperial China: Aspects of Social Mobility, 1368–1911*. New York: Columbia University Press.

———. N.d. *Zhongguo Huiguan Shilun* (The History of Chinese Huiguan). Taipei: Student Book Publisher.

Holston, James, and Arjun Appadurai. 1999. "Introduction: Cities and Citizenship." In James Holston, ed., *Cities and Citizenship*, 1–18. Durham, N.C.: Duke University Press.

Honig, Emily. 1986. *Sisters and Strangers: Women in the Shanghai Cotton Mills, 1919–1949*. Stanford, Calif.: Stanford University Press.

———. 1992. *Creating Chinese Ethnicity—Subei People in Shanghai 1850–1980*. New Haven, Conn.: Yale University Press.

———. 1996. "Regional Identity, Labor, and Ethnicity in Contemporary China." In Elizabeth Perry, ed., *Putting Class in Its Place: Worker Identities in East Asia*, 225–43. Berkeley: Institute of East Asian Studies, University of California.

Hsieh, Winston. 1993. "Migrant Peasant Workers in China: The PRC's Rural Crisis in an Historical Perspective." In George T. Yu, ed., *China in Transition: Political and Social Development*, 89–97. Lanham, Md.: University Press of America.

Huang Jinghong, and Ning Quanchen. 1987. "Dao Guangzhou 'Zhaofanwan' de Waidiren" (Outsiders Who Look for "Rice Bowls" in Guangzhou). *Guangzhou Wenyi* (Journal of Literature and Art of Guangzhou), no. 7: 2–11.

Huang, Philip C. C. 1985. *The Peasant Economy and Social Change in North China*. Stanford, Calif.: Stanford University Press.

Humphrey, Caroline. 1991. "'Icebergs,' Barter, and the Mafia in Provincial Russia." *Anthropology Today*, no. 7: 8–13.

Jameson, Fredric. 1997. *Postmodernism, Or, the Cultural Logic of Late Capitalism*. Durham, N.C.: Duke University Press.

Jeong, Jong-Ho. 2000. *Renegotiating with the State: The Challenge of the Floating Population and the Emergence of New Urban Space in Contemporary China*. Ph.D. dissertation, Yale University.

Ji Dangsheng et al. 1995. "Beijing Shi Liudong Renkou Xianzhuang yu Duice Yanjiu" (A Study on the Current Condition of and Strategies for Beijing's Floating Population). *Renkouxue yu Jihua Shengyu* (Population Studies and Birth Planning) 5: 75–82.

Jing, Jun. 1996. *The Temple of Memories*. Stanford, Calif.: Stanford University Press.

———, ed. 2000. *Feeding China's Little Emperors: Food, Children, and Social Change*. Stanford, Calif.: Stanford University Press.

Jones, Susan Mann. 1974. "The Ningpo Pang and Financial Power at Shanghai." In Mark Elvin and G. William Skinner, eds., *The Chinese City Between Two Worlds*, 73–96. Stanford, Calif.: Stanford University Press.

Judd, Ellen. 1994. *Gender and Power in Rural China*. Stanford, Calif.: Stanford University Press.

Kearney, Michael. 1986. "From the Invisible Hand to Visible Feet: Anthropological Studies of Migration and Development." *Annual Review of Anthropology* 15: 331–61.

Kipnis, Andrew B. 1997. *Producing Guanxi: Sentiment, Self, and Subculture in a North China Village*. Durham, N.C.: Duke University Press.

Kondo, Dorinne K. 1990. *Crafting Selves: Power, Gender, and Discourses of Identity in a Japanese Workplace*. Chicago: University of Chicago Press.

Koselleck, Reinhart. 1985. "The Historical-Political Semantics of Asymmetric Counterconcepts." *In Futures Past: On the Semantics of Historical Time*. Cambridge, Mass.: MIT Press.

Kuhn, Philip A. 1990. *Soulstealers: The Chinese Sorcery Scare of 1768*. Cambridge: Cambridge University Press.

Lang, Olga. 1946. *Chinese Family and Society*. New Haven, Conn.: Yale University Press.

Lee, Ching Kwan. 1998. *Gender and the South China Miracle: Two Worlds of Factory Women*. Berkeley: Unversity of California Press.

Lee, Sing, Shatin Kong, and Arthur Kleinman. N.d. "China Seen Through the Window of Mental Health." Unpublished manuscript.

Lefebvre, Henri. 1991. *The Production of Space*. Oxford: Blackwell.

Leong Sow-Theng. 1997. *Migration and Ethnicity in Chinese History: Hakkas, Pengmin, and Their Neighbors*. Stanford, Calif.: Stanford University Press.

Levi-Strauss, Claude. 1969. *The Elementary Structures of Kinship*. Boston: Beacon.

Li Haoran. 1996. *Wenzhou Xin Yueqian* (The New Leap and Transformation of Wenzhou). Shanghai Shehui Kexu Xueshu Chubanshe (Shanghai Social Science Publisher).

Li, Lianjiang, and Kevin J. O'Brien. 1996. "Villagers and Popular Resistance in Contemporary China." *Modern China* 22(1): 28–61.

Li, Minghuan. N.d. "To Get Rich Quickly in Europe!—Reflections: A Study of Migration Motivation of the People in Wenzhou *Qiaoxiang*." Unpublished paper.

———. 1998. "Transnational Links Among the Chinese in Europe: A Study on European-wide Chinese Voluntary Associations." In Gregor Benton and Frank Pieke, eds., *The Chinese in Europe*, 21–41. Houndmills, England: Macmillan.

Li Yanhong. 1995. *Chengxiang Jiehebu Shehui Guanli Tizhi de Xintansuo: Dui Zhejiangcun Jing-Wen Aixinshe de Chubu Yanjiu* (A New Exploration of the Social Regulation System in the Rural-Urban Transitional Zone: A Preliminary Study of the Jing-Wen Love Heart Society in Zhejiang-cun). Master's thesis, Department of Sociology, Peking University.

Liang, Zai, and M. J. White. 1996. "Internal Migration in China: 1950–1988." *Demography* 33(3): 375–84.

Lim, Linda. 1983. "Capitalism, Imperialism, and Patriarchy: The Dilemma of Third-World Women Workers in Multinational Factories." In J. Nash and M. P. Fernández-Kelly, eds., *Women, Men, and the International Division of Labor*, 70–91. Albany: SUNY Press.

Lin Guozheng, ed. 1992. *Zhejiang Sheng Jingji Dili* (The Economic Geography of Zhejiang Province). Xinhua Chubanshe (Xinhua Publishing House).

Lin, Nan, and Chih-jou Jay Chen. 1999. "Local Elites as Officials and Owners: Shareholding and Property Rights in Daqiuzhuang." In Jean Oi and Andrew Walder, eds. *Property Rights and Economic Reform in China*, 145–70. Stanford, Calif.: Stanford University Press.

Liu Manyuan. 1993. "Liudong Renkou Mianmian Guan" (Viewing the Multiple Aspects of the Floating Population). *Zhongguo Funu Bao* (The Newspaper of Chinese Women), February.

Liu Xiuhua. 1996. "Liudong Renkou dui Beijing shi Fazhan de Yingxiang" (The Impact of the Floating Population on Beijing's Development). *Renkou Yanjiu yu Jihua Shengyu* (Population Studies and Birth Control), no. 1.

Liu, Yia-Ling. 1992. "Reform from Below: The Private Economy and Local Politics in the Rural Industrialization of Wenzhou." *China Quarterly* 130: 293–316.

Live, Yu-Sion. 1998. "The Chinese Community in France: Immigration, Economic Activity, Cultural Organization, and Representation." In Gregor Benton and Frank Pieke, eds., *The Chinese in Europe*, 96–124. Houndmills, England: Macmillan.

Logan, Kathleen. 1981. "Getting By with Less: Economic Strategies of Lower Income Households in Guadalajara." *Urban Anthropology* 10(3): 231–46.

Lowe, Lisa. 1996. *Immigrant Acts*. Durham, N.C.: Duke University Press.

Lu, Hanchao. 1999. *Beyond the Neon Lights: Everyday Shanghai in the Early Twentieth Century*. Berkeley: University of California Press.

Lu, Xiaobo, and Elizabeth J. Perry, eds. 1997. *Danwei: The Changing Chinese Workplace in Historical and Comparative Perspective*. Armonk, N.Y.: M. E. Sharpe.

Luo Maochu et al. 1986. "Beijingshi Liudong Renkou Diaocha." (Investigation of the Floating Population in Beijing). *Renkou Yanjiu* (Population Studies), no. 3.

Ma, Laurence J. C., and Biao Xiang. 1998. "Native Place, Migration and the Emergence of Peasant Enclaves in Beijing." *China Quarterly* 155 (Sept.): 546–81.

Ma, Ming. 1995. *Guanshang Zhijian* (Between Officials and Merchants). Tian-jing Renmin Chubanshe (Tianjing People's Publishing House).

Malkki, Liisa. 1992. "National Geographic: The Rooting of People and the Territorialization of National Identity Among Scholars and Refugees." *Cultural Anthropology* 7(2): 24–44.

———. 1995. *Purity and Exile: Violence, Memory, and National Cosmology Among Hutu Refugees in Tanzania.* Chicago: University of Chicago Press.

———. 1996. "Speechless Emissaries: Refugees, Humanitarianism, and Dehis-toricization." *Cultural Anthropology* 11(3): 377–404.

Mallee, H. 1988. "Rural-Urban Migration Control in the People's Republic of China: Effects of the Recent Reform." *China Information* 11(4): 12–22.

Mann, Susan. 1987. *Local Merchants and the Chinese Bureaucracy, 1750–1950.* Stanford, Calif.: Stanford University Press.

———. 1996. "Work in Chinese Culture: Historical Perspectives." Paper presented at the conference "Gender, Households, and Boundaries of Work," University of North Carolina at Chapel Hill, October 25–27.

Marx, Karl. 1977. *Capital: A Critique of Political Economy.* Ben Fowkes, trans. New York: Vintage Books.

———. 1978. "Manifesto of the Communist Party." In Robert C. Tucker, ed., *The Marx-Engels Reader,* 469–500. New York: W. W. Norton.

Marx, Karl, and Frederick Engels. 1988. *The German Ideology.* New York: International Publishers.

Massey, Doreen. 1994. *Space, Place, and Gender.* Minneapolis: University of Minnesota Press.

Meisner, Maurice. 1977. *Mao's China: A History of the People's Republic.* New York: Free Press.

Mills, Mary Beth. 1999. *Thai Women in the Global Labor Force: Consuming Desires, Contested Selves.* New Brunswick, N.J.: Rutgers University Press.

Mintz, Sidney. 1985. *Sweetness and Power: The Place of Sugar in Modern History.* New York: Penguin.

Mitchell, Timothy. 1991. "The Limits of the State: Beyond Statist Approaches and Their Critics." *American Political Science Review* 85(1): 77–96.

Moore, Henrietta L. 1988. *Feminism and Anthropology.* Minneapolis: University of Minnesota Press.

Moore, Sally Falk, ed. 1993. *Moralizing States and the Ethnography of the Present.* American Ethnological Society Monograph Series, no. 5.

Munn, Nancy. 1986. *The Fame of Gawa: A Symbolic Study of Value Transformation in a Massim Society*. Cambridge: Cambridge University Press.

Naquin, Susan, and Evelyn Rawski, eds. 1987. *Chinese Society in the Eighteenth Century*. New Haven, Conn.: Yale University Press.

Nathan, Andrew. 1973. "A Factionalism Model for CCP Politics." *China Quarterly* 53 (Jan.–Mar.): 34–66.

Nee, Victor, and Frank W. Young. 1990. "Peasant Entrepreneurs in China's 'Secondary Economy': An Institutional Analysis." Center for International Studies at Cornell University, no. 4.

Norman, Jerry. 1988. *Chinese*. Cambridge: Cambridge University Press.

Oi, Jean C. 1989. *State and Peasant in Contemporary China: The Political Economy of Village Government*. Berkeley: University of California Press.

O'Laughlin, Bridget. 1975. "Marxist Approaches in Anthropology." *Annual Review of Anthropology* 4: 341–70.

O'Neill, Mark. 1998. "Migrant Workers a Threat to the Urban Unemployed." *South China Morning Post*, January 9, 1998.

Ong, Aihwa. 1987. *Spirits of Resistance and Capitalist Discipline: Factory Women in Malaysia*. Albany: State University of New York Press.

———. 1991. "The Gender and Labor Politics of Postmodernity." *Annual Review of Anthropology* 20: 279–309.

———. 1996 "Citizenship as Subject Making: New Immigrants Negotiate Racial and Ethnic Boundaries." *Cultural Anthropology* 37(5): 737–62.

———. 1999. *Flexible Citizenship: The Cultural Logics of Transnationality*. Durham, N.C.: Duke University Press.

Ortner, Sherry. 1974. "Is Female to Male as Nature Is to Culture?" In M. Z. Rosaldo and L. Lamphere, eds., *Woman, Culture, and Society*, 67–87. Stanford, Calif.: Stanford University Press.

———. 1995. "Resistance and the Problem of Ethnographic Refusal." *Comparative Study of Society and History* 37: 173–93.

Ownby, David. 1993. "Chinese *Hui* and the Early Modern Social Order: Evidence from Eighteenth-Century Southeast China." In David Ownby and Mary S. Heidbues, eds. *"Secret Societies" Reconsidered: Perspectives on the Social History of Early Modern South China and Southeast Asia*, 34–67. Stanford, Calif.: Stanford University Pres.

Oxfeld, Ellen. 1996. *Blood, Sweat, and Mahjong: Family and Enterprise in an Overseas Chinese Community*. Ithaca, N.Y.: Cornell University Press.

Papademetriou, Demetrios G. 1989. "Uncertain Connection: Labor Migration and Development." Working Paper, Commission for the Study of International Migration and Cooperative Economic Development, no. 9.

Parris, Kristen. 1993. "Local Initiative and National Reform: The Wenzhou Model of Development." *China Quarterly* 134: 242–63.

Pearson, Margaret. 1997. *China's New Business Elite: The Political Consequences of Economic Reform*. Berkeley: University of Caifornia Press.

Perlman, Janice E. 1976. *The Myth of Marginality: Urban Poverty and Politics in Rio de Janeiro*. Berkeley: University of California Press.

Perry, Elizabeth J. 1980. *Rebels and Revolutionaries in North China, 1845–1945*. Stanford, Calif.: Stanford University Press.

———. 1989. "State and Society in Contemporary China." *World Politics* (July): 579–91.

———. 1993. *Shanghai on Strike: The Politics of Chinese Labor*. Stanford, Calif.: Stanford University Press.

———. 1994. "Trends in the Study of Chinese Politics: State-Society Relations." *China Quarterly* 139: 704–13.

Pieke, Frank N. 1995. "Bureaucracy, Friends, and Money: The Growth of Capital Socialism in China." *Comparative Study of Society and History* 37(3): 494–518.

Portes, Alejandro. 1983. "The Informal Sector: Definition, Controversy, and Relation to National Development." *Review* 7(1): 151–74. Research Foundation of SUNY.

Portes, Alejandro, and Robert L. Bach. 1985. *Latin Journey*. Berkeley: University of California Press.

Potter, Sulamith H. 1983. "The Position of Peasants in Modern China's Social Order." *Modern China* 9(4): 465–99.

Potter, Sulamith H., and Jack M. Potter. 1990. *China's Peasants: The Anthropology of a Revolution*. Cambridge: Cambridge University Press.

Povinelli, Elizabeth. 1993. *Labor's Lot: The Power, History, and Culture of Aboriginal Action*. Chicago: University of Chicago Press.

Pun, Ngai. Forthcoming. *Becoming Dagongmei: New Subjectivities and New Forms of Transgression in Reform China*. Durham, N.C.: Duke University Press.

Putnam, Robert D. 1995. "Bowling Alone: America's Declining Social Capital." *Journal of Democracy* 6(1): 65–78.

Rabinow, Paul. 1977. *Reflections on Fieldwork in Morocco*. Berkeley: University of California Press.

Rankin, Mary Backus. 1986. *Elite Activism and Political Transformation in China, Zhejiang Province, 1865–1911*. Stanford, Calif.: Stanford University Press.

Research Team of the CCP School. 1998. "Guoyou Qiye Zhigong Xiagang Fenliu he Zaijiuye Wenti Yanjiu" (A Study of the Unemployment of State-Owned Enterprise Workers and Their Re-employment Problems). *Zhonggong Zhongyang Dangxiao Xuebao* (Journal of the Chinese Communist Party School), no. 4: 45–54.

Ries, Nancy. 1998. "The Many Faces of the Mob: Mafia as Symbol in Postsocialist Russia." Paper presented at the American Anthropological Association Annual Meeting, Philadelphia, December 4.

Rofel, Lisa. 1999. *Other Modernities: Gendered Yearnings in China After Socialism*. Berkeley: University of California Press.

Rosaldo, Michelle Z. 1974. "Woman, Culture, and Society: A Theoretical Overview." In M. Z. Rosaldo and L. Lamphere, eds., *Woman, Culture, and Society*, 17–42. Stanford, Calif.: Stanford University Press.

———. 1980. "The Use and Abuse of Anthropology: Reflections on Feminism and Cross-Cultural Understanding." *Signs* 5(3): 389–417.

Roseberry, William. 1989. *Anthropologies and Histories: Essays in Culture, History, and Political Economy*. New Brunswick, N.J.: Rutgers University Press.

———. 1991. "Marxism and Culture." In Brett Williams, ed., *The Politics of Culture*, 19–43. Washington, D.C.: Smithsonian Institution Press.

Rouse, Roger. 1991. "Mexican Migration and the Social Space of Postmodernism." *Diaspora* (Spring): 8–23.

———. 1992. "Making Sense of Settlement: Class Transformation, Cultural Struggle and Transnationalism among Mexican Migrants in the United States." *Annals of the New York Academy of Sciences* 645: 25–52.

———. 1995. "Thinking Through Transnationalism: Notes on the Cultural Politics of Class Relations in the Contemporary United States." *Public Culture* 7(2): 353–402.

Rowe, William. 1979. "Urban Control in Late Imperial China: The Pao-chia System in Hankow." In Joshua Fogel and William Rowe, *Perspectives on a Changing China*, 89–112. Boulder, Colo.: Westview.

———. 1984. *Hankow: Commerce and Society in a Chinese City, 1796–1889*. Stanford, Calif.: Stanford University Press.

Rubin, Gayle. 1975. "The Traffic in Women: Notes on the 'Political Economy' of Sex." In R. Reiter, ed., *Toward an Anthropology of Women*, 157–210. New York: Monthly Review Press.

Sabin, Lora. 1994. "New Bosses in the Workers' State: The Growth of Non-State Sector Employment in China." *China Quarterly* 140: 944–70.

Sacks, Karen. 1974. "Engels Revisited: Women, the Organization of Production, and Private Property." In M. Z. Rosaldo and L. Lamphere, eds., *Woman, Culture, and Society*, 207–22. Stanford, Calif.: Stanford University Press.

Sahlins, Marshall. 1976. *Culture and Practical Reason*. Chicago: University of Chicago Press.

Sampson, Steven. 1991. "Is There an Anthropology of Socialism?" *Anthropology Today* 7(5): 16–19.

Sangren, P. Steven. 1984. "Traditional Chinese Corporations: Beyond Kinship." *Journal of Asian Studies* 43: 391–415.

———. 1987. *History and Magical Power in a Chinese Community*. Stanford, Calif.: Stanford University Press.

———. 1996. "Value Transformation/Appropriation and Gender in Chinese Local Ritual Organization and Practices." Paper presented at the Annual Meeting of the Association for Asian Studies, Honolulu, April 11–14.

Santiago-Irizarry, Vilma. 1996. "Culture as Cure." *Cultural Anthropology* 11(1): 3–24.

Scharping, Thomas, ed. 1997. *Floating Population and Migration in China: The Impact of Economic Reforms*. Hamburg, Germany: Institut für Asienkunde.

Schein, Louisa. 1997. "Gender and Internal Orientalism in China." *Modern China* 23(1): 69–98.

Schmidt, Steffan W., et al., eds. 1977. *Friends, Followers, and Factions: A Reader in Political Clientelism*. Berkeley: University of California Press.

Schneider, Jane, and Peter Schneider. 1976. *Culture and Political Economy in Western Sicily*. New York: Academic Press.

Scott, James C. 1985. *Weapons of the Weak: Everyday Forms of Peasant Resistance*. New Haven, Conn.: Yale University Press.

Selden, Mark. 1993. *The Political Economy of Chinese Development*. Armonk, N.Y.: M. E. Sharpe.

———, ed. 1979. *The People's Republic of China: A Documentary History of Revolutionary Change*. New York: Monthly Review Press.

Sen, Gita, and Caren Grown. 1987. *Development, Crises, and Alternative Visions: Third World Women's Perspectives*. New York: Monthly Review Press.

Shen Yimin and Tong Chengzhu. 1992. *Zhongguo Renkou Qianyi* (Population Migration in China). Zhongguo Tongji Chubanshe (Chinese Statistics Publisher).

Shi Xianmin. 1993. *Tizhi de Tupo: Beijingshi Xichengqu Getihu Yanjiu* (Structural Breakthrough: A Study of Private Business in Beijing's West District). Zhongguo Shehui Kexue Chubanshe (Chinese Social Sciences Publisher.)

Shue, Vivienne. 1988. *The Reach of the State: Sketches of the Chinese Body Politic*. Stanford, Calif.: Stanford University Press.

———. 1995. "State Sprawl: the Regulatory State and Social Life in a Small Chinese City." In Deborah Davis et al., eds., *Urban Spaces and Contemporary China*, 90–112. Cambridge: Cambridge University Press.

Siu, Helen. 1989. *Agents and Victims in South China: Accomplices in Rural Revolution*. New Haven, Conn.: Yale University Press.

———. 1990. "The Politics of Migration in a Market Town." In Deborah Davis and Ezra F. Vogel, eds., *Chinese Society on the Eve of Tiananmen: The Impact of Reform*, 61–82. Cambridge, Mass.: Harvard University Press.

Siu, Paul. 1987. *Chinese Laundryman: A Study of Social Isolation*. New York: New York University Press.

Skinner, G. William. 1958. *Leadership and Power in the Chinese Community of Thailand*. Ithaca, N.Y.: Cornell University Press.

———. 1964–65. "Marketing and Social Structure in Rural China." *Journal of Asian Studies* 24: 3–43, 195–228, 363–99.

———. 1968. "Overseas Chinese Leadership: Paradigm for a Paradox." In Gehan Wijeyewardene, ed., *Leadership and Authority*, 191–207. Singapore: University of Malaya Press.

———. 1976. "Mobility Strategies in Late Imperial China: A Regional System Analysis." In Carol Smith, ed., *Regional Analysis*, Vol. 1, 327–64. New York: Academic Press.

———. 1977a. "Cities and the Hierarchy of Local Systems." In G. William Skinner, ed., *The City in Late Imperial China*, 275–351. Stanford, Calif.: Stanford University Press.

———. 1977b. "Introduction: Urban and Rural in Chinese Society." In G. William Skinner, ed., *The City In Late Imperial China*, 219–60. Stanford, Calif.: Stanford University Press.

Skinner, G. William, and Edwin A. Winckler. 1961. "Compliance Succession in Rural Communist China: A Cyclical Theory." In Amitai Etzioni, ed., *A Sociological Reader on Complex Organizations*, 410–438. New York: Holt, Rinehart and Winston.

Smith, Carol A. 1976. "Regional Economic Systems: Linking Geographic Models and Socioeconomic Problems." In Carol Smith, ed., *Regional Analysis*, Vol. 1, 3–63. New York: Academic Press.

Soja, E. W. 1989. *Postmodern Geographies: The Reassertion of Space in Critical Social Theory*. London: Verso.

Solinger, Dorothy. 1984. *Chinese Business Under Socialism: The Politics of Domestic Commerce, 1949–1980*. Berkeley: University of California Press.

———. 1992. "Urban Entrepreneurs and the State: The Merger of State and Society." In Arthur L. Rosenbaum, ed., *State and Society in China: The Consequences of Reform*, 121–41. Boulder, Colo.: Westview.

———. 1995a. "The Floating Population in the Cities: Chances for Assimilation?" In Deborah Davis et al., eds., *Urban Spaces and Contemporary China*, 113–39. Cambridge: Cambridge University Press.

———. 1995b. "China's Urban Transients in the Transition from Socialism and the Collapse of the Communist 'Urban Public Goods Regime.'" *Comparative Politics* (January): 127–46.

———. 1997. "The Danwei Confronts the Floating Population." In Xiaobo Liu and Elizabeth J. Perry, eds., *The Danwei: The Changing Chinese Workplace in Historical and Comparative Perspectives*, 195–222. Armonk, N.Y.: M. E. Sharpe.

———. 1999a. *Contesting Citizenship in Urban China: Peasant Migrants, the State, and the Logic of the Market.* Berkeley: University of California Press.

———. 1999b. "Laid-Offs in Limbo: Unemployment, Reemployment, and Survival in Wuhan, Summer 1999." Paper prepared for the conference "Wealth and Labour in China: Cross-Cutting Approaches of Present Developments," Centre d'Etudes et de Recherches Internationales, Paris, December 6–7.

Stacey, Judith. 1983. *Patriarchy and Socialist Revolution in China.* Berkeley: University of California Press.

Stark, David, and Laszlo Bruszt. 1998. *Postsocialist Pathways: Transforming Politics and Property in East Central Europe.* Cambridge: Cambridge University Press.

Stevenson-Yang, Anne. 1999. "Farewell to Xinjiang Alley: Xinjiang Style Restaurants Make Way for Beijing's 50th Anniversary City-Improvement Plan." *City Edition,* Feb. 13–Mar. 4, p. 12.

Strand, David. 1989. *Rickshaw Beijing: City People and Politics in the 1920s.* Berkeley: University of California Press.

Sun Yuesheng. 1989. *Dongfang Xiandaihua Qidongdian—Wenzhou Moshi* (The Starting Point of the Oriental Modernization—Wenzhou Model). Shehui Kexue Wenxian Chubanshe (Social Science Documentary Publishing House).

Swartz, Marc. 1969. "Introduction." In Marc Swartz, ed., *Local-Level Politics,* 1–46. London: University of London Press.

Taussig, Michael. 1992. "Maleficium: State Fetishism." In *The Nervous System,* 111–40. New York: Routledge.

Taylor, J. 1988. "Rural Employment Trends and the Legacy of Surplus Labor." *China Quarterly* (December) 116: 736–66.

Thomas, Nicholas. 1992. "The Invention of Tradition." *American Ethnologist* 19(2): 213–32.

Tilly, Charles. 1990. "Transplanted Networks." In Virginia Yans-McLaughlin, ed., *Immigration Reconsidered: History, Sociology, and Politics,* 79–95. New York: Oxford University Press.

Tsai, Kellee S. 1999. *Banking Behind the State: Private Entrepreneurs and the Political Economy of Informal Finance, 1978–1998.* Ph.D. dissertation, Department of Political Science, Columbia University.

Turner, Terence S. 1980. "The Social Skin." In *Not Work Alone: A Cross-Cultural View of Activities Superfluous to Survival.* Beverly Hills, Calif.: Sage.

Turner, Victor. 1967. *The Forest of Symbols.* Ithaca, N.Y.: Cornell University Press.

van Gennep, Arnold. 1960. *The Rites of Passage.* Trans. Monika B. Vizedom and Gabrielle L. Caffee. Chicago: University of Chicago Press.

Verdery, Katherine. 1991. "Theorizing Socialism: A Prologue to the 'Transition.'" *American Ethnologist* 18(3): 419–39.

———. 1996. *What Was Socialism, and What Comes Next?* Princeton, N.J.: Princeton University Press.

Vermeer, Eduard. 1999. "Shareholding Cooperatives: A Property Rights Analysis." In Jean Oi and Andrew Walder, eds., *Property Rights and Economic Reform in China*, 123–44. Stanford, Calif.: Stanford University Press.

Vincent, Joan. 1971. *The African Elite: The Big Man of the Small Town*. New York: Columbia University Press.

Wakeman, Frederic, Jr. 1975. "Introduction: The Evolution of Local Control in Late Imperial China." In Frederic Wakeman and Carolyn Grant, eds., *Conflict and Control in Late Imperial China*, Berkeley: University of California Press.

Walder, Andrew G. 1984. "The Remaking of the Chinese Working Class, 1949–1981." *Modern China* 10(1): 3–48.

———. 1986. *Communist Neo-Traditionalism: Work and Authority in Chinese Industry*. Berkeley: University of California Press.

Wan, G. H. 1995. "Peasant Flood in China—Internal Migration and Its Policy Determinants." *Third World Quarterly* 16(2): 173–96.

Wang, Bernard. 1982. *Chinatown: Economic Adaptation and Ethnic Identity of the Chinese*. New York: Holt, Rinehart and Winston.

———. 1987. "The Chinese: New Immigrants in New York's Chinatown." In Nancy Foner, ed., *New Immigrants in New York*, 243–71. New York: Columbia University Press.

Wang Chunguang. 1995. *Shehui Liudong he Shehui Chonggou—Jingcheng Zhejiangcun Yanjiu* (Social Mobility and Social Restructuring: A Study of Zhejiangcun in Beijing). Zhejiang Renmin Chubanshe (Zhejiang People's Publishing House).

Wang, Feng, and Xuejin Zuo. 1996. "Rural Migrants in Shanghai: Current Success and Future Promise." Paper presented at the International Conference on Rural Labor Mobility in China. Beijing, June 25–27.

Wang Hansheng and Chen Zhixia. 1998. "Zaijiuye Zhengce yu Xiagang Zhigong Zaijiuye Xingwei" (Re-employment Policy and the Re-employment Behaviors of Laid-off Workers). *Shehuixue Yanjiu* (Sociological Studies), no. 4: 13–30.

Wang Ju et al. 1993. "Beijingshi Liudong Renkou de Zhuangkuang ji Guanli Duice" (The Situation and Regulation Strategies of the Floating Population in Beijing). *Renkou yu Jingji* (Population and Economy) 79(4): 35–39.

Wang Shuxin and Feng Litian. 1986. "Jingji Tizhi Gaige zhong de Beijingshi Liudong Renkou" (Beijing's Floating Population in the Reform of the Economic System). *Renkou yu Jingji* (Population and Economy), no. 1.

Wang Ying, Zhe Xiaoye, and Sun Bingyao. 1993. *Shehui Zhongjianceng: Gaige yu Zhongguo de Shetuan Zuzhi* (The Mediating Social Strata: Reform and China's Mass Organizations). Zhongguo Fazhan Chubanshe (China Development Publishing House).

Wang Yuesheng. 1991. "Qingdai Beijing Liudong Renkou Chutan" (Exploring Beijing's Floating Population in the Qing Dynasty). *Renkou yu Jingji* (Population and Economy).

Wang Zhenzhong. 1996. *Mingqing Huishang yu Huaiyang Shehui Bianqian* (Anhui Merchants in the Ming and Qing Period and Social Changes in Huaiyang). Shenghuo-Dushu-Xinzhi Sanlian Shudian (Union Publisher of Life-Reading-New Knowledge).

Wank, David L. 1999. *Commodifying Communism: Markets, Trust, and Politics in a South China City*. Cambridge: Cambridge University Press.

Watson, James L. 1975. *Emigration and the Chinese Lineage: The Mans in Hong Kong and London*. Berkeley: University of California Press.

Watson, Rubie S. 1994. "Memory, History, and Opposition Under State Socialism: An Introduction." In Rubie S. Watson, ed., *Memory, History, and Opposition Under State Socialism*, 1–20. Santa Fe, N.M.: School of American Research Press.

Watts, Michael J. 1992. "Space for Everything (a Commentary)." *Cultural Anthropology* 7(1): 115–29.

Weber, Max. 1958. *The Protestant Ethic and the Spirit of Capitalism*. Trans. Talcott Parsons. New York: Charles Scribner's Sons.

———. 1981. *From Max Weber: Essays in Sociology*. Ed. and trans. H. H. Gerth and C. Wright Mills. New York: Oxford University Press.

Wenzhou Statistics Bureau. 1995. *Wenzhou Nianjian* (Statistical Yearbook of Wenzhou).

White, Gordon. 1993. *Riding the Tiger: The Politics of Economic Reform in Post-Mao China*. Stanford, Calif.: Stanford University Press.

Whiting, Susan. 1999. "The Regional Evolution of Ownership Forms: Shareholding Cooperatives and Rural Industry in Shanghai and Wenzhou." In Jean Oi and Andrew Walder, eds., *Property Rights and Economic Reform in China*, 171–200. Stanford, Calif.: Stanford University Press.

Whyte, Martin King, and William L. Parish. 1984. *Urban Life in Contemporary China*. Chicago: University of Chicago Press.

Willis, Paul. 1977. *Learning to Labor—How Working Class Kids Get Working Class Jobs*. New York: Columbia University Press.

Winckler, Edwin A., ed. 1999. *Transition from Communism in China: Institutional and Comparative Analyses*. Boulder, Colo.: Lynne Reinner.

Wolf, Arthur P. 1978. "Gods, Ghosts, and Ancestors." In Arthur Wolf, ed.,

Studies in Chinese Society, 131–82. Stanford, Calif.: Stanford University Press.

Wolf, Arthur P., and Chieh-shan Huang. 1980. *Marriage and Adoption in China, 1845–1945*. Stanford, Calif.: Stanford University Press.

Wood, Charles. 1981. "Equilibrium and Historical-Structural Perspective on Migration." *International Migration Review* 16(2): 298–319.

Xiang Biao. 1994. "Beijing You Ge 'Zhejiang Cun.'" (There is a "Zhejiang Village" in Beijing). *Chengshi Jingji Quyu Jingji* (Urban Economy and Regional Economy), no. 1: 33–50.

———. 1994–95. "Zhejiangcun Zhaji" (Notes on Zhejiangcun). *Zhongguo Nongmin* (Chinese Peasantry), nos. 7–12, 1994; nos. 3, 5, 7, 8, 9, 10, 11, 12, 1995.

———. 1996. "How to Create a Visible 'Non-State Space' Through Migration and Marketized Traditional Networks: An Account of a Migrant Community in China." Paper presented at the International Conference on Chinese Rural Labor Force Mobility, Beijing, June 25–27.

Xu Gang. 1993. *Meng Bali* (Dreaming Paris). Zhongguo Wenlian Chuban Gongsi (Chinese Art Association Publishing House).

Yan Fan. 1993. *Da Chuanlian* (Great Political Traveling). Jingcha Jiaoyu Chubanshe (Police Education Publisher).

Yan Yayu. 1994. *Zhongguo Nongmin de Shehui Liudong* (Social Mobility of Chinese Peasantry). Sichuan Daxue Chubanshe (Sichuan University Publisher).

Yan, Yunxiang. 1996. *The Flow of Gifts: Reciprocity and Social Networks in a Chinese Village*. Stanford, Calif.: Stanford University Press.

Yanagisako, Sylvia Junko. 1979. "Family and Household: The Analysis of Domestic Groups." *Annual Review of Anthropology* 8: 161–205.

Yang, Mayfair Mei-hui. 1988. "The Modernity of Power in the Chinese Socialist Order." *Cultural Anthropology* 3(4): 408–27.

———. 1994. *Gifts, Favors, and Banquets: The Art of Social Relationships in China*. Ithaca, N.Y.: Cornell University Press.

———. 1996. "Tradition, Traveling Anthropology and the Discourse of Modernity in China." In Henrietta L. Moore, ed., *The Future of Anthropological Knowledge*, 93–114. London: Routledge.

Yang, Xiushi. 1993. "Household Registration, Economic Reform, and Migration." *International Migration Review* 27(4): 796–818.

———. 1996. "Patterns of Economic Development and Patterns of Rural-Urban Migration in China." *European Journal of Population* 12(3): 195–218.

Yi Dangsheng and Shao Qing, eds. 1995. *Zhongguo Renkou Liudong Taishi yu Guanli* (The Floating Pattern and Regulation of China's Population). Zhongguo Renkouxue Chubanshe (China Demography Publishing House).

Yi Dangsheng et al. 1995. "Beijingshi Liudong Renkou Yanjiu" (A Study of Beijing's Floating Population). In Yi Dangsheng and Shao Qing, eds., *Zhongguo Renkou Liudong Taishi yu Guanli* (The Floating Pattern and Regulation of China's Population), 142–165. Zhongguo Renkouxue Chubanshe (China Demography Publishing House).

Young, Susan. 1995. *Private Business and Economic Reform in China.* Armonk, N.Y.: M. E. Sharpe.

Yuan Yue et al. 1996. *Luoren: Beijing Liumin de Zuzhihua Zhuangkuang Yanjiu Baogao* (The Naked Men: A Research Report on the Organizational Condition of Beijing's Floaters). Manuscript prepared for the International Conference on Chinese Rural Labor Mobility, Beijing, June 25–27.

Zhang, Li. 1998. "City as Market, City as Gold: Social Imagination and Mobility Strategies in China's Floating Population." Paper presented at the Annual Meeting of the Association for Asian Studies, Washington, D.C., March 26–29.

———. 2001. "Migration and Privatization of Space and Power in Late Socialist China." *American Ethnologist,* 28(1): 179–205.

———. Forthcoming. "Identity and Urban Belonging among Rural Migrants in China." In Perry Link, Paul Pickowicz, and Richard Madsen, eds., *Popular China II.* Lanham, Md.: Rowman and Littlefield.

Zhang Qingwu. 1983. "Dangqian Zhongguo Liudong Renkou Zhuangkuang he Duice Yanjiu" (A Study of the Current Situation of China's Floating Population and Tactics). *Renkou yu Jihua Shengyu* (Population and Family Planning), no. 4.

———.1988. "Basic Facts on the Household Registration System." *Chinese Economic Studies* 22(1): 22–85.

———, ed. 1994. *Zhongguo 50 Xiangzhen Liudong Renkou Diaocha Yanjiu* (Studies on the Census of the Floating Population in 50 Chinese Townships). Zhongguo Renmin Gongan Daxue Chubanshe (The Chinese People's Public Security University Press).

Zhang Youyi and Wang Zhilin. 1991. "Liudong Renkou yu Huji Guanli" (The Floating Population and Hukou Regulation). *Renkou yu Fazhan* (Population and Development), no. 4.

Zhang Zaixing and Han Zixiang. 1993. "Zouchu Hundun—Wailiu Mingong Xintai Genzong Caifang Shouji" (Coming Out of Chaos—Interview Notes on the Inner World of Migrant Peasant Workers). In Wang Linxu, ed., *Dushi li de Moshengren* (Strangers in the Metropolises), 377–411. Shanghai Shehui Kexue Chubanshe (Shanghai Social Sciences Publishing House).

Zhang Zhenzhong. 1985. *Wenzhou Wenshi Ziliao* (Wenzhou's Historical Materials).

Zhang Zhiren. 1989. *Wenzhou Chao* (Wenzhou Waves). Wenhua Yishu Chubanshe (Cultural and Art Publishing House).

Zheng Dajiong. 1991. *Wenzhou Gaige* (Wenzhou Reform). Shanghai: Fudan University Publisher.

Zhong Shuiying. 1998. "Renkou Liudong yu Chengzhen Zhigong Xiagang Wenti de Jiejue" (Population Movement and the Solutions to the Unemployment Problems of Urban Workers). *Renkou yu Jingji* (Population and Economy), no. 6: 45–48.

Zhou Houcai. 1990. *Wenzhou Gangshi* (History of the Port of Wenzhou). Renmin Yunshu Chubanshe (The People's Transportation Publisher).

Zhou, Kate Xiao. 1996. *How the Farmers Changed China*. Boulder, Colo.: Westview.

Zhou Yuming and Shao Yong. 1993. *Zhongguo Bang Hui Shi* (History of Chinese Gangs and Associations). Shanghai People's Publishing House.

Zhu Xiaoyang. 1987. "Mangliu Zhongguo" (Blind Migration Flow in China). *Zhongguo Zuojia* (Chinese Writers), no. 4.

Zito, Angela, and Tani E. Barlow. 1994. *Body, Subject, and Power in China*. Chicago: University of Chicago Press.

Index